The Managerial State

The Managerial State

Power, Politics and Ideology in the Remaking of Social Welfare

John Clarke and Janet Newman

SAGE Publications
London • Thousand Oaks • New Delhi

© John Clarke and Janet Newman 1997

First published 1997

SAGE Publications Ltd
6 Bonhill Street
London EC2A 4PU

SAGE Publications Inc
2455 Teller Road
Thousand Oaks, California 91320

SAGE Publications India Pvt Ltd
32, M-Block Market
Greater Kailash – I
New Delhi 110 048

British Library Cataloguing in Publication data

A catalogue record for this book is available
from the British Library

ISBN 0 8039 7611 9
ISBN 0 8039 7612 7 (pbk)

Library of Congress catalog record available

Typeset by Photoprint, Torquay, Devon
Printed in Great Britain by Redwood Books, Trowbridge,
Wiltshire

Contents

Preface   vii

Introduction   ix

1   From the Cradle to the Grave: the Crises of the Post-War
    Welfare Settlements   1

2   Towards the Managerial State?   18

3   A Change for the Better? The Tyranny of Transformation   34

4   The Making of Management: Regimes of Power   56

5   Incentives, Institutions and Identities: Shaping the Managerial
    State   83

6   Capturing the Customer: the Politics of Representation   107

7   Reinventing the Public   123

8   An Unstable State?   140

    Bibliography   160

    Index   170

Preface

We begin in a rather conventional way by saying who we are, because where we come from has shaped the evolution of this book in important ways. Our current roles, one working in social policy, the other in public policy and management, imply different starting points for analysing the changes that have occurred at the intersection of management and the welfare state. But such differences matter less than what we have in common. We are both products of the 'old way of life' – we were children of the welfare state who learned and practised our trades within it. We have occupied the roles with which the arguments of this book are concerned: we have been workers in public service organisations and professionals in the 'professional bureaucracies' of local government and education. We have been both managers and managed within them. More recently, we have worked individually and together with groups of staff in a range of public service settings. These pressures have engaged us – and them – in the problems of making sense of what has happened.

We have arrived at this book through a number of academic routes – including the study of social policy, sociology, feminist analysis, public policy and management. Despite our different trajectories through these perspectives, we share a common experience of being formed by cultural studies. This has left us with an awareness of the social and political importance of symbols, language and meaning and the ways in which they are struggled over and contested. More than anything else, this concern informs the way we have approached the remaking of the welfare state in this book. This intellectual starting point is also one that seems appropriate to the task in more mundane ways. What is most striking about the processes of change around and in the welfare state is the pervasive importance – and elusiveness – of the language used to describe, explain and justify them. People talk about 'cultural' change or the impact of the 'contract culture'. They feel 'lost for words' or are baffled by 'empty rhetoric'. The exemplary moment for our concern with language came when some middle level social services managers explained that – in their area at least – there was no 'unmet need'. Their director had informed them that there was now only 'unmet demand'. Our intention in writing this book has been to make these issues more than merely words – to treat words, languages and cultures as central and active parts of the struggles to remake the welfare state.

In writing this book, we have incurred a variety of debts. Most of all we want to thank those working in the field of public services for trying to explain to us the pain and pleasure of working in a 'world turned upside down' and for discussing our attempts to interpret it. This debt has been accumulating through a whole range of organisational visits, interviews, courses, programmes and workshops over the past few years. Particular thanks are due to the students on the Public Services MBA at the University of Birmingham. At the same time, our friends and colleagues have supported our obsessions, informed our thinking and argued with us when they saw fit. We have certainly benefited from the process and we hope that they will think that this book has, too. In particular, we would like to thank Allan Cochrane, Eugene McLaughlin, Gail Lewis, Gordon Hughes, Paul du Gay, Maureen Mackintosh, Fiona Williams, Vivien Lowndes, John Stewart and the late Kieron Walsh for their capacity to keep these conversations going.

We must also express our thanks to Stephen Barr at Sage for thinking that this book was a worthwhile investment and for remaining patient during the delays when, for one reason or another, we were being patients – or health care consumers.

Introduction

Why 'the managerial state'? This term registers the fact that the state has been the focus of change during the past two decades. From attempts to control public spending, through Civil Service reforms, to the creation of new delivery systems for welfare services, the state has been at the centre of attention. For those working in public services, the experience has been one of 'permanent revolution'. At times, it has seemed that not a week has gone by without another reform, a new White Paper, a further initiative. There has always been a next step to be taken. The depth and breadth of change has led to a proliferation of terms intended to capture and explain these processes: globalisation, post-Fordism, modernisation, the post-bureaucratic organis-ation, the 'new' public management, the mixed economy of welfare, plus a whole host of terms identifying change in the nature of the state itself: the contract state, the hollow state, the enabling state, the surveillance state, the evaluative state, the minimal state, the skeleton state, the strong state and more.

We talk about the *managerial* state because we want to locate mana-gerialism as a cultural formation and a distinctive set of ideologies and practices which form one of the underpinnings of an emergent political settlement. The book sets out to explore the impact of managerialism on key sets of relationships: those between state and citizen, between public and private, between the providers and recipients of social welfare, and between 'management' and 'politics'. These changing relationships are mediated through a range of structural and institutional realignments: the introduction of markets, the rise of contracting, the changing balance of power between central government and local and regional agencies of governance and so on. But the ideologies and institutions of managerialism provide a coherent field that underpins and legitimates these shifts. Managerialism, we argue, is shaping the remaking of the British state – its institutions and practices as well as its culture and ideology.

Our analysis concentrates on the changes in the *British* welfare state. The emergence of a 'new public management' is often portrayed as a global phenomenon – a core element in a process of convergence between states, overriding distinct political and cultural characteristics. We think that the nature of change in specific nations cannot be understood simply in terms of global forces and trans-national economic retrenchment. Nor can it merely be read as the local effect of a global set of ideas about how to run public organisations (Flynn and Strehl, 1996). The effects of world recession were particularly sharply felt in Britain because of the relative structural weakness of the British economy. The succession of New Right influenced governments which dominated British politics from the end of the 1970s were central to the process of rethinking the role of the state. But as Mishra and others have pointed out, the consequences of these conditions of crisis were not inevitable. Countries pursued different solutions to economic crises, ranging from maintenance to retrenchment of welfare provision (Mishra, 1990). These solutions – and even the definition of what the problem was – depended on specific national circumstances, and the policies, ideologies and politics of particular national governments. As a result, our efforts here are directed at understanding the peculiarities of the British welfare state.

Engaging with the managerial state

Much of the impetus to write this book has come from our work with people in public service organisations. We have been struck by the contradictory nature of their experience of change. They have talked about the difficulties of constantly being asked to make efficiency savings, the problems of responding to a 'can do' climate of policy making and of working in a context of low and declining trust between public, politicians and managers. Those working in public services are having to manage not just budgets and people in the pursuit of greater efficiency, but the tensions and dilemmas of rapid and unpredictable change. The results are frequently high levels of stress and overload which tend to spill over into 'personal' life. At the same time, however, these managers have engaged with the challenge of building more responsive, flexible and user oriented public services. Many have welcomed the opportunities for innovation, or come to enjoy the challenge of competition. Some have sought to modernise what they see as outdated organisations and institutions in the pursuit of a new sense of public purpose. Others have been more cautious, expressing concern about the impact of change on users and communities and doubtful about the future of 'public service' values in a culture which they see as dominated by the values of the business world. Despite the diversity of individual responses, common issues and agendas have emerged around the need to develop solutions to a number of core dilemmas: doing more for less in pursuit of the holy grail of efficiency; trying to be 'strategic' while juggling an ever increasing number of injunctions and restrictions from central government; managing the problems arising from overlapping, fast changing and often contradictory policy agendas; and struggling to balance all this with living a life beyond the workplace.

These experiences tell us that the nature of change has not been smooth and linear, but has been uneven and contested. The diversity of responses and the downright messiness of change suggests that social actors are not shaped unambiguously by large scale trends or forces. It is possible to *over-read* the logic of change, seeing forces such as globalisation, institutional fragmentation, the adoption of business ideas and practices in public service delivery, as cascading down from the global level of new economic pressures to the world of individual experience and action in a way which suggests simple and linear sequences of cause and effect.

In writing this book, we have tried to distinguish between different levels of analysis in tracing the impact of managerialism on state restructuring. In the early chapters (1–3) we deal with the social, political and ideological conditions of the 'crisis of the welfare state' and the attempts to resolve it through restructuring and reform. Chapter 1 deals with the changing social formations and political conjunctions which constituted the conditions of crisis. Chapter 2 explores the reconfiguration of state power and the redrawing of the boundaries between the public and the private in the process of reconstruction. Chapter 3 identifies a conjunction between New Right and managerial ideologies in producing and embedding the process of 'transformational' change.

In later chapters we consider the changing nature of organisational regimes and some of the micro-politics through which managerialism has been enacted. Chapter 4 identifies managerialism as a distinct 'regime of power' through which internal and external organisational relationships are ordered. Chapter 5 looks at the contradictory and uneven ways in which this regime is experienced, drawing on institutional theory to explore the ways in which social actors create and adapt a range of different forms of managerialism. Chapter 6 explores managerialism as a site of 'micro-politics' which are played out in struggles around consumerism. Chapter 7 then moves back to the broader political arena and explores the contemporary struggles to address some of the deficits of managerialism through attempts to reinstall wider notions of the public, expressed through the concepts of a new public management, stakeholding and communitarianism. The final chapter reviews the 'story so far', assessing whether the processes of restructuring have produced new settlements that resolve the crisis of the welfare state.

However this is not a simple matter of moving from one level of analysis to another in a direct sequence of either topics or theoretical approaches. It is clearly tempting to identify an economic level (the global changes of a world capitalist system), a political level of analysis (the strategies of specific nation states and governments) and an organisational level (the institutions and practices of management), with analysis of their impact on users or the wider society as the output of these processes. Such a structure is attractive, but it compartmentalises analysis in a peculiar way (that's the 'economic', now for the 'political', then the 'organisational') and at least implies a rather linear sequence of determinations down this series of levels. The process of this book is rather different. It loops back on itself because of an insistence on the interconnectedness of different levels of analysis. As a result, many topics (such as markets) or themes (for example social diversity) recur in different chapters. We want to stress this interconnectedness because at each level there are specific forms of theory that we draw on to build our overall analysis. Each level of theory, on its own, tends to bracket off other levels. Studies of economic, social and political change do not deliver the means of understanding the specific ways in which their effects are played out in particular organisational sites. Institutional theories explore the ways in which rules, norms and conventions are shaped in the interplay of external imperatives and the actions of individuals and groups, but do not offer ways of adequately theorising the broader cultural and political processes which inform this. Our argument in this book works *through* these and other approaches in trying to develop an understanding of the managerial state which goes beyond them.

This insistence on working with and through theories is the source of some problems. Writing about theory in the late 1990s has become difficult for two important reasons. The first is that it is somewhat unfashionable to do so. As we shall suggest later in the book, moving forward has become more important than understanding where you have been, and practical action more important than reflection and analysis. Managerialism itself provides a substantial part of this momentum, being oriented towards means rather than ends, and towards action rather than reflection. The 'can do' culture of management has a strong preference for practical prescriptions over mere academic analysis. Despite that, we are committed to the necessity of theorising the changes to which the state and those working in the provision of services to the public have been subjected – and especially the place of management itself in those processes.

The second difficulty lies in the fragmentation of theory itself as the 'grand theories' of Marxism and other perspectives have been challenged. Disciplines have come to follow their own trajectories of theoretical development in what often appears to be a fairly insular fashion. This means that attempts to pursue analysis across disciplines, as we wish to do here, is less than easy. We have attempted not to fall into the pit of eclecticism, but want to respond to the challenge of revaluing the importance of theory against the prevailing climate of pragmatic realism. We believe that it is impossible to deal with questions about the future of relationships between citizen and state, public and private, from within the paradigms offered by single disciplines, whether the discipline be economics, politics, or (especially) public management itself. Indeed, we are not sure that *a* theory in the singular finished sense exists (or even should exist) that could account for the phenomenon. Nevertheless, we have tried to produce something more than an *ad hoc* collection of insights culled from different perspectives. The argument of this book has taken shape around a set of core ideas and concerns.

Language, ideology and discourse

This has emerged as an important theme not because we think this is all there is – the changes we are concerned with are lived and felt in a very material way – but because many of the struggles we are concerned with are conducted through these symbolic forms. For example, the shifts in language around and between notions of 'customers', 'citizens' and 'communities' that we consider in Chapters 6 and 7 signify different sets of roles, expectations and relationships. But language can be appropriated by different groups for different sets of purposes: it forms a distinct terrain of political contestation. This terrain is of critical importance because of its place in the struggle for legitimacy. The success of any change project, whether initiated by government legislation or by organisational managers, depends on the success of its claims for legitimacy and its ability to win the 'hearts and minds' of those on whom it impacts.

Power

We see power as the 'absent presence' of many of the existing analyses of change. Where it occurs, it tends to focus on analyses of the 'coercive power' of legislation, the increasing centralisation of power in the hands of central government, or the shift of power to non-elected bodies (quangos). We think that power is both more important and more complex than these formulations suggest. Power is, firstly, always contested. This means that the analysis of how power is mobilised by different groups and interests as alliances are shaped or dismantled forms an important part of our analysis. Secondly, power occurs in many forms, existing not only in the coercive power of particular groups, but also underpinning the ways in which decisions are framed through the logics and legitimating frameworks of different forms of knowledge. Our use of discourse theory at various points of the book suggests the ways in which power may be 'constitutive' as well as coercive. Thirdly, we see power as 'relational', and explore the dynamics of how power is distributed in the context of the dispersal of state power to a range of bodies and agencies. In particular we are concerned with the consequences of this dispersal for the shifting balances of power between state and citizen, between organisations and their users, and between 'old' professionals and administrators and 'new' managerial roles and identities.

Diversity

We use the concept of diversity in two different ways. The first is used to suggest that, although we are talking about what seems to be a very general concept – the 'managerial state' – it is experienced in practice in a diversity of forms. We have tried to highlight the variations, tensions and contradictions within it. Many of these are as yet unresolved, and one of the questions to which we shall return in the final chapter is how far we can talk of the emergence of new settlements in place of the old political, social and organisational certainties which provided the underpinnings of the post-war welfare state.

  The second sense in which we use the term diversity is in the sense of social differentiation. Analyses of state and public sector change are rife with undifferentiated concepts such as 'citizens', 'customers', 'users', 'the public', 'communities', and more recently 'stakeholders'. We think that these terms mask important forms of differentiation around 'race', gender, class and other social formations. We argue that the crisis of the welfare state was based partly on the dismantling of the *social* settlement on which it was founded, and explore tensions in contemporary attempts to 'reinvent' the public in new settlements between state and civil society.

Theorising change

The concept of change lies at the heart of this book, but talking about change raises a number of difficulties. What struck us in reading and talking to people was that the very pervasiveness of the word is itself a problem – it is used to mean everything, and so in the end means very little. If everything is changing, how do you get a grip on understanding any particular change? How can you assess the relationship between 'macro' and 'micro' forces? Does the pervasiveness of the language of change itself have an ideological effect in establishing its own necessity? Our fascination with these questions resulted in us devoting a whole chapter (Chapter 3) to exploring the discourse of change itself. Rather than attempting to describe what has happened in terms of a series of changes, our analysis is based on a concern with the specific features of particular historical *conjunctures* (see also Hall, 1996a). We are not convinced by images of change presented in terms of 'from–to' dualisms (such as from Fordist to post-Fordist, or from hierarchies to markets). Rather, we treat change in terms of attempts to resolve the ambiguities and the contradictions of political agency. Antonio Gramsci once suggested that 'the life of the state is conceived of as a continuous process of formation and superceding of unstable equilibria' (1971: 182). The book explores the attempts to create a new 'equilibrium' that supercedes the old social democratic settlements and traces some of its instabilities.

These commitments guide our analysis, and motivate the way in which we negotiate other theories and perspectives. We draw on their 'good sense' where they add to or illuminate these issues, but also attempt to move beyond their limitations. Our approach may, of course, be a source of frustration to readers: the analysis we present may disappoint those in search of a Theory, and our appropriation of certain perspectives (discourse theory for example) may annoy those who believe in theoretical purity. But our primary concern is not to produce or exemplify a specific unified theoretical statement; it is to engage with the pressing problems of understanding the conditions and consequences of radical transformations in the form of the state.

1

From the Cradle to the Grave: the Crises of the Post-War Welfare Settlements

The remaking of the state has been a continuing strand in British politics for the past twenty years. Hardly any institutional arrangement has been left untouched by the waves of reforms, revolutions and realignments, from the Civil Service to community organisations providing local services. This remaking has not only changed the internal organisational forms of the state, but the relationships between the state and the economy, the state and society and the state and the citizen. Much of the drive towards institutional reform has been based on a perceived 'crisis of the welfare state'. This crisis carries with it issues about the proper role of the state.

The shape and dimensions of this crisis were predominantly constructed through the ideological terms of reference established by the New Right. As Gramsci observed, crises 'create a terrain more favourable to the dissemination of certain modes of thought, and certain ways of posing and resolving questions involving the entire subsequent development of national life' (1971: 184). Much of this book examines the consequences of how 'certain modes of thought' posed and tried to resolve the problem of the welfare state. This chapter begins by examining the conditions of this crisis.

The post-war welfare state was legitimated and sustained by a range of settlements. Hay has summarised these as 'the relationship between the state, the economy, civil society and the public sphere that was to emerge and become institutionalised in post-war Britain' (1996: 44). We want to pull this apart by examining three separate but overlapping types of settlement: the political–economic, the social and the organisational settlement. The political–economic settlement has been defined in a number of ways: as the compromise between capitalism (and the free market) and socialism (and public provision through the state) or the compromise between the principles of inequality (market-driven) and equality (state guaranteed citizenship). It has been regarded as the settlement between the class forces of 'Capital' and 'Labour', and as the basis of a consensus politics establishing a more or less grudgingly accepted common framework of policy direction for parties of the Right and Left. Most accounts of the problems of the welfare state have focused on these political and economic dimensions. For example, Mishra (1990) describes the dismantling of the commitment to a mixed economy based on Keynesian principles of macro-economic planning; the benevolent role of the state in managing the economy; and public spending on social and welfare services. Attention has concentrated on the global economic crisis of the mid-1970s and its consequences for the economies of the West. In particular, this crisis exposed the costs of public spending to political scrutiny and debate. Some discussions of the crisis have stressed an attempt by Capital and its representatives to redraw the post-war settlement in ways that enhance profitability, cutting the costs of taxation, freeing labour markets from state interference and removing the burdens of regulation from corporate capitalism. Other accounts have highlighted the successes of parties of the Right – and the New Right, in particular – in breaking up consensus politics and pursuing policies that were anti-statist and in favour of the free market.

All of these elements were visible in the crisis of the welfare state in Britain – and in particularly intense forms. But the focus on the political and economic crises has tended to overshadow other dimensions that have played a significant part. The political and economic settlement of the post-war welfare state was enmeshed with two other settlements – a social settlement and an organisational settlement – whose character contributed to the overall shape of the crisis and to the solutions proposed to resolve it. The intersection of problems in all three settlements produced the crisis of the welfare state.

The social settlement

The welfare state was erected around a framework of assumptions about the nature of British society, the needs of its citizens and how these should be met.

An emerging body of work best, but not only, represented in the writings of Fiona Williams (1989, 1992, 1993, 1994) has traced what might be called the 'social settlement' associated with the welfare state. Her concern has been with the ideological formations and social relations that have been produced and reproduced in the policies and practices of the welfare state. These focal points emerged from a concern to move social policy analysis beyond its preoccupation with income, work and class.

> A solution is to see the notions of **Family** and **Nation**, as well as **Work**, as three central and interconnected themes in the development of welfare. In other words welfare policies have both appealed to and reinforced (as well as occasionally challenged) particular ideas of what constitutes family life, national unity and 'British culture', although the notions and reality of Family, Nation and Work themselves change over time . . .
>
> Although the themes Family, Nation and Work could be applied to most industrialised societies, in the context of Britain the above model is about an analysis of the welfare state within a patriarchal and racially structured capitalism. As such the model broadens the production focus of social policy to include social reproduction and its particular impact on women and it widens the context to an internationalist understanding of imperialism and its impact on the lives of black and minority ethnic welfare users and workers. (Williams, 1992: 211–12)

Family and work intersect first in the assumptions about the organisation of waged and unwaged work. The precondition of the expanded welfare role for the state was the maintenance of full – male – employment, since such employment was to underpin the organisation of social welfare. It would ensure that most people's needs would be met through the earned income of a male head of household. The state would only come into play in the absence of wages (through unemployment benefit or pensions, for example). The maintenance of full employment was also essential for the financial foundations of state welfare, since it would be funded primarily by insurance contributions from the economically active.

This conception of full employment as the province of male wage earners both drew on and reinforced conceptions of the family as the site of a naturalised sexual division of labour, where, in Beveridge's oft-quoted phrase, 'housewives as mothers have vital work to do in ensuring the adequate continuance of the British Race and British ideals in the world' (1942: 52). The family – in this heterosexual and patriarchal guise – was to be the corner-stone of the system of social welfare. The wage-earning husband laboured in the public realm to provide the economic means for the housewife as mother to perform that vital work of reproduction within the private sphere of the home. The structure of welfare benefits reflected this assumption about the sexual division of labour, such that married women *and other dependants* would gain benefits in times of need via the male head of household (Land, 1995). This model of the family also projected a world in which the state would only be a support for welfare needs where 'the family failed', since caring for children, the sick and the elderly would be a natural function of families and, in particular, of women's role within the family (Finch, 1987; Finch and Groves, 1983; Graham, 1993).

Beveridge's remarks about the British Race also serve to signify the other dimension of the social settlement of the post-war welfare state: the ethnicity of the 'citizen' in relation to the nation state. This was, above all, a British welfare state, construed as serving British citizens with a known and predictable pattern of life and well understood welfare needs. This British citizen was – almost incidentally – white, with at least the residue of an imperial status and mission. The subsequent growth of the citizenship test for eligibility for welfare, in which 'race', nationality and citizenship would become compounded, was not an issue in the 1940s when it was simply presumed that everyone knew who a British citizen was. The implications for the social character of the universalism of the welfare state involved the unspoken inscription of a singular set of patterns of life, values and needs into the heart of welfare services as if they were universal.

In all its facets, this social settlement of the welfare state created a structure of different positions in relation to welfare benefits and services. This structure naturalised a set of social arrangements based on gender (the sexual divisions of welfare); age and able-bodiedness (the structuring of dependency) and 'race' (the identity of citizenship) and fixed them as the principles of state welfare. As Langan and Clarke have argued:

The 'universalism' of citizenship is, in these ways, deeply circumscribed – a highly conditional universalism which presumes a family-based social and economic structure. It addresses an indigenous population at whose heart are wage earning males supporting families surrounded by a set of dependent populations positioned by age (both young and old), by gender (the 'anomaly of the married woman'), by infirmity and by 'race' (the 'alien' non-citizen). (1993a: 28)

This structuring of citizenship was not only significant for the ways in which it shaped social policies and their implementation. It also played a wider ideological role in defining the relationship of the public and the state. It produced a unifying imagery of 'the people' which aligned them with the state in mutual defence against disruptions to their individual and collective stability (birth, illness, death, etc.) and joined them in collective investment in their future (the promise of social improvement). In this imagery, patterns of social divisions were naturalised: treated as something other than social. Thus gender divisions belonged to the realm of biology, as did racialised divisions of ethnicity and the distinction between the able-bodied and the 'handicapped'. The tensions between natural and social conceptions of these divisions were to become significant in the subsequent break-up of the social settlement.

This identification of the people and the state drew on particular historical images which provided legitimating narratives for the construction and expansion of the welfare state. Some of these narratives were about class and the failures of old elites. Some concerned the dangers of the free market, pointing to the social consequences of unregulated capitalism in the 1920s and 1930s. Others dealt with the role of the state, contrasting pre-1940s failures of governance with the enlarged role of the war-time state. These narratives combined to present the limitations and failures of pre-1940s national and local provision in the field of social welfare as necessitating a reinvention of the state's relationship to the people. The post-war state promised to replace old elites, patronage, partiality and the mixture of *laissez-faire*, charity and means testing that had dominated earlier conceptions of social welfare in Britain. The creation of the welfare state as a distinctive political and ideological entity – with its amalgam of Keynesian and Beveridgean commitments – required an organisational form or regime of the state in which people could see themselves represented.[1] This points to the third settlement associated with the welfare state – the organisational settlement.

The organisational settlement

The organisational construction of the British welfare state was structured by a commitment to two modes of coordination: bureaucratic administration and professionalism (for fuller discussions, see, *inter alia*, Cousins, 1987; Hoggett, 1994; Newman and Clarke, 1994). It is through the settlement between these different modes of coordination that notions of *public service* – as a set of values, a code of behaviours and forms of practice – became institutionalised. By modes of coordination, we refer to the complex of rules, roles and regulatory principles around which the social practices of organisations are structured – which generate typical patterns of internal and external social relationships and which, among other things, privilege certain types of knowledge. We have used the term modes of coordination partly because it undercuts the naturalising effect of the word 'managing' in which the common-sense meaning of 'running things' is elided with the more specific prescriptions of a *managerialist* mode of coordination.

The first mode of coordination embedded at the heart of the new welfare state was that of *bureaucratic administration*. At one level, the adoption of bureaucratic approaches to the administration of social welfare can be traced to the simple fact that this was the model which the architects of the new system had at hand (Hall, 1984). The development of 'public administration' in Britain since the nineteenth century reform of the Civil Service had taken the form of rational bureaucracy, designed to promote the efficient and impartial administration of public business of all kinds. Although there is a large and complex literature on the sociology of bureaucracy, we want to concentrate here on the attractions of the bureaucratic mode of coordination for the structuring of public services. The first of these is the capacity of bureaucratic coordination to deliver *routinised or predictable outputs*. The structuring principles of bureaucratic administration – emphasising the appropriate application of a body of rules and regulations by trained staff – turn complex tasks of assessment or calculation into routinised processes and guarantee that the outcomes of those calculations are stable or predictable. For the administration of complex systems of benefits, for example, the bureaucratic mode promised that each 'case' would be treated according to a set of common rules and that the results of such administrative processing would ensure that each case would be treated fairly.

This idea of equitable treatment is also the key to the second desirable feature of bureaucratic administration – that it is *socially, politically and personally neutral*. In the light of contemporary critiques of bureaucracy, it is easy to forget that bureaucracy emerged as a progressive alternative to corrupt and oppressive systems of governance in which patronage, nepotism and corruption were endemic (du Gay, 1994a). Bureaucracy was intimately linked to the development of public administration precisely because it promised a system of governance in which members of 'the public' would be treated impartially rather than in ways which reflected their social status, wealth or place in social networks of influence. In the field of social welfare, such rational administration had a distinctive appeal because of the contrast with the ways in which social welfare had been delivered by organisations such as Poor Law Boards of Guardians or the Charity Organisation Society in which social and moral evaluations of worth or desert had been embedded.

The principles of bureaucracy also guaranteed insulation of public policy from the effects of personal whims, enthusiasms and commitments. What is often described as the 'depersonalising' effect of bureaucracy is, in fact, the result of a commitment to separate personal commitments from the administration of the public realm. The elaborate structures of the 'machine bureaucracy' (Mintzberg, 1983), involving complex task divisions, long hierarchical structures of supervision and control and the formality of rules, records and communication, aim to embody this separation of the person and the position in the most minute features of organisational life. The development of bureaucratic administration of the public realm was also viewed as a means of balancing the stable running of the state's activities with the potential uncertainties and perturbations of democratic politics. Although the convention of separating 'policy' and 'implementation' as the respective concerns of politicians and administrators has always been sustained in theory, in practice the bureaucratic machinery of government has disciplined the development and implementation of policy initiatives through the provision of advice and the procedural control of implementation.

However, bureaucratic administration was not, by itself, sufficient for the public provision of social welfare. It needed to be tempered by forms of 'expertise' which were more than administrative competence and which drew on distinctive bodies of knowledge and skills about the causes and solutions of social problems. This marks the point at which bureaucratic administration and professionalism met in the development of the welfare state (Cousins, 1987: ch. 5). This second mode of coordination – *professionalism* – was also part of the welfare inheritance, most obviously in the tortuous negotiations about the place and role of medical power in the formation of the National Health Service. But it also underpinned the expansion of public education, based on a view of the curriculum as the province of 'professional expertise' possessed by teachers and academics, and the growth of personal social services, based on the small but growing 'semi-professions' that would eventually become social work (Clarke, 1993, 1996a).

As a mode of coordination, professionalism provides a sharp contrast with bureaucratic administration. Where bureaucracy is concerned with predictability and stability, professionalism stresses the indeterminacy of the social world as necessitating the intervention of expert judgement. Problems are only responsive to expert knowledge and lay perspectives lack such expertise. Where bureaucracy operates through the standardisation of work processes in the tight formal specification of roles and responsibilities, professionalism is based on the standardisation of skills through externally controlled training and qualification (Mintzberg, 1983). Professionalism lays claim to an irreducible autonomy – the space within which professional judgement can be exercised and must be trusted. In addition, welfare professionalism seeks a different balance of the 'personal' and 'impersonal' from that of bureaucracy. While all professions place a premium on behaving professionally which is intended to preclude personal biases, prejudices or 'becoming emotionally involved', professional power and practice is nevertheless distinctively embodied in the person of the professional. It is personalised in the professional–client relationship and the processual nature of professional intervention – whether at the bedside, in the classroom or in the case work relationship.

Professionalism operates both as an occupational strategy, defining entry and negotiating the power and rewards due to expertise, and as an organisational strategy, shaping the patterns of power, place and relationships around which organisations are coordinated. The pre-existence of significant groups of professionalised workers (particularly in health and education) meant that the development of an expanded welfare state had to 'come to terms' with professionalism. It was impossible to conceive of a national health service that was not organised around medical knowledge and practice – even though negotiating the precise conditions of medical power was a complex process. Similarly, the expansions of both secondary and tertiary education required a settlement with teachers and academics about levels of autonomy and control – particularly over the curriculum and the classroom.

Nevertheless, the place of professionalism in the welfare state was not simply the result of grudging concessions made to professional power. It was also an actively sought principle. Social problems and social needs were, in this view, complex entities and not responsive to simple political or administrative solution. Professionals, then, were indispensable partners in the great national task of social reconstruction and, within limits, they were to be trusted and encouraged to apply their expertise for the public good. In this positive recruitment of professionals to state welfare, we can see the influence of Fabian ideology in which knowledge and expertise are positively valued as the means for promoting rational social development through the machinery of the state. For the Fabians, the state – viewed as a neutral power standing above society – could provide the engine of social progress and ensure that such progress was ordered and rational (by contrast with the inchoate unpredictability of the marketplace). This view of the neutrality of the state coincided with the neutrality of professionalism (or, more accurately, the neutrality proclaimed in professional ideologies). Just as bureaucratic administration promised impersonal fairness, so professionalism promised disinterested service. Bound by professional values and codes, the professional placed his or her skills and expertise at the state's disposal in the pursuit of social improvement. While administrators could be trusted because their purpose was merely to implement rules, professionals could be trusted because their neutrality was guaranteed by an ethos of service (exemplified in the Hippocratic oath).

The welfare state, then, developed around a double logic of representation of the public. On the one hand, bureaucratic knowledge (either of rules or specific expertise) is invoked in the service of the 'public interest'. On the other, professional knowledge is constituted as the engine of social progress and improvement which would enhance the 'public good'. These *organisational* modes of representing the public intersect with the formal *political* processes of democratic representation through which different social interests were mediated and reconciled. Between the late 1940s and the mid-1970s, then, it is possible to see the welfare state as being sustained by a triple social neutrality: first, the bi-partisan political settlement which proclaimed the welfare state (more or less enthusiastically) as above party political differences; second, bureaucratic administration which promised social impartiality; and third, professionalism which promised the application of valued knowledge in the service of the public. This is a relatively general argument about the character of the welfare state as a whole. At more particular levels of analysis, these three principles – of political representation, bureaucratic administration and professionalism – combined in different ways and with different balances of power in specific institutional arrangements. Thus, professional power held a very strong position within the NHS; bureaucratic administration provided the central principles of income maintenance systems; while political representation operated unevenly at the levels of national and local government.

The combination of bureaucracy and professionalism supported a particular ideological representation of the relationship between the state and the people in which they served as the institutionalised guarantors of the pursuit of the public good. The value base of the welfare state (as many management texts now refer to this formation) was one which constantly cross referred the claims about 'public service' to the organisational regime – bureau-professionalism – of the welfare state itself. Public service was embodied in both the rhetoric and the structure of practices of this organisational regime through which the post-war political settlement was institutionalised.

In highlighting the social and organisational settlements, we have tried to show how the welfare state was constructed as a popular institution – that is, one in which 'the people' were represented. The combination of the three settlements provided the foundation for the post-war construction and subsequent expansion of the welfare state (Langan and Clarke, 1993a). We have deliberately used the word settlements here to indicate that these are limited and conditional reconciliations of different interests. They established the frameworks of reference within which considerable conflict, negotiation and shifting alliances took place. They also served to exclude or marginalise a range of interests, issues and arguments that were defined as irrelevant or inappropriate. Taken together, these three settlements, political–economic, social and organisational, form the distinctive character of post-war British social democracy. The overlapping ways in which these settlements came apart formed the conditions of the crisis of the British welfare state.

Dismantling the settlements

The crisis of the welfare state is conventionally located in the intersection of economics and politics. The underlying weakness of the British economy in the context of both global recession and capital restructuring exposed public spending, particularly on social welfare, to pressures for retrenchment from the mid-1970s onwards. Such pressures were often articulated through a new economic calculus which treated public spending as a drain on the competitive viability of individuals, corporations and nations. The 'death of Keynesianism' – at least in terms of government policy – marked a shift from a view of public spending as collective or social investment to an emphasis on public spending as unproductive cost: a view promulgated vigorously both nationally and internationally (e.g., Bacon and Eltis, 1976). Although different interpretations of the mid-1970s crisis can be offered, the undoubted effect was to dislocate the economic settlement – the commitment to managed growth and full (male) employment – which had formed one of the fragile foundations of the expanded welfare state. The idea of the welfare state as part of a settlement between labour and capital was equally disrupted, as both national and international capital began to renegotiate the conditions – and even availability – of employment. The symbolic moment of a Labour government cutting back public spending at the behest of the IMF marked the exhaustion of bi-partisan political consensus on the desirability of the welfare state. The subsequent antipathy of the New Right to the welfare state has been extensively discussed by social policy analysts and others (e.g., Johnson, 1990; Loney, 1985; Mishra, 1990). Such accounts capture the ways in which the economic and political settlements associated with the social democratic or Keynesian Welfare State came apart, but they are often less attentive to the conditions of crisis in the social and organisational settlements of the welfare state.

The social settlement, formed in the intersection of 'family, work and nation', had proved no more stable than its economic and political counterparts. The interplay of social changes – in the make-up of households, workers and the people – and new forms of social, cultural and political movements destabilised the social settlement profoundly. Particular lines of social differentiation became a focus for collective action and political conflict. Many of these centred on divisions which had previously been treated as natural categories (such as 'race', gender and sexuality) where collective action sought to redefine them as socially produced and constructed. These struggles arose partly from contradictions inherent in different features of the social settlement of the post-war years. For example, the 1945 settlement had assumed a white British citizenry: the conception of the nation attempted to cast 'race' out into the realms of biology (and colonial geography). Welfare universalism had subsequently been assumed to extend unproblematically to minority ethnic groups through the mechanisms of social assimilation. But the stumbling attempts at assimilation in British social policy highlighted the contradictions of trying to sustain a racialised conception of citizenship in the context of a multi-ethnic populace. As Britain moved uneasily out of Empire, so the social character of citizenship became exposed as a contested issue. Attempts to narrow its range and accessibility encountered struggles against the racialised status of 'second class' citizens. Growing evidence of, and struggles for, divergent 'needs' made uneven impacts upon the system of welfare (see, for example, Ahmad, 1993). At points, such differences were recognised in the form of relatively limited multi-cultural approaches or in the recruitment of minority ethnic staff more representative of, and better 'attuned' to, the needs of the populations they were expected to serve (see, for example, Taylor, 1993; Lewis, 1997). But, in other respects, cultural diversity exposed minority ethnic groups to the repressive dimensions of state welfare – not merely in the form of discriminatory policing, but to diagnoses of 'maladjustment' of various kinds in respect of education, social work and health visiting which necessitated greater intervention or surveillance. These tensions were framed by the overarching approach to 'race' in Britain which structured policy around the twin goals of immigration control and the fostering of 'good race relations' through assimilationist policies (Anthias, 1992). In practice, though, such policies were increasingly supplemented by a concern with regulating and policing the 'unassimilated' in the 1980s and 1990s.

During the same period, the family emerged as something other than the happy coincidence of God and Nature. Material shifts in the alignment of family and work and the rise of feminism exposed gendered divisions of labour and power where once only biology had been discerned (Wilson, 1977). These changes included the growing involvement of married women in paid employment (alongside their 'vital role' as housewives and mothers); the rise of divorce and remarriage producing serial families; the rise in lone-parent families; the spread of alternatives to the family form – communal living, gay or lesbian households, and so on. In all these ways, conventional patriarchal assumptions about the stability of the family form became increasingly detached from social reality. At the same time, other assumptions about the family were being challenged. These concerned the interior life of families, conventionally understood as the intimate and tranquil 'haven', protecting its members from the rigours of the public world. Led by women's movement campaigns, a less protective interior was revealed – whether in the form of economic and power inequalities between men and women or the capacity of the family to both produce and conceal abuse of its members (wife-battering, marital rape and the physical and sexual abuse of children). These developments challenged the assumption of the normality of the family as the focal point of state welfare (as something that contributed to welfare and as something to be maintained by welfare provision). Williams has pointed to the ways in which social movements around 'race' and gender developed complex critiques of state welfare:

> the struggles of many of these groups against relations of dominance have themselves focused on welfare provision. . .What was also important about these social movements was that they were not simply concerned with the distributional politics of welfare, but with the very way welfare was organised. Racism and sexism operate at state, institutional and personal levels and in so far as these specific movements struck a new universal demand it was over who controlled

welfare and in whose interests. In these terms the campaigns of the Women's Movement not only linked conditions within the private sphere of domestic and personal relations but also sought to replace the bureaucratic and professionally controlled relations of welfare with non-hierarchical, non-sexist, non-racist relationships where users of welfare exercised control over the nature and delivery of welfare services. (1994: 64)

Similar challenges were developed in relation to disability and sexuality, again insisting on the *social* character of such identities and refusing the dependent and pathologised statuses attributed by biological or psychological essentialism and enshrined in social policy (see, for example, Carabine, 1992; Oliver, 1990; Oliver and Barnes, 1991). The cumulative effect of such challenges, sometimes referred to as the 'new social movements' (Pierson, 1993, ch. 3), might be seen as the 'return of the repressed' in social policy. Those elements of social relations which had been expelled to the realm of the natural in the structuring assumptions of welfare provision became the focus for collective social action aimed not just at the enlargement of social welfare but at the transformation of its principles of provision and delivery. In the process, the ideological assumptions of social policy were exposed, challenged and, at points, modified.

As the above quotation from Williams suggests, these challenges also called into question the nature of the welfare state's neutrality as embodied in its bureau-professional organisational regimes. Critics argued that this neutrality did not extend to the sexual division of labour nor the racialised structuring of social relations. Equally, it was not impartial in relation to disablement or sexuality. Each of these dimensions of inequality and division had been ideologically consigned to the realm of the extra-social: they were simply the more or less unfortunate effects of nature. The struggles to re-socialise them opened up new dimensions of bias, partiality and discrimination to critical attention. Instead of neutrality, both the formal and informal rules of bureaucracies and the practices of professionalism were revealed as contributing to the production and reproduction of power and inequality. Policy formation and implementation, employment practices and the characteristic organisational cultures of welfare institutions were all implicated (Newman and Williams, 1995).

These challenges bore particularly on the 'front lines' of state welfare, even though they were also directed at the commanding heights of policy making. Welfare workers, by virtue of the fact that they carried the day to day contact between the people and the state, were prone to being captured or coopted by these 'challenges from the margins' and their demands for greater equity or redress (e.g., Taylor, 1993). Welfare professionalism was at least partially open to the attempts by the new social movements to socialise definitions of social problems, and became one of the sites in which issues about 'discrimination', 'empowerment' and inequalities of different kinds were played out. The effects were unevenly distributed: professions based in more essentialist conceptions of problems, such as medicine, proved relatively impervious by comparison with occupations like social work. The results were often limping and uneasy compromises: 'matching' black clients with black workers; multi-culturalist policies; commitments to 'anti-discriminatory practice'; bureaucratised equal opportunities statements and so on. Nevertheless, the crisis of the social penetrated deeply into the organisational and occupational worlds of the 'old' welfare state.

Indeed, the crisis of the 'external' settlements – political–economic and social – imploded into the organisational settlement, making it a central site for the playing out of the multiple problems and conflicts. The way in which state practices had come to reinforce a thoroughly racialised and patriarchal set of norms, embedded in legislation, regulations and professional practice, was exposed. Internal tensions were magnified as welfare organisations attempted to adapt to or compromise with such challenges – expressed in the search for and struggles over feminist, multi-cultural, anti-racist, anti-homophobic or non-discriminatory forms of welfare practice. Some of these tensions involved splits within the bureau-professional regime itself, as professionals were seen to be vulnerable to excessive 'client-centredness' and in need of tighter organisational regulation and control (see Johnson, 1973, on the characteristic tensions of mediating professions).

This collapse of trust in the neutrality of bureau-professional regimes of state welfare intersected with other emerging tensions. Although they overlap, it is convenient to separate these into internal and external problems. From the outside, bureaucracy was coming to be defined as an inappropriate and inefficient organisational form – ill-adapted to the demands of complexity and change in the modern world. By the time the state sector had discovered 'corporate management' as an approach to coordinating large scale organisational forms in the early 1970s, the avant-garde of business management was already looking to new ways of organising enterprises. At a more popular level, welfare bureaucracies were increasingly being perceived as both inefficient and impersonal. Welfare professionalism was coming under attack for its detachment from the 'real world'. Trendy theories and liberal or permissive values were seen as eroding both effectiveness and social authority. Teachers were castigated for their adoption of 'child-centred' teaching methods and social workers for their inability to prevent child abuse tragedies.

The complaints about welfare bureau-professionalism were generated from very divergent starting points and addressed very different problems. It has become conventional wisdom to assimilate these challenges to a 'consumerist' critique of the impersonality and lack of choice offered by welfare agencies. In our view, this does a profound disservice to the diversity of popular disenchantment with the welfare state – and feeds rather too conveniently into the New Right's appropriation of that disenchantment. The challenges to the welfare state involved arguments about access, power, rights, levels of benefits and services, the conditions under which they were provided, questions of structural bias and inequality as well as the forms of service delivery. The consumerist critique also underestimates the internal sources of tension in the bureau-professional regime. The shift from growth to restraint in welfare agencies in the 1970s, combined with growing criticisms of and demands on these agencies, unsettled the compromises between bureaucratic and professional modes of coordination. Professionalism continued to develop new and expansive agendas of intervention (such as the emergent commitment to anti-discriminatory practice in social work, 'access' in education or the development of new medical technologies) while administrative concerns with control were intensified by new problems of disciplining professional autonomy (the bureaucratisation of social work intervention in child abuse as part of 'defensive practice', for example). At the same time, bureau-professional regimes also proved to be relatively weak institutional arrangements for the exercise of the fiscal discipline thought to be needed after 1976. Hoggett argues that because the welfare state was a 'mongrel' organisation, based on an uneasy marriage between a pre-Fordist craft (professional) productive system and a Taylorised (rational-bureaucratic administrative) system, it proved relatively weak in its attempts to keep state spending under control.

> it was precisely because human services were so difficult to rationalise, that, if costs were to be kept under some kind of control, the need to rationalise them was so great. But the attempt to control professional service workers in this way was almost doomed to failure, given the discrepancy between bureaucratic and professional modes of control. (1994: 42–3)

Attempts to impose such discipline frequently provoked increasing lines of internal fracture, especially between administrators and professionals. Such shifts exposed tensions between professional discretion and administrative control more explicitly. These tensions were overlaid with the effects of the decline of political neutrality both at national and local level, producing new conflicts over the direction of welfare policy and the control of its implementation.

The truces between political representation, bureaucratic administration and professional discretion which formed the uneasy but stable condition of the organisational settlement of the post-war welfare regime were becoming de-stabilised in the face of the complex pressures of public spending restraint, growing politicisation, increasing social diversity and challenges to the neutrality of representations of the public and its needs. The effect of these multiple tendencies was to produce 'the crisis of the welfare state' – not merely in the collapse of the political consensus but in the intersection of crises in all three settlements: political-economic, social and organisational. The conditions of crisis – in the reshaping of the world economy, the collapse of the Keynesian consensus and the break-up of the social settlement – can be seen as organic features: the consequence of long standing tensions and contradictions which were integral to the character of the post-war welfare state. Nevertheless, it is the way in which these conditions disrupted the organisational settlement by the late 1970s that marked it out as the conjunctural focus of the reconstruction of social welfare in the 1980s and 1990s. The bureau-professional regime of the old welfare institutions emerged as the major battleground for the new welfare order.

'Speaking for the people': the New Right and the welfare state

The special contribution of the New Right in Britain was to tell a particular
– and particularly effective – story about these conditions of crisis and to lay
the ground for the reconstruction of the relationship between the state and
social welfare. This story was constructed around three central themes: the
costs of state welfare, the effects of state welfare and the problem of the
welfare state itself. These themes embody different strands of New Right
ideology: neo-liberalism and its revival of economic individualism, and neo-
conservatism with its commitment to the revitalisation of traditional morality and social authority (Clarke, 1991: ch. 6; Hall, 1988; Levitas, 1986).
Neo-liberal economics in Britain and the USA stressed the supremacy of
markets as mechanisms of social distribution of goods, services and
incomes. From this point of view, the state represented an unnatural
intrusion into the workings of the market. The state distorted markets in
three main ways. The growing levels of personal and corporate taxation
needed to sustain the activities of the state (and the level of public debt)
were identified as an inhibition to competitiveness and enterprise in the
nation, individual companies and individuals. Excessive taxation (described
as 'theft' by some neo-liberal economists) had the effect of stifling enterprise. Markets were further distorted by the state's role as an employer of
labour (taking people away from 'wealth creating jobs'), by its excessive
regulation of labour markets, guaranteeing unreasonable employment rights
or setting wage levels and finally by the state's provision of welfare benefits
at levels which created a disincentive to taking paid employment.

This neo-liberal critique of the economic costs of welfare also informed
the assault on public services as monopoly providers through the development of what has become known as public choice theory (see, for example,
Niskanen, 1971). The monopoly position of state providers was viewed as
denying users of such services the opportunity to exercise customer choice.
State monopolies – whether public utilities such as gas and water or welfare
services such as housing and education – were contrasted with the dynamic
and enterprising qualities of markets in which competition would guarantee
effective choice for consumers. The public choice critique of state provision
draws attention to a combination of political and organisational factors
which were seen as distorting the market for public goods and producing an
inefficient use of public resources. It focused the growing concern about the
costs of welfare, but also contributed to the second theme of the New Right
story – the neo-conservative attack on pernicious effects of the welfare state
itself.

While the citizen as taxpayer (and ratepayer) was being subjected to
excessive levels of taxation to pay for the welfare state, and the citizen as
consumer was being denied effective choice in service provision, the other
citizen – the one dependent on welfare services and benefits – was being
demonised as a 'scrounger', using public handouts to avoid responsibility
(Clarke, 1996c). The scrounger has been through a number of incarnations

during the 1980s and 1990s – at one point, the term refers to 'lone parents' encouraged in their sexual fecklessness by state support, and at another to the demoralised 'underclass'. The scrounger is an image in which neo-liberal and neo-conservative strands of New Right thinking meet. Neo-liberalism views the scrounger as the inevitable product of levels of welfare benefits that fail to provide incentives to work by not being set sufficiently below prevailing labour market wages. In these circumstances, the rational 'economic man' will make the simple and predictable calculation that it is better not to work. This calculative assumption has been developed more widely in the idea of the 'perverse incentives' or 'moral hazard' of welfare benefits (Parker, 1982), which implies that where situations are insured against by the existence of benefits, they are more likely to occur – such that providing benefits that support lone parents makes women more likely to choose to be lone mothers. At the same time, neo-conservative critics of state welfare developed a view about the demoralising effects of welfare provision which overlaps with neo-liberalism but places a greater emphasis on the collapse of culture or morality resulting from state welfare (Murray, 1984, 1990). In this view, a traditional morality which placed a premium on personal and familial responsibilities had been undermined by the expectation that the state will provide, producing the demoralised underclass or the 'dependency culture'. The collapse or disorganisation of the family (and of gender roles within the family) is seen as a further effect of this state-driven process of demoralisation.

The New Right in Britain and the USA amalgamated these different strands of critique (sometimes in rather contradictory and unstable ways) to produce a potent challenge to the post-war consensus and the symbolic place of the welfare state within it (Clarke, 1991: ch. 6; Langan and Clarke, 1993b). In the process, they targeted the welfare state as an active agency in the process of national decline, rather than simply an economic drain on the country's resources. This was conducted through a sustained dismantling of the 'neutrality' of the organisational regime of the welfare state. Bureaucrats were identified as actively hostile to the public – hiding behind the impersonality of regulations and 'red tape' to deny choice, building bureaucratic empires at the expense of providing service, and insulated from the 'real world' pressures of competition by their monopolistic position. Professionals were arraigned as motivated by self-interest, exercising power over would-be customers, denying choice through the dubious claim that 'professionals know best'. Worse still, welfare professionals were often the product of 1960s and 1970s 'liberalism' which was viewed as undermining personal responsibility and family authority and as prone to trendy excesses such as egalitarianism, anti-discrimination policies, moral relativism or child-centredness. Such attacks undercut the implicit claim of the 1945 organisational settlement that the professional bureaucracies of the welfare state could be trusted to represent the 'public interest'.

To these attacks on welfare bureau-professionalism, the neo-conservatives added a continued assault on political representation at the level of the local state – most developed in the demonisation of municipal socialism as the 'loony left' but more widely in an argument that political dogma and interference undermined the possibility of efficiently run local services. During the 1980s, tight financial controls were combined with the abolition of particularly troubling local authorities (the GLC and metropolitan counties) and the gradual erosion of local authority control over a range of services. The identification of political 'dogma' as a problem points to a distinctive ideological paradox at the heart of the New Right. Committed as it was to the overthrow of consensus politics, the New Right created the most self-consciously ideological and dogmatic politics in the post-war period. At the same time, its populist character – in particular its claim to be rooted in 'common-sense' – allowed it to speak as if others were dogmatically political (Hall and Jacques, 1983). The New Right continually positioned itself throughout the 1980s and 1990s on the side of the people 'against the state', even though it has been in government throughout that period.

This anti-statist character of New Right ideology highlights the way in which it has consistently treated the institutions of the post-war state as a problem to be overcome – or as a potential blockage to the remaking of Britain as a competitive and enterprising society. The welfare state – in all its national and local complexity – represented a series of institutional points of connection between citizens and social democracy. However flawed the practice might have been, these points of connection were deeply embedded in the imagery of the nation. Such imagery was uneven, but nevertheless formed a non-marketised (or de-commodified) field of symbolism and relationships in which social democratic notions of 'citizenship' and collectivist views of society were enmeshed.

In addition, public service workers at all levels formed a potential political force – identified with the state in terms of their careers, occupational and social ideologies and likely voting patterns. Collectively, such employees were unlikely to be sympathetic to a New Right project of 'rolling back the state', either from narrow self-interest or from their ideological commitments to the state as an embodiment of public service or agency of social progress. In the USA, neo-conservative critics argued that public service bureau-professionals formed a 'new class', using the state to pursue their class interests against the 'people'.[2] In Britain, the terms of condemnation were usually less elevated, but particular hostility was reserved for the liberal welfare professions staffed from the expansion of higher education in the late 1960s and 1970s.

These issues serve as a reminder that the New Right programme of transforming the welfare state was never simply a question of how to cut the costs of public spending or make services more responsive and efficient. It was also directed at the organisational regimes of the welfare state because they constituted a field of relationships and symbolism that embodied (in bricks and mortar as well as 'vocations') an alternative social formation to that being pursued by the New Right. Conservative political and ideological hostility to the welfare state as an institutional articulation of social democracy meant that the 'crisis of welfare' was also necessarily a 'crisis of the organisational regime'. The financial discipline of controlling public spending would never, by itself, be enough to unlock this particular blockage. The state itself needed to be restructured.

Notes

[1] It should be noted that the 'welfare state' was a political *representation* not an organisational reality, since the welfare state was embodied in practice in a number of state agencies (departments or ministries) and in different tiers of the state, particularly in the distribution of responsibilities between the central and local state (see Cochrane, 1993b).

[2] This argument drew heavily on Djilas's writings about state bureaucracies in communist societies (Djilas, 1957).

2

Towards the Managerial State?

The New Right attempted to resolve the crisis of the welfare state through a continuous programme of reconstruction. Its effects were to change both the character and content of social welfare, and the institutional forms of the state. These changes have tended to be analysed separately, reflecting the focus of different specialisms. As a consequence, this chapter explores both the 'welfare' focus of social policy and the 'institutional' focus of public administration and management. Nevertheless, the programme of reconstruction has not just changed these twin elements of welfare and the state, it has also changed the relationship *between* them. This remade relationship underlies contemporary public and academic discussions about whether it is still possible to speak of a 'welfare state' in Britain. The problem of how to make sense of these complex – and contradictory – processes of change is the main focus of this chapter.

Welfare without the state?

Studies of social policy during the 1980s and 1990s have emphasised a strikingly diverse series of changes involved in the restructuring of the welfare state. Some studies of these have stressed the social objectives of New Right social policy – in particular the intensification of inequalities. For example, Johnson argues that 'inequality has unquestionably grown under the Conservatives. This has not just happened through drift or as the unintended consequences of policies. Inequality has been used as a deliberate strategy' (1990: 26). Social policy studies have examined different dimensions of the production and reproduction of forms of inequality – the changing nature and social composition of poverty (Oppenheim, 1993), and the impact of policy changes on gendered, racialised and other dimensions of inequality (Williams, 1993). Some commentators have suggested that this has involved a politics of 'two-nation Toryism', with intensified divisions between rich and poor (Hay, 1996: ch. 8; Walker and Walker, 1987). A related focus in social policy has been renewed attention to the politics of policy formation induced by the self-consciously ideological politics of the New Right (see, for example, Deakin, 1994). This has included attention to the ideological assumptions and social objectives of Thatcherite social policies – their views of social inequality, the causes of poverty, their pro-family rhetoric and their free market predilections (e.g., Levitas, 1986; Loney et al., 1986).

These concerns with policy formation and outcomes have been supplemented by a growing interest in the forms of service organisation. The choice between the state or the market posed by New Right ideology and its translation into marketising reforms of welfare services has led to a growing interest in the study of such market or 'quasi-market' arrangements (e.g., Hudson, 1994; Johnson, 1995; Le Grand and Bartlett, 1993). Similarly, attention to ideas about 'welfare pluralism' or the 'mixed economy of welfare' has developed as a means of analysing the diminution of direct service provision by public agencies and the split between public financing of welfare and service provision by agencies located in other sectors (e.g., Glennerster, 1992; Rao, 1996; Wistow et al., 1994). In broad terms, social policy studies of the restructuring of the welfare state have been more focused on the 'welfare' part of this term, rather than the 'state'. With a few exceptions, social policy has been little concerned with the changing nature of the state form during the past two decades. In addition, we might also note that the rise of managerialism – the focus of this book – has been a relatively marginal subject (though with some notable exceptions: Cutler and Waine, 1994; Taylor-Gooby and Lawson, 1993a; Pollitt, 1993). Social policy studies have certainly tracked the changing scale and scope of welfare policy, and its social effects, but the state has tended to be treated as the agency through which New Right policies have been delivered. This reflects the relatively underdeveloped conception of the state in social policy (see also Clarke, 1996b).

There are some significant limitations that result from starting from the vantage point of social policy. Because the primary focus is on welfare policies, changes in the institutional forms and structures of the state and their consequences for policy outcomes have tended to receive less attention. Thus, in the area of income maintenance, most studies have concentrated on the changing levels of and eligibility for benefits, and the social consequences for income distribution. The changing organisational form of the Department of Social Security and the construction of the Benefits Agency are rarely seen as connected to such changes. Where they are addressed, such changes have tended to be treated in the context of specific policy fields: for example, in the creation of internal markets in the NHS or the introduction of contracting in social care. As a consequence, continuities in the restructuring of the state that extend *beyond* its welfare functions tend to be missed. So, the construction of Civil Service Agencies and the introduction of marketised relations and forms of contracting have had impacts across the state as a whole and not simply in social policy. We now turn to analyses of changing organisational forms of the state in order to identify these tendencies.

Remaking state institutions

The main focus of those concerned with public administration and management is on a succession of structural changes. Most studies take a sequential view, with organisational reform (such as the devolution of finance through the Financial Management Initiative – FMI) being followed by broader attempts to bring about cultural change (e.g., Citizen's Charter, consumerism) and with later stages bringing a greater use of market mechanisms (Jervis and Richards, 1995; Metcalfe, 1993; Pollitt, 1993). The first wave of reform, dominant in the 1980s, was concerned with improving the efficiency of public services within the existing 'planning' framework. The reforms were directed to overcoming the deficits of the bureaucratic model, and included the introduction of devolved budgeting and management in the Civil Service, rate capping in local authorities and attempts to strengthen management control in the NHS by the introduction of general management.

Many accounts have distinguished between this early stage of reforming the machinery of government and the later, market-based phases of reform. Markets were introduced in a variety of ways, including direct privatisation, contracting out selected services and the introduction of charging for services. More recently there have been the development of a range of partnerships between private and public sectors in joint ventures, and the capitalisation of new ventures through the Private Finance Initiative. Where this has included the outsourcing not only of support services (cleaning, catering) but of core services (such as nursing) the result has been 'a significant blurring of the boundary between public and private sectors' (Jervis and Richards, 1995: 6).

Such accounts draw attention to the way in which government thinking has evolved, and suggest the importance of the dynamic interplay between policy changes and successive attempts to reform the machinery of government. However, a problem with such sequential analysis is that it can tend to underplay the continuity of earlier themes (especially the overriding focus on controlling costs) in the later stages. Attempts to periodise complex change also mask some of the differences in the reforms process in specific sectors (the Civil Service, NHS, local government and so on). Managerialism has been a central thread in these changes, taking on different inflections in each of these 'stages' and processes. For example, Pollitt views the initial period of changes in the UK, characterised by cost control and decentralised management, as underpinned by a 'neo-Taylorist' form of managerialism:

> The central thrust, endlessly reiterated in official documents, is to set clear targets, to develop performance indicators to measure the achievement of those targets, and to single out, by means of merit awards, those individuals who get 'results'. The strengthening and incentivising of line management is a constant theme. . . . In official terms, what seems to be required is a culture shift of a kind that will facilitate a more thoroughgoing functional/neo-Taylorist management process. (1993: 56)

Pollitt views the later reforms as a 're-evaluation' of neo-Taylorism, leading to the introduction of quasi markets, a greater emphasis on decentralisation, a constant emphasis on the need to improve quality, and insistence on greater attention being given to meeting the wishes of the individual service users. Much of this explicitly drew on the work of Peters and Waterman (1982) and other management writers who established some of the main directions of what has become known as the 'new managerialism'. As the application of market mechanisms became the dominant strand of reform, managerialism as an array of business techniques came to be seen as offering the possibilities of creating 'public entrepreneurship' (Osborne and Gaebler, 1992).

Pollitt and others have described the later stages of reform in terms of a shift towards what has been (often confusingly) termed a 'New Public Management' which is contrasted with 'old' public administration. The features of this are summarised by Dunleavy and Hood (1994: 9) as follows:

- Reworking budgets to be transparent in accounting terms, with costs attributed to outputs not inputs, and outputs measured by quantitative performance indicators.
- Viewing organisations as a chain of low cost principal/agent relationships (rather than fiduciary or trustee-beneficial ones), network of contracts linking incentives to performance.
- Disaggregating separable functions into quasi-contractual or quasi-market forms, particularly by introducing purchaser/provider distinctions, replacing previously unified functional planning-and-provision structures.
- Opening up provider roles to competition between agencies or between public agencies, firms, and not-for-profit bodies.
- Deconcentrating provider roles to the minimum feasible sized agency, allowing users more scope to 'exit' from one provider to another, rather than relying on 'voice' options to influence how public service provision affects them.

These changes are seen by Dunleavy and Hood in terms of two overall shifts in the 'design co-ordinates' of public sector organisations: the first being a shift in the degree to which the public sector is distinctive from the private; and the second a change in the extent to which the discretionary powers of managers are limited by uniform and general rules of procedure. Both these shifts have important implications both for the making of welfare policy and for the recipients of social welfare. For example, the devolution of 'discretionary' management responsibility, linked to tight budgets, highlights the problems of rationing and choice in service delivery, especially in the NHS. Unfortunately, while there are some interesting exceptions (e.g., Jervis and Richards, 1996) most studies of institutional change have tended to be the mirror image of the social policy approach that we discussed earlier. Where social policy has focused on welfare reform but has underplayed the remaking of the structures of the state, this focus on the remaking of the machinery and processes of government has had little to say about its policy consequences. Evaluations of the New Public Management from within the public administration traditions have tended to focus on the benefits or drawbacks of these, and other, design changes for the *delivery* of public services. One recent survey of welfare changes concluded that 'a system based upon the practices and values of public administration is being replaced by a new set of practices and values, based upon a language of welfare delivery which emphasises efficiency and value for money, competition and markets, consumerism and customer care' (Butcher, 1995: 161). The problem here is that these systems 'based on practices and values' are separated from the content and character of the welfare services that they deliver. So for all the examination of greater efficiency or better operational management, it is difficult to see these reforms as linked to a massive rise in the numbers of people living in poverty, growing health inequalities, increasing homelessness or any of the other indicators of deepening welfare problems.

Post-Fordism: state restructuring with a mission?

There has been one influential – though much criticised – line of analysis which promises to overcome this split between changes in welfare policy and the institutional restructuring of the state. This is the attempt to develop and apply analyses of the transition to a post-Fordist economy to the changes in the welfare state (e.g., Burrows and Loader, 1994). This approach locates such changes in the global tendencies towards the greater internationalisation of economic production and distribution. It identifies the development of new organisational forms of corporate enterprise and labour processes intended to overcome the constraints and contradictions of Fordist systems. The state is implicated in these trends in a number of ways. For example, Jessop (1993, 1994) has drawn a distinction between the old Keynesian Welfare State (KWS) and the (possibly) emergent Schumpeterian Workfare State (SWS), which he identifies as having the potential to form 'the best possible shell' for post-Fordist economic development (1993: 7). The SWS is characterised as having a commitment to promoting innovation, flexibility and economic competitiveness and its social policies are subordinated to economic objectives. It promotes market development and market forms and its welfare agenda is subordinated to the interests of capital:

> the transition to a post-Fordist paradigm is prompting a reorientation of the state's primary economic functions. For the combination of the late Fordist trend towards internationalisation and the post-Fordist stress on flexible production has encouraged states to focus on the supply-side problem of international competitiveness and to attempt to subordinate welfare policy to the demands of flexibility. (1994: 26–7)

Pitched at this general level and informed by references to examples of marketising reforms or the promotion of labour flexibility, the post-Fordist explanation of change looks relatively plausible. So, too, does the claim that the nation state is being progressively 'hollowed out' by a double movement of power away from it – on the one hand by decentralising forces towards regional and local institutions and on the other hand by the appropriation of power by supranational institutions such as the European Union (Peters, 1993; Rhodes, 1994).

Such arguments have been explored in relation to both local government (e.g., Stoker, 1989, 1990; see also Cochrane, 1993b, ch. 5) and the National Health Service (Harrison et al., 1992; Mohan, 1995: ch. 2) as examples of new organisational systems which have moved away from highly integrated and bureaucratic service structures. However, the pattern of change is not as simple as the post-Fordist argument suggests. While there are clearly examples of tendencies which have shifted power to supra-national organisations and institutions and those which have embodied decentralisation producing a 'hollowing out' of the nation state, there are contradictory trends towards the greater centralisation of some forms of power. Control over public spending and the resourcing of welfare services has been increasingly tightened at the level of central government subject to increased Treasury influence (see Deakin and Parry, 1993). Similar issues can be raised in the context of the creation of a national curriculum and the aggregation of other powers in the hands of the Secretary of State for Education (Fergusson, 1994) and the more general (if unstable) distinction between 'policy' and 'operational management' associated with the creation of Civil Service Agencies.

Attention to decentralising tendencies needs to be balanced by an examination of contradictory movements, which raise issues about the nature of devolved power in the current shape of public services. While not wanting to go as far as Taylor-Gooby and Lawson's argument that 'Power over the essentials is retained centrally while management of inessentials is decentralised' (1993b: 133) since it assumes that what is essential is known in advance, we share their stress on the *tendency* to centralisation that has been visible in social and public policy. In addition, the structures *through* which power has been decentralised or devolved have not remained untouched. Indeed the traditional intermediate institutions of the local state have been much reduced and, to a large extent, supplanted by new forms of control: particularly non-elected boards and agencies (TECs, Trusts, Housing Associations, etc.). These changes raise questions about the nature of state power as it is exercised through indirect rather than direct agency.

A related strand in the application of post-Fordism to state restructuring has emphasised the changing *organisational forms* of the state. This has stressed the role of new technologies of control in creating new organisational structures which may be analogous to the move from Fordist to post-Fordist forms of organising production (e.g., Hoggett, 1990). There are, however, difficulties associated with this analysis. One concerns the designation of old welfare state forms as 'bureaucratic monoliths', constructed by Murray (1991) as the analogy between Fordist mass production and consumption and state welfare. It is, we think, highly arguable whether the welfare state was ever Fordist (except possibly by virtue of existing in

Fordist economies). Certainly, many of its organisational structures and labour processes remained resolutely pre- or non-Fordist (Clarke, 1996a; Mohan, 1995: ch. 2; Rustin, 1994). Equally, we are not persuaded that the delivery of *universalist* welfare services can be constructed as an equivalent to *mass* consumption. Such services involved the elaborate construction of complex forms of differentiation and categorisation of users, needs and 'treatments'. Cochrane has drawn attention to the problems that this recognition of complex labour processes poses for those who would construct an analogy between Fordist industrial production and welfare delivery:

> Superficially, the analogy is quite attractive, but there is a real danger of exaggerating the significance of a metaphor of this sort which does not hold up very well under sustained scrutiny . . . A key point about 'street level bureaucrats' – to borrow Lipsky's eloquent phrase – such as teachers and social workers, is precisely that they are expected to make judgements based on individual discretion where bureaucratic rules do not apply very well. They are trapped between their 'clients' and their 'employers', with only their 'professionalism' to pull them through. The detailed differences and discretion make it difficult to process people en masse, according to rational-bureaucratic rules. (1993b: 85)

We would want to argue that the processes of restructuring have involved attempts to realign a series of relationships – between the state and the citizen; between the state and the economy; and between the state and its institutional or organizational forms (including its labour processes). Even if these realignments take place in the context of a global recomposition of capitalism, it remains necessary to understand their specific national and political conditions, processes and outcomes rather than treat them as epiphenomenal reflections of 'deep' processes elsewhere (see also Mohan, 1995: ch. 1). The analyses of post-Fordism point to significant issues and tendencies. However, these need to be assessed alongside other (and potentially contradictory) directions in the recomposition of the British state. We would suggest that one central task for the analysis of the new welfare order is to understand the contradictory movements that have been taking place.

Post-Fordist analyses have tended to be relatively selective in the welfare policy examples that they use – stressing those with obvious labour market or economic objectives. However, this tends to leave more complex and contradictory reforms out of the picture or to reduce them to simple cost-saving or privatising measures. As a result, little attention is given to the issue of the tensions between neo-liberal and neo-conservative social agendas articulated around the competing conceptions of freedom and discipline. So the Child Support Agency might be seen as framed by multiple objectives: the reduction of welfare costs; the regulation of deviant family forms; and the restoration of parental responsibility and patriarchal norms via the agency of the state. As Fiona Williams (1994) and others have argued, post-Fordist analyses seem to have difficulty remembering that there are social relations other than class and that these have a specific bearing on the welfare state and the forms of its reconstruction.

One dominant concept for talking about post-Fordist shifts in the form of the state and its associated organisational forms has been that of 'fragmentation'. This refers to the breaking up of large scale and integrated corporate structures into new forms of core–periphery elements and to processes of externalisation through sub-contracting. Like other post-Fordist concepts such as 'flexibility', we find fragmentation a little imprecise (Sayer and Walker, 1992: ch. 5). Fragmentation unites a number of processes (decentralisation, delegation, devolution, sub-contracting, and more) in an overly general category. As a result, it is difficult to see anything but fragmentation (just as the world is now full of flexibilities). But fragmentation as a concept gives a specific weight to *centrifugal* directions – the processes of splitting away from the centre (whether the nation state or the corporate 'core'). It leaves open the issue of how such fragments are integrated – or what *centripetal* processes are involved (see Hoggett, 1996).

We think it may be more useful to descibe these movements as *dispersal* rather than fragmentation. The concept of dispersal signals such processes as the effect of strategic calculation rather than inevitable occurrences. These are processes through which 'agency' is being distributed from and by a strategic centre. The state delegates – through a variety of means – its authority to subaltern organisations that thus are empowered to act *on its behalf*. The idea of dispersal does not carry the intrinsically disintegrative connotations of fragmentation. The effects of dispersal may well be perceived and experienced as fragmentation and disintegration of services and institutions, but that is not the same as identifying the process. Dispersal draws attention to the relations of power that both underpin and act through these processes, not least the means by which the centre attempts to maintain command while distributing power to the periphery. This stress on the 'relations of power' means that it is necessary to examine not just what sorts of power are held in different places but also what the flows of power are that allocate positions and places in this field. It may, for example, be possible to trace the shifts in who exercises different types of decision-making power in specific policy fields (e.g., Winstanley et al., 1995). However, such redistributions need to be contextualised in the larger field of relations between the state and its empowered agent.

Power flows: reconstructing and traversing boundaries

These processes of dispersal can be seen in the shift to a more 'mixed economy' of welfare with expanded roles for the private, voluntary and informal sectors. In most social policy analysis, the idea of a mixed economy of welfare has tended to emphasise the boundaries that differentiate the sectors. Most analyses of community care policy have stressed the reduction in direct provision by local authority social services departments and the accompanying growth in the provision by other sectors – with local authorities playing a purchasing or commissioning role in relation to these service providers. The concentration on sectors allows the movement *outwards* of tasks, duties and responsibilities from the state to other agencies to be traced. However it pays less attention to the new relationships and new flows of power that are constructed in these processes. What from one angle can be viewed as the diminution of the state's role can be seen from another as the extension of state power, but through new and unfamiliar means. At its crudest, this involves new relations of financial regulation – evidenced by the anxieties of the commercial residential care sector or by the fears in the voluntary sector about dependency induced by participation in the 'contract culture' (Lewis, 1993).

More elaborately, it raises questions about the nature of power exercised through regulation, contracting, monitoring and surveillance. These are not just technical arrangements, specified in statutes, contracts or service level agreements between different agencies. They are also the means through which inter-organisational relationships are ordered and conducted and within which power is exercised. While the rhetoric of diminishing direct public provision may stress the 'independence' of non-state providers, the relationships that are involved in acting as sub-contracted or delegated agents of the state produce an *expansion* of state power. Waine has argued that the expanded role for voluntary organisations involved tensions between their 'desirable' features and the emergent pattern of relationships:

> Of central importance is the objective of directly linking both the volume and character of public funding [to the voluntary sector] to the priorities of government departments ... The consequences of these trends for many voluntary organisations were that receipt of government funding, on terms determined by government, distorted their objectives ... [T]he use of contracts is likely to have contradictory results, as they will favour groups which are large and well organised. The structures of such groups will need to adapt to the contract culture, which will require the input of expertise and professional knowledge. Opportunities for volunteers, both on management committees and in service provision, may be severely restricted. (1992: 84–6)

It is worth noting the significance of Waine's reference to the need for voluntary groups to be 'well organised', since this involves expectations that voluntary sector organisations will adapt themselves to the new requirements of 'being businesslike' in relation to contracting, developing their internal accounting and management capabilities (Charlesworth et al., 1996; Waine, 1992: 82–3). The more general point is that treating sectoral boundaries as if they were essential and unchanging features of the landscape of welfare provision risks missing the dynamics of changing internal and inter-organisational relationships (see also Mackintosh, 1995a).

There are also problems about changing definitions of what the term public sector means in such mixed economies. The public sector itself now embodies a range of functions and forms which range from semi-autonomous organisations (Agencies, Trusts, etc.) involved in service delivery to 'enabling' or 'purchasing' activities. Sometimes, such functions have been organisationally separated (as in the distinction between purchasers and providers in the NHS) but elsewhere purchasing and provision may be located within the same agency (in Social Services Departments or 'Fund

Holding' General Practitioners). Even if we treat public provision as one sector in a new mixed economy, there remain questions about the relationship *between* the state and public sector provision. The concept of the mixed economy requires a notion of a state which organises or directs the balance and structure of relationships of state and non-state institutions. It might be more appropriate to think of the mixed economy as a 'structure in dominance' in which one element of the combination (the state) both performs its own functions (purchasing and providing through the public sector) and allocates the places of other elements (sectors) within the combination. The 'managerial state' involves all of these elements, and requires us to think in terms of a field of power relations and not just the distribution of tasks or functions between sectors. The new form of state is not just about the organisational systems through which services are delivered. It involves reconfigurations of power in the pattern of provision, and changing definitions of individual and collective responsibility, which lie at the core of the policy changes themselves. Changing notions of 'public' and 'private' are at the heart of these shifts and exemplify the ways in which relationships traverse boundaries between different sectors.

Reconfiguring the 'public' and the 'private'

There are a number of different meanings of public and private that circulate in contemporary political debate. For example, in relation to the production and delivery of welfare services, these terms have tended to be used as references to different economic sectors – where the 'public' stands for state institutions and the 'private' for commercial enterprises. However, in other areas of policy debate the public and the private are distinguished by reference to the inside and outside of the family. Thus, 'private' is used to refer to the sphere of the household, comprising family relationships, roles and responsibilities, while the public realm is that which is external to the family (including all the other 'sectors'). We think it is worth distinguishing between three forms of changes in the relationship between 'public' and 'private' in the restructuring of welfare policy and provision which are associated with the idea of privatisation. First, there is privatisation as the direct sale of public assets to the private/commercial sector, as in the case of public utilities like gas, water and electricity (Swann, 1988). This has not been the model for social welfare restructuring, despite exploratory considerations of privatising the pension system, for example. However, aspects of welfare services have been privatised through sub-contracting in various forms and through the sponsored expansion of markets for the personal (or corporate) purchase of benefits and services in pensions and health care. It has, though, performed a significant ideological function, providing a reference point against which welfare reforms have been measured. Such assessments have ranged from neo-liberal complaints about the 'failure' to privatise sufficiently to social democratic warnings of 'creeping' privatisation.

The second form of 'privatisation' can be found in the processes of undermining the boundaries between public and private sectors by means of sponsored competition and restructuring. Such changes form the core of the arguments around whether the NHS has been privatised. It has not, in the first sense of privatisation; but the changes in competition, trading rules, financing and organisational structures have had the effect of blurring the boundaries between public and private. In part, these are the result of introducing marketising or pseudo-competitive relationships into service provision, but they are also the consequence of isomorphic injunctions that public sector organisations should learn to 'become businesslike' in more general terms (Cutler and Waine, 1994; Pollitt, 1993). These processes have been intensified by more recent developments such as the Private Finance Initiative which enable or encourage more forms of public–private 'partnership' and the loosening of trading rules so as to allow NHS trusts to offer private health care packages (1996). This second sense of privatisation involves a degree of *de-differentiation* – a reduction, though not necessarily removal, of some of the distinctions between the state and the market (or the public and private sectors) through the requirement that public organisations come to behave 'as if' they were commercial corporate entities.

The third, and rather different, sense of privatisation is the shift of responsibilities from public to private understood as the familial domain (or the 'informal sector'). This is most visible in the fields of health and social care where the family or the community has been expected to take on a greater role in the provision of care (see, for example, Brown and Smith, 1993). In these changes it is now well established that the community-as-carer has primarily meant the family, and that within the family the gendered division of labour has meant that caring work has primarily fallen on women as mothers, daughters and wives. This is an important reminder that, in addition to pursuing neo-liberal economic and social policies, the New Right in both Britain and the USA has also been profoundly influenced by neo-conservative obsessions with restoring the traditional family (Clarke, 1991: ch. 6).

This meaning of privatisation is also part of a wider agenda about the transfer of resources (via taxation policies), choices (empowering the welfare consumer) and duties (enforcing parental responsibilities) away from the state to the private realm of the family. This too cannot be understood as movement in a single direction: it is more than a shift towards expanded roles for the family and reduced responsibilities for the state. The redrawing of the public/private distinction in the 1980s and 1990s has also produced greater state involvement in the private domain. The shift of responsibilities to families has been accompanied by the subjection of households to greater state surveillance, regulation and intervention. For example, the Child Support Act, while being rhetorically defined as making parents 'responsible', has also created an apparatus of investigation and regulation. The 'criminalisation' of parents of delinquent children through the 1991 Criminal Justice Act has subjected familial relations to judicial intervention. The integration of 'primary carers' into the organisation of community care is not just a transfer of tasks and responsibilities to the private realm of the family. It also brings carers and their household arrangements into the realm of state assessment, evaluation and surveillance. Like the dual movements of centralisation and decentralisation in public policy, the reshaping of the public/private divide is a complex, not a simple, process. While the state has withdrawn in some ways, its powers and apparatuses have been extended in others – transferring 'responsibilities' but simultaneously creating the capabilities of surveillance and enforcement to ensure that such responsibilities are being fulfilled.

Analyses of restructuring which emphasise sectoral boundaries between the public and private (in its different forms) may miss the dynamic relationships which both reconfigure and traverse such boundaries. An emphasis on the transfer of tasks, roles and responsibilities outwards from the state risks neglecting the processes by which the dispersal of power in these processes engages these other agents in the state's field of relationships. These dispersals – of tasks, responsibilities and power – have the effect of 'enabling' or 'empowering' different agents to provide social welfare: commercial enterprises, trusts, voluntary organisations, primary carers and so on. But at the same time they subject these agents to new constraints and demands through processes of assessment, contracting and evaluation. The capacity of these agents to act or make choices is not their intrinsic property but an effect of their relationship with the state in which they are both empowered and disciplined.

Managerialised dispersal

Dispersal has been a political strategy for reconstructing both the state itself and the coordination of its welfare functions. It is a strategy that amounts to more than the specific mechanisms through which it has been implemented. The dispersal of power forms a uniting thread that underpins a variety of new systems and mechanisms, linking the introduction of marketising processes, the expansion of other non-state sectors, processes of centralisation and decentralisation and varieties of privatisation and externalisation. Dispersal has meant the simultaneous shrinking of the state and the enlargement of its reach into civil society (through its engagement of non-state agents). As a strategy of state reconstruction, dispersal has realigned relations of power in a complex way. Above all, it has sought to discipline and transform the old institutional sites of power in the state – the bureau-professional regimes of the welfare state.

Dispersal subjected them to forms of power dispersed beyond them – to the citizen-as-consumer empowered to make choices, press demands and be informed about service standards and performance. At the same time, it subjected them to intensified forms of centralised power and control, through tighter fiscal control, new policy directions and an expanding apparatus of audit and evaluation. These vertical reconfigurations of power have been

overlaid with changes in the horizontal axes of inter-organisational relationships. These have increasingly been re-cast in the form of pseudo-
competitive relationships, involving either direct competition for customers
or contracts or indirect performance evaluation systems measuring relative
success in meeting specified objectives. Each organisational agency has thus
been positioned in a new field of forces. The vertical axis aligns agencies as
delegated authorities between the centralised power of the nation state and
the 'consumer' power of the periphery, while subjecting them to more
rigorous forms of financial and performance evaluation. The horizontal axis
characteristically repositions them in a nexus of marketised or quasi-
competitive relationships. Within this field of forces agencies are typically
given the 'freedom to manage' (Birchall et al., 1995; Hoggett, 1996). This
freedom is intended to recruit such agencies to the practice of 'self-
discipline' through the internalisation of financial and performance targets.

The concept of the 'freedom to manage' is a reminder that the coordinating principle of this dispersal is managerialism. Managerialism is the
ideology that makes sense of such dispersed power in a practical way. It
actively seeks 'responsibility' and seeks to further disperse it as a corporate
and individual good. It promises 'transparency' within a complex field of
decision-making. It is committed to the production of 'efficiency' in the
pursuit of super-ordinate objectives. Managerialism represents the cement
that can hold together this dispersed organisational form of the state and, in
its customer orientation, claims to be able to represent and service an
individuated public (see Chapter 6). Managerialism promises to provide the
discipline necessary for efficient organisation, particularly in relation to
welfare professionalism's claims to exercise discretionary judgement. These
promises articulate a new basis for discretion as a managerial rather than
professional prerogative – the freedom to 'do the right thing' (Clarke, 1995;
Clarke and Newman, 1993a).

We have witnessed striking changes in the organisational form of the state
and the way state power works. Much analysis has framed these changes in
terms of the retreat or withdrawal of the state – pointing to a diminished
public sector operating in the context of a mixed economy. In this view, the
state is now mainly conceived of as a combination of policy making and
financing functions increasingly separated from service delivery. Nevertheless, we think it can be argued that far from being shifts towards a 'rolling
back' of the state, these changes involve a 'rolling out' of state power but in
new, dispersed, forms. These new forms both cross and reorganise the
conventional boundaries of public and private (or state and non-state).
Dispersal engages more agencies and agents into the field of state power,
empowering them through its delegatory mechanisms and subjecting them
to processes of regulation, surveillance and evaluation. This process brings
the contemporary state form closer to what might be described as the
Foucauldian conception. It relies less on direct control through state apparatuses of the conventional kind and more on 'productive subjection' through
new discourses and practices. In this sense, the new flows of power resemble

the concept of power as relational and productive developed by Foucault and writers exploring his approach in relation to social and organisational governance (e.g., Rose, 1989).

Nevertheless, it is important to stop and insert a brief health warning. The Foucauldian conception has some dangerous tendencies towards idealism. Too many of the analyses of the productivity of power and discursive subjection have treated such strategies as though they worked rather than as *attempts to achieve* their desired results. It is, we think, important to insist that attempted 'subjections' are not always accomplished and that 'discursive strategies' do not always achieve their objectives. This is an issue at the micro-level (organisations persistently fail to produce the ideal worker and new technologies of control still have a few bugs in the system) and at the macro-level of the state. If this is a new field of state power, it is also a rather unstable one where contradictions and forms of contestation are not resolved simply by being expelled from integrative discourses. The dispersal of power and the development of managerialised coordination are, then, strategies rather than accomplishments. Neither the attempt to delegate responsibility nor the effort to represent decision making as the domain of technocratic managerialism have been entirely successful – particularly, but not only, in the case of the NHS. It is important to recognise that not everyone wishes to be empowered, while others insist that the empowerment being experienced is all too partial. The contradictory consequence of dispersal is that while it aims at the breaking up of the institutionalised centres of power characteristic of the old state form, it also multiplies new sites of potential resistance by increasing the number of decision-making nodal points. Although these are dispersed by contrast with the centralised power exercised at the heart of the state, they are nevertheless open to potential cooption by localised interests and alliances. Dispersal makes the exercise of managerialised power and decision-making unstable in a number of ways.

At one level, the delegation of state power engages a range of agents who are not formally part of the state – associations, groups, corporate entities and individuals who gain part of their new legitimacy precisely from the fact that they are separate from the state. But at the same time, such agents are able to mobilise forms of social power at the points of their intersection with the state. Their power is not simply that delegated by the state but stems from other sources. These range from economic power (in contracting processes especially), through aspects of social or representational power (users' groups, community leaders, the local business world, etc.) to the more or less effective power of individual consumers. This structured instability is sometimes referred to in management texts (particularly public sector management ones) as the issue of 'multiple stakeholders' (e.g., Smith, 1994): those individuals or groups who can make a claim on an organisation's attention or resources. However, we want to insist that this issue needs to be treated as a structural feature of the strategy of dispersal and as a process which is framed by the centralised power of the state. The latter frames the limits of what is negotiable at such nodal points and tends to identify the 'legitimate interests' – or more accurately the *hierarchy* of legitimate interests – that can be taken account of in such negotiations. It is possible to trace the patterns of prioritization that have taken place in the identification of more or less desirable 'partners' with whom the state should work: the private sector, the family, the parent-governor, the consumer and so on (see Cochrane, 1993b). As a result, this new state form is unstable at this intersection of centralised prioritisation and local negotiation.

A further site of instability is to be found in the attempt to discipline the old centres of bureau-professional power. In part this reflects a concern about the vulnerability of 'front-line' workers to the demands of different groups for rights or services. Becoming businesslike was expected to restrain this socialising tendency towards 'ologies and isms' that was visible in the old welfare state. What has emerged is a more complex set of conflicts and compromises that we explore further in Chapters 4 and 5. Here, though, we can note that this potential for instability derives partly from the limitations of managerialism itself. Notwithstanding its penchant for missions and visions, managerialism is essentially a subordinate function, plying its trade in the service of others' super-ordinate goals. As a consequence, it is vulnerable to competing definitions of the service mission that may be articulated by professional groups, user groups or other lay perspectives. Managerialised dispersal may have changed some of the conditions in which the core issues of welfare policy and practice now appear (subjecting them to the requirements of business planning, market positioning and fiscal rectitude). It may also have produced new images of the relationship between welfare services and social differentiation as matters of consumer choice or more 'responsive' organisations (Williams, 1996). Nevertheless, the tensions involved remain potent ones for the organisation of social welfare. In particular, they are the basis for continuing resistance to the conception of an individuated – or consumerised – public as the recipient of welfare services. We return to these issues in Chapters 6 and 7.

In this chapter we have concentrated on the New Right project for restructuring the welfare state that took place during the 1980s and 1990s. We have argued that assessments of these changes must pay attention to the ways in which both social welfare and the state itself were transformed. The strategic dispersal of power that we have highlighted has involved complex realignments of the state and other agencies and has combined the considerable centralisation of power with its decentralisation. Managerialism has played a central role in this restructuring both as an ideology that legitimates the development of new organisational forms and relationships and as the *practical* ideology of being businesslike that promises to make the new arrangements work. While the dominant view of these new arrangements is that they are *dynamic* – able to adapt and respond to change – our view is that they are structurally *unstable*, built around forms of relationships and power that institutionalise new sites of resistance, contestation and contradiction. In the following chapter we examine the ways in which the New Right project of restructuring coalesced with managerialism in the construction of a discourse of change that has driven the remaking of public service organisations.

3

A Change for the Better?
The Tyranny of Transformation

The reconstruction of the state has been shaped by the intersection of two ideologies: those of the New Right and of managerialism. Both have constructed definitions of the problems of the old regime and provided visions of the new. This chapter examines how the articulation of these two ideologies created a discourse about change that announced its necessity and its direction. Ideas of 'transformation', 'revolution', 'reinvention' and 'cultural change' have become a sustained theme in government pronouncements and political rhetoric ever since Thatcherism signalled the displacement of the political left by the political right as the source and agency of radicalism. Old assumptions were to be challenged; old alliances dissolved; old power bases weakened. This was to be accomplished not only through enforced change driven through by government but by winning consent to the idea that change itself was a virtue, necessary for Britain's survival in the emerging global economy, and an essential precondition for its renewal as a nation. A new role for, and new approaches to, management were central to this project:

> Efficient management is the key to the [national] revival . . . And the management ethos must run right through our national life – private and public companies, civil service, nationalised industries, local government, the National Health Service. (Heseltine, 1980, quoted in Pollitt, 1993: vi)

In part, this new role for management derived from the New Right's insistence on the innate superiority of the market over the state as a mechanism of allocation, but this was not the only legitimation. Managerialism was presented as the means through which more rigorous *discipline* could be introduced to the public sector to produce more cost-effective services (and thus limit public spending). This identification of management as being business-like, as the driving force for greater productivity, efficiency or 'value for money' is based on a fairly general conception of management as a progressive social force. Below this level of generality, there are, as Pollitt has observed, a more diverse array of 'middle level' managerialisms:

> While the broad assumptions of managerialism may change only slowly, the more specific content of management thought has developed rather fast. The managerialism of the 1980s and 1990s is therefore not simply a set of broad assumptions about the unique potentials and rights of management. It is also a much more specific set of models of efficient organisational functioning and of techniques

through which such smooth functioning may be realized. There is, then, a middle level to the ideology of managerialism, one subject to variety, controversy and sometimes quite rapid change ... (1993: 11)

What is striking about the 1980s and 1990s is the growing social salience of the general ideology of managerialism and the proliferation of these middle level models. At the general level, managerialism became increasingly influential as more and better management was promoted as the way forward for Western economies experiencing economic decline and stagnation in the face of global change and competition. This general ideology was directed at both private and public sector organisations. It was reflected in the growth of management certification (MBAs, Diplomas, etc.) and the explosion of both inspirational and technical management books, videos and consultancy. The huge stress on remaking management as a practice has served to rescue it from its low public and political valuation. Its current potency might be reflected in the contrasting fortunes of types of social authority. As social scientists were describing a 'post-modern condition' in which traditional forms of authority (monarchies, politicians, professional elites, etc.) were losing public confidence and trust, so managers began to take on public roles as authoritative sources of opinion and advice on how to run the world (not just organisations). Peters and Waterman's *In Search of Excellence* (1982) was reputed to be the best selling management text of all time. Management 'gurus' proliferated, dispensing wisdom not just to other managers but to everyone (and some, such as Sir John Harvey Jones and Charles Handy, even came to have their own TV and radio programmes).

At the same time, managerialism was being revived, if not re-invented, by the emergence of new 'schools', of excellence, culture management, Human Resource Management, Total Quality Management, and re-engineering (to name but a few). Each of these promised a more or less coherent philosophy of and approach to managing and all testified to the potency and rewards of doing management. They changed the face of managers away from their previous image as dull organisational time-servers to those of entrepreneurial and inspirational change agents. Like all good discourses, the new managerialism announced the conditions of its own necessity – elaborating a tale of the failings of the old management and their dire consequences. The new manager was born out of a climate of crisis and disillusionment – located in the start of a long drawn out crisis of US capitalism in the late 1970s and more specifically in its competitive failure in the face of the industrialising Pacific Rim. This climate of American failure was the precondition for the new managerial literature's promise of salvation. It announced the possibility of a way forward which linked the fortunes of the individual manager, the corporation and the nation. The born-again manager could rescue the situation brought about by the failure of the old corporate mentality: the 'playing safe' organisation man; the ossified corporation; and the over-regulatory state produced by the politics of 'corporate liberalism' (Clarke, 1991: ch. 6; Swann, 1988).

The new managerialism promised liberation for managers (at least those who keep the faith) from their past oppressions. It was expressed through an inspirational literature whose rhetoric proclaims that success is achievable by self-transformation from bureaucratic time-server to dynamic leader. This prospect of liberation is echoed in the transformation of corporations from top-heavy and ossified structures to flexible entities driven by values, missions, visions and charismatic personal example. The literature is centred on tales of managerial heroism and the transformational miracles which such heroes have performed in 'turning round' troubled or failing enterprises. Like most theologies it is dogmatic and sectarian, requiring the existence of unbelievers (bureaucrats) and heretics or dissenters (those who fail to see the vision). It also presents its own version of damnation – the fires of business failure. This liberatory rhetoric provided important affinities between the ideology of managerialism and the transformational project of the New Right.

Transforming the state

Managerialism intersected with the New Right project of reshaping state institutions in several ways. Decentralisation, contracting, the creation of 'quasi-markets', privatisation and other processes integral to state restructuring have all placed a new emphasis on managerial and business skills. However, there is a risk of treating management as merely the technical means of accomplishing new political objectives in these processes. We want to suggest that managerialism has also played a substantial role in legitimising change and heralding a new order. This was not just a process of organisational restructuring, but a large scale process of *cultural* change through which 'hearts and minds' could be engaged. The Rayner era of civil service reform and subsequent initiatives have been directed towards bringing about fundamental changes of attitudes as well as of practices. 'Culture' – as something to be *managed* – rapidly entered political discourse:

> Rayner coined the phrase 'the culture of Whitehall' to draw attention to the inbuilt limitations of civil service thinking about management . . . Changing the culture of Whitehall has been a theme of the Efficiency Strategy since the first days of Raynerism. In public and professional discussion of Raynerism, the scrutiny programme has received the lion's share of attention. Nevertheless, in Rayner's view, lasting reforms of civil service management depend on changing the culture of Whitehall to instil a more managerial outlook from the top down. (Metcalfe and Richards, 1990: 16)

The means through which change was to be accomplished have varied over time, with financial devolution and restructuring in the early years of reform being supplemented by the later stress on competition and market mechanisms. The emphasis moved to designing changes which aimed to produce new incentives rather than simply being enforced. Change then becomes a task to be 'self-managed' rather than a series of centrally driven restructurings. Although these by no means disappeared, the focus moved to creating the conditions which require (or 'enable') everyone to become a 'change agent'. For example, Harrow and Talbot note that the strategy for implementation of the Citizen's Charter was 'clearly more about shaking up public services management culture, rather than direct intervention' (1994: 61) and that this approach was reinforced by the employment of a specialist in organisational psychology and cultural change management as adviser to the Prime Minister. They go on to illustrate the transformational hopes surrounding the introduction of the Citizen's Charter:

> Mr Waldegrave himself has talked about the Charter as being 'a genuine revolution in Whitehall' that has 'introduced the spirit of entrepreneurship into the corridors of power'. Westminster City Council has even stated that: 'the image of the faceless bureaucrat will be banished forever' as a result of Charter based initiatives. A senior Civil Servant has called the Charter 'the cultural challenge', saying that 'changes in structures and systems will need to be accompanied by changes in culture and management style'. (1994: 61)

The concern with cultural change has been through various phases. Initial attention focused on installing a managerial culture in which concerns for efficiency and costs were pre-eminent. Later variants (including the Citizen's Charter) have been redolent with progressive and visionary images of change: becoming customer-driven, empowering staff, delivering quality services and so on. These are, however, 'progressive' within a limited terrain. Old notions of progress, based on the state and its professionals 'solving' social problems, have been displaced by a more limited vision of 'more effective service delivery' or 'improved customer responsiveness'. The images of the future in the transformational discourse are simultaneously more visionary and more circumscribed.

Nevertheless, they have implied a new spirit, captured in phrases such as 'reinventing government' – giving the idea of government a positive inflection in contrast to the negative images of wasteful bureaucracy with which it had been characterised in the early years of restructuring and efficiency programmes. The case for reinvention was set out by Osborne and Gaebler (1992) and has since flourished in the USA where reinvention has itself become big business (with, for example, the setting up of a non-profit 'Alliance for Redesigning Government' and a consultancy firm, the 'Reinventing Government Network') as well as being closely associated with the Clinton administration itself through the national Performance Review process. The reinvention thesis was welcomed in Britain, too. There were meetings between Gaebler and William Waldegrave, then minister responsible for the Citizen's Charter Unit, and positive attention from government and from key public sector chief executives. Gaebler himself traced analogies between the principles of 'reinventing government' and those embedded in the Citizen's Charter, with 'eight or nine of the Charter's main aims being shared' (Interview, *Independent on Sunday*, 13 December 1992).

The vocabulary of reinvention has, like its predecessors, percolated downwards to be installed in specific organisational conceptions and projects of change:

> The decade through to 2005 is suggested as that within which HE will need 'to reinvent itself' – if, by this, the pundits suggest a dynamic re-appraisal, a re-focus of intent and method, an over-arching aim to develop and renew, then we would accept it as a text. (Higher Education organisation senior management team briefing, 1994)

The 'reinvention' case is that in order to respond creatively to problems such as crime, failing schools and the health care crisis, a fundamental transformation in ways of thinking about the role of government is required. Osborne has argued that 'many of the same tools used to improve the performance of companies – employee empowerment, internal competition, and measurement – can be marshalled to "reinvent" government itself' (quoted in Posner and Rothstein, 1994: 133). There are clear links between the political project of cultural change and the discourses of managerial transformation and business process re-engineering. The visionary rhetoric of Tom Peters and others in the 1980s, and of the 'reinvention' experts of the 1990s, set out the progressive possibilities of large scale transformations from unresponsive, paternalistic and leaden bureaucracies to the customer-driven, flexible, quality oriented and responsive organisations of the future. Managerialism and entrepreneurship were seen as the agency through which such a transformation could be accomplished (du Gay, 1996: ch. 3).

Many parts of the public sector, as well as the expanding range of organisations operating across the boundaries of public and private, came to welcome the possibilities of becoming more responsive and flexible and took the new language of missions, visions, customers, business units, strategic management and so on as its own. The style and language of these developments also offered a more attractive alternative to the impoverished organisational cultures associated with the experience of managed decline in public services. For example, many local authorities launched internal culture change programmes and decentralisation initiatives in order to make themselves more responsive to customers and local communities. Modernisers within the Civil Service welcomed the progressive possibilities of new management approaches. Many in the NHS enthused about the possibilities which the change to Trust status has brought: 'The idea of the local control and management of services liberates all sorts of energies and abilities you never knew were there. It is a very creative process. The focus on the patient and the GP has revolutionised services' (Chief Executive of NHS Trust, quoted in *The Health Service Journal*, 28 March 1996: 29). For a range of different reasons, then, acceptance of the new arrangements has been established in many areas. But this has been both accompanied and promoted by a distinctive political inversion of definitions of radical and conservative. The radical progressive terminology of values and visions, of transformation and revolution, of empowerment and liberation, now belongs to Tom Peters and other management experts. The need to 'love change' and to 'thrive on chaos' has helped to constitute a *tyranny of transformation* which has served to legitimate the processes of state restructuring. It is through the power of these discourses of change, we argue, that the unthinkable became thinkable; the unspeakable became speakable; and things which at first appeared to be terrifying inversions of older certainties came to be a normal part of everyday practice. Management has not just been the means through which change is to be delivered: managerialism as a discourse has energised the very process of change.

Ministerial pronouncements, Audit Commission and Civil Service documents and managerial texts have often had a remarkable similarity of both content and tone over the last decade or more. For example, the Audit Commission notes that 'Local Authorities are in the throes of a revolution' (Audit Commission, 1988) and suggests that 'Changing from a traditional role requires a cultural revolution; and any failure to grasp the extent of the changes needed can be in itself a considerable obstacle to progress' (Audit Commission, 1992: 19). 'We' – the audiences subjected to these discourses – are told by both that change is now everywhere and is at the heart of everything: whether we are addressed as 'business men' (sic), public sector staff, citizens or welfare consumers, we encounter attempts to persuade us that we must welcome change, learn to love it, and indeed thrive on it. We must rise to the challenge of the global marketplace. We have to accept the new reality of what the state can and cannot provide for its citizens. We have to change our expectations of relations between employer and employee, throwing away outdated notions such as 'career' and the state as a 'good employer'. Above all we have to accept the necessity, inevitability and universality of change.

Accounting for change: normalising narratives

In the sections that follow, we focus on change as a discourse in the contemporary world of public services and, in particular, on its functions as a rhetorical device in the reshaping of those services. As a consequence, we are not primarily concerned with questions of empirical accuracy (is this change described accurately?), with explanatory capacity (does this change account for that change?) or with technical evaluations of effectiveness (has this change brought about the intended results?). While these may be important issues in their own terms, they do not address what seems to us to be the most striking feature about change – its pervasive presence in the languages of public sector reconstruction. To pursue this issue means treating language as more than descriptive (a more or less accurate representation of the social world). Rather we will be treating language as rhetorics, discourses and ideologies which aim to be *productive*. Discourses seek to mobilise – to build alliances and support for specific social projects. They aim to establish themselves as normalised 'truths', the self-evidently correct frameworks of thought and action (see, *inter alia*, Burr, 1995; Rose, 1989; Wetherell and Potter, 1994).

The significance of the discourse of change is not simply to be found in its role as a point of affinity and interchange between political and managerial ideology. There is also a question of how the imperative of change has been deployed in the construction of specific social projects. The discourse of change has legitimated and mobilised support for *particular* changes. Narrative forms – whether management texts, political pronouncements or strategic plans – present accounts which attempt to establish the inevitability or necessity of the specific changes which they endorse. Increasingly, particular changes have come to be legitimated in and through narratives which place them in globalised contexts of change. The elementary structure of such narratives is familiar: the World has changed . . . Britain has changed . . . the Sector has changed . . . We must change . . .

There are, of course, a variety of narrative forms. Some (as in many management books) centre on heroic formulations, associating change with charismatic or transformational leadership which creates visions, directions, values and purposes capable of inspiring and motivating followers. Some are 'cautionary tales', centred on the bleak prospects of failure. They tell of the fate that befalls those who do not heed the imperative of change. Others are structured around promise, opportunity and possibility: the pleasures of change. Despite this diversity, we have tried in what follows to identify some of the typical narrative structures which carry the imperative of change in what follows. Each of these draws on a particular set of images and is constructed around a different set of associations or oppositions. In practice most statements – whether by politicians, management experts or senior managements within organisations – draw on more than one kind of image in the way they construct the imperative of change.

Change as natural

The first narrative represents change as a natural process of growth and development. For example, in a section titled 'The need for change', the Griffiths Report begins to set out its case as follows:

> Throughout the 1980s the Government has thus presided over a massive expansion of the NHS. It has ensured that the quality of care provided and the response to emergencies remain among the best in the world. But it has become increasingly clear that more needs to be done because of rising demand and an ever-widening range of treatments made possible by advances in medical technology. (1988: 2)

Here, change is presented as common sense, as natural, as part of the normal development of the healthy organism. The metaphors are organic and evolutionary, and draw on the concept of equilibrium and balance. The organism itself (in this case the NHS) is able to retain its integrity of identity and purpose through a process of adaptation to its changing conditions of existence. Continuity will be assured only if change is accepted. There is also, we should note, one of the characteristic rhetorical devices which establishes the *obviousness* of change in the relationship between the text and its audience – 'but it has become increasingly clear that'. The absence of an active subject (there is no 'we' who think/argue this) establishes this clarity as a pervasive social fact. It articulates the imperative of change as a set of environmental conditions to which organisations must adapt – or die.

This naturalising imagery of change has been central to managerial discourse. The dominant paradigm of scientific management was partially displaced in the post-war years by more humanistic approaches, in which organisations were represented as organic systems. 'Organisational development', the process through which an organisation could achieve greater health both for itself (its own survival) and for the individuals who worked within it, became established as a management discipline in its own right. In some ways this organic imagery is little more than a residual element in contemporary narratives of change. Nevertheless it played a central role in early critiques of public sector organisations, which were recurrently identified as inert or unadaptive. Their lack of capacity to change was seen as the result of such organisations being too internally focused – obsessed with themselves rather than paying attention to their environment and the changes within it. Now that organisations have become more externally focused – or at least capable of producing strategic plans that note a long list of external factors requiring a response – this view of change has moved from centre stage. Organic and adaptive images fall short of the experience of rapid and dislocatory transformations in the public sector. The processes of restructuring towards more competitive and contractual relationships between organisations required new modes of legitimation, bringing with them, we argue, a shift in the type of narratives deployed to legitimate change. Principal among these is the idea of survival in a hostile environment.

Change as defence against hostile forces

Here the environment is represented in terms of a series of dangers and threats which require active responses rather than mere adaptation. The imagery is likely to be military and strategic rather than organic and natural. The discourse is rife with battles and wars, strategic responses and alliances. The outcome is concerned with 'repositioning' rather than 'adaptation'. This representation of change is based on strong boundaries between inside and outside, between 'us' and 'them'. The environment is composed of actively or potentially hostile forces which threaten 'us'. In the face of such dangers, organisations must act assertively: 'Strategy can be viewed as building defences against the competitive forces or as finding positions in the industry where the forces are weakest' (Porter, 1989: 141). This environment may also be represented as something which increasingly needs to be controlled:

> This new world order adds to an increasingly voracious business environment that punishes organisations that fail to make the grade ... Managers are urged not

simply to gather information on environmental characteristics in order to plot a successful strategy; but to develop innovative strategies that create a new environment in which the organisation has an advantage. (Hardy, 1994: 13)

'We' – as a corporate entity – can have continuity of existence and purpose only by successfully knowing the enemy and ensuring our own dominance. Notions of nationhood at bay in the new 'global economy' mirror the imagery of corporate competitiveness in this narrative form. Pat Kane's report of a motivational workshop run by Jack Black captures this xenophobic sense of threat:

> The folk devil of the day is the 'wee man from China' who lives in a tiny room, works 12 hours a day in a factory, does repetitive labour for minimum wages and gets one weekend off a year with his betrothed. Jack Black saw him on a nightly news programme, presented as a horror story. 'But you know what they missed?' he muses. 'They missed the fact that he had a smile on his face. He loved his job and he loved his wife. When that wee man from China finally wakes up, he is coming after us. And he will wipe us out. Destroy us. Unless we change our way of thinking and living completely.' (Kane, 1996: 22)

This view of organisations and nations engaged in a struggle for survival establishes the necessity of change.

Transformative change

This more expansive view of change is carried through narratives which centre on organisational (and social) transformation. Here change is viewed as not merely necessary because of the pressure of external forces, but as a progressive force for transformation and the development of a new order. The key metaphors are 'reinventions' of the old and 'visions' of the new. The focus is on bringing about paradigm shifts involving the unravelling or dismantling of old bureaucratic, ossified companies or the old social order of the welfare state settlement and the ways of thinking that sustained them.

Recent job advertisements illustrate the prevalence of this trans-formational discourse. Many attempt to attract managers through self-representations as radical, leading edge, innovative, progressive or visionary organisations. In recent editions of the *Guardian* jobs pages we found an organisation seeking managers for a 'brand new department' whose task would be to turn the 'vision into a reality'; another seeking 'progressive professionals committed to change'; another wanting potential chief executives of a new unitary local authority to imagine the delights of 'beginning with a clean sheet of paper'; and another headlined: 'Change demands a different perspective' and which begins 'XXX is changing and changing fast. We are committed to a fundamental reassessment of our organisation . . . The extent of our change programme demands people who can look differently at service delivery. Top quality managers who have the vision, imagination and drive to impact far reaching improvements.' Yet another – for a housing department – was accompanied by an artist's image of an idealised environment. The text read: 'There's a new look to Housing in XXX . . . the [Department] is at the forefront of new initiatives which are gradually transforming the face of the borough and improving the quality of life for our residents. ... A radical reorganisation of our managerial structure will create X new housing neighbourhoods each headed by a team of entirely new managerial posts.'

In each case the vision is organisational or managerial. In only one case was there reference to social goals, and that a rather vague reference to improved 'quality of life'. The dynamic role for management is repeatedly established through the kind of language used. This is in marked contrast to the occasional exception which drew on other discourses of change. For example, an advert for a social services team leader was headlined 'Evolution Through Experience'. Transformational discourse is, then, distinct from the 'organic' imagery in which evolution is still possible. It is also distinct from the defensive imagery of some variants of the strategic planning discourse. It requires more than a cognitive shift in the way managerial subjects are to understand the world: it requires personal, as well as organisational, transformations.

Change as uncertainty and turbulence

Transformational imagery has links with a still more comprehensive conception of change, where the predominant metaphors are discontinuity, instability, fluidity and chaos. There are links with the defensive imagery in that change is often legitimated by the threat of external realignments. Rather than defensiveness, however, this discourse deploys the language of turbulence and chaos to challenge previous cognitive frameworks through which the world is to be understood. 'We' need to view these apparently threatening or disturbing phenomena as positive developments rather than try to protect ourselves against them. They need to be actively embraced as new ways of working, thinking and *being* in the world. 'Learning to love change' or 'Thriving on chaos' are the characteristic managerial prescriptions and the talk is of revolution:

> So this book is about a revolution – a necessary revolution. It challenges everything we thought we knew about managing, and often challenges over a hundred years of American tradition. Most fundamentally, the times demand that flexibility and love of change replace our long standing penchant for mass production and mass markets, based as it is upon a relatively predictable environment now vanished. (Peters, 1987: xi)

The idea of discontinuous change was also a core feature of popular management texts in Britain. The cover of Charles Handy's *The Age of Unreason* carries the quote:

> We are entering an Age of Unreason, a time when the future, in so many areas, is to be shaped by us and for us; a time when the only prediction that will hold true is that no predictions will hold true; a time, therefore, for bold imaginings in private life as well as public; for thinking the unlikely and doing the unreasonable. (1989: front cover)

Handy stresses that discontinuous change requires discontinuous or 'upside-down' thinking 'even if both thinkers and thoughts appear to be absurd at first sight' (1989: 5). We have to learn to think differently, not just do different things. Control is no longer possible. We have to move, flow, dance, recognise the instability of everything (including cherished notions of career or profession). We have to rethink our careers in 'post-entrepreneurial' terms, shifting from concepts of 'climbing' to 'hopping' (Moss Kanter, 1989). We have to learn to work in and with 'virtual' organisations and arrangements, supported by the power of new technology. We can hardly see the enemy, let alone control our environment, so change has to mean change in ourselves. These arguments are not just telling us 'how to manage': they are selling the very *idea* of change itself, and so establishing part of the legitimating basis for the 'new' approaches to management. The discourse is evangelical, designed to challenge the 'established church' of traditional management (Hopfl, 1992). It is not for nothing that the new writers are often termed management 'gurus'.

Change as re-engineering

The transformational discourse has close associations with the languages of re-engineering organisations and reinventing government. Re-engineering is one of the more recent of a series of management fashions. 'Business Process Re-engineering is the fundamental rethinking and radical redesign of business processes to achieve dramatic improvements in critical contemporary measures of performance' (Hammer and Champy, 1993). Organisations producing goods and services must be re-engineered because tinkering with them, making change at the margins, is just not enough. The authors highlight the critical importance of the idea of change as fundamental, radical, and dramatic. This has parallels with notions of transformation, but involves a much sharper and more dramatic curtailment of old realities and practices. It is also more enforced. BPR is essentially a top-down exercise, not reliant on the uncertain processes of inspiring people through visions and leadership to change themselves. It is usually led by management 'experts' rather than being based on the more participatory discourses of transformation which rely on everyone being 'on board'. Re-engineering organisations has close affinities with the notion of 'reinventing' government, which makes similar claims to fundamental, radical and dramatic reassessments of the role of the state and the means of delivery of public services. Indeed, 're-engineering' was the language chosen by Peter Lilley, Secretary of State, to present the latest approach to reforming the benefits system (Radio 4 'Today' programme interview, 6 February 1996).

  The narratives we have delineated here play different roles in the process of legitimating change. They are not mutually exclusive or contradictory, but in practice constitute different layers of the imperative of change. They have a cumulative effect. The first (organic) installs the idea of change as healthy. The second (defence against hostile forces) represents change as necessary for survival. In both of these, though new tasks, goals and skills are required, the 'self' who is managing the change can remain intact. The third – the discourse of transformation – tells us we have to transform ourselves in a new image, and the fourth – the discourse of turbulence, chaos and uncertainty – reminds us that nothing is certain, not even the idea of the state or a public sector. It requires cognitive change and personal readjustment to the 'new reality' where the only continuity is change itself. The final discourse – reinvention – takes this further by telling us that we have to participate in building this new order of things.

Each of these has the capacity to operate separately, being based on particular discursive structures and narrative frameworks, some of which we explore below. In practice, however, they are often overlaid on each other, with the final three (uncertainty, transformation and reinvention) operating powerfully together as an discursive nexus which articulates the imperative of change. It is around this nexus that the 'remaking of management' by the management experts meets the 'reinvention of government' by the New Right. The affinities that made this alliance possible can be seen around three central themes: the customer focus; the mutual antipathy to bureaucracy; and the commitment to transformative change. It is important to see how these affinities legitimated the role which managerialism was given in the restructuring of the welfare state. Being 'customer-centred', in the new managerialist discourse, was the principle which drove and guaranteed organisational dynamism, while for the New Right it was the principle through which the provider power of the old welfare monopolies could be challenged. These affinities were most clearly expressed in the shared hostility towards bureaucracy. For the new managerialism, bureaucracy embodied and exemplified the worst features of corporate ossification: an approach to corporate organisation that systematically privileged stability over adaptation, repetition over innovation, rules over responsiveness, hierarchy over performance, and roles over people. In all these ways, bureaucracy stifled the possibilities of creativity, dynamism and competitiveness. The imperative of change constitutes public entrepreneurship as the antithesis of bureaucracy. As du Gay comments, 'the identity of entrepreneurial governance is constituted in relation to that which it is not – namely the public service bureaucracy' (du Gay, 1994a: 141). Finally, the commitment to organisational transformation underpinned the extension of managerial power (understood as leadership) and was necessitated by a reading of global changes that identified old corporate structures as the cause, not the solution, of declining competitiveness. For the New Right, old organisational regimes represented a blockage to their programme of economic and social modernisation.

The radical political agenda of social transformation in the 1980s has been both reflected in, and articulated through, the transformational discourse of the new managerialism. This mutual interaction of politics and management is partly sustained by the ways in which the radical and transformative agendas of each are represented through common discursive structures and strategies. We want to explore three such strategies: the common *narrative structures* of the discourses, which provide legitimation for change; the structuring of the discourses around *oppositions*, which serve to represent discontinuities between past and future; and the presentation of *prescriptions* in the form of goals to be pursued. Each of these, we argue, creates structures of meaning and imaginary identifications through which change is both represented and realised.

From the global to the local: the cascading imperative of change

The development of a global economy has formed one of the meta-narratives which has legitimised change, at the level of the state itself and in terms of the management of organisations (for a more sceptical view, see Hirst and Thompson, 1996). At the level of the state, the narrative concerns the competitive positioning of nations in the global economy. It sets out the need to construct 'Great Britain plc' in the image of a company competing in a hostile and aggressive marketplace, where its traditional status and role are being inexorably eroded by 'new entrants' from the Pacific Rim nations and elsewhere. There is a strong articulation between the discourses of the New Right and managerialism here around notions of strategy and of responses to competition. Neo-liberal ideology constituted the British state as unwieldy, overburdened and inefficient and thus an impediment to Britain's economic survival in the face of global competition.

> With the arrival of Thatcher came a great determination to do what was 'necessary' to rescue Great Britain from the perceived national decline for which the civil service was partly to blame. Reducing public expenditure, eliminating waste, rolling back the frontiers of the state, lifting the dead hand of bureaucracy, cutting the public payroll were the objects of a crusade given authority by a clear electoral victory and leadership of a peculiarly visionary and dogmatic kind. (Grocott, 1989: 119)

At the same time, a new managerial discourse, based on Peters and others, emerged with strong messages about the reasons for the declining competitiveness of US corporations in the global marketplace. This discourse represented large organisations as top heavy, bureaucratic and unresponsive, and as needing to change in order to survive in the marketplace.

> The global economy in which American business now operates is like a corporate Olympics – a series of games played all over the world with international as well as domestic competitors. The Olympic contests determine not just which business team wins but which nation wins overall . . . there are common overall characteristics in those teams that can compete and win again and again – the strength, skill and discipline of the athlete, focused on individual excellence, coupled with the ability to work well within a well organised team. (Moss Kanter, 1989: 18–19)

This draws on many of the different imageries of change we have discussed. The survival and legitimacy of both nations and institutions is represented as under threat unless change is delivered. But this defensive discourse is overlaid by the discourse of turbulence and uncertainty, and both are deployed to legitimate the need for transformation. The mythic happy ending of the globalisation narrative is one in which both nations and companies become faster and more agile in developing responses to new forms of competition. In relation to the public sector, this narrative of globalisation has a double purchase. Not only must the state enable British business to become more competitive (by reducing the iron hand of regulations and excessive taxation), it must also become more lean and agile itself. Both imply a reduction in the size and cost of the public sector and 'being businesslike' is presented as the means of achieving these objectives. Indeed, being business-like (understood both in the personification of 'businessmen' and the application of techniques derived from commercial organisations) is seen as the means of delivering fundamental change to the institutions of the state itself.

These narratives come together in political conceptions of the need for organisational change. Setting out the case for 'more radicalism' in the reform of the Civil Service, Barry Legg MP argued that:

> British society is no longer capable of being administered by a bureaucratic, hierarchical civil service as may have been the case in an immediate post-war Britain. The manner in which the civil service now needs to act has dramatically altered, this will require internal reform to provide the structures necessary to promote this new attitude. The critical issue is that the UK has undergone significant economic restructuring. The deregulation of financial markets, the breaking up of labour market rigidities, the encouragement of private provision and private ownership, the privatisation of many former state owned industries, the growth of self employment has created, at least partially, an enterprise society. This new society sits oddly besides Whitehall.
>
> The new demands for flexibility and a general recognition that many of the lessons of the private sector can be learned and utilised in the public sector need to be acted on. This is not a case of dogmatism. Rather, with the rise of a far freer, more liberalised post-GATT trading order in which the East Asian Giants are making the running, it is imperative that Britain should make herself as flexible as ever in order to be able to fully share in the greatest potential explosion of wealth creation resulting from the new Pacific Rim dynamism. (1994: 22)

This quotation indicates some of the ways in which links are forged between the global and the local to establish the changed economic and social conditions at a national level which are both the effect of global shifts and the forces which necessitate change to the state. Such stories serve both to simplify and make sense of complex phenomena and form the myths through which meaning is institutionalised. These narratives appear in different forms, linking different domains – academic theories (e.g., of post-Fordism), political projects, and the theory and practice of managing organisations. They all point to the need to dissolve the old arrangements and seek new solutions. The imperative of change is a cascading one – from global competition to corporate and individual success – and at each level there is a set of constraints and conditions that can be identified as requiring change. This point is highlighted by du Gay in his analysis of the isomorphic effects of the managerial discourse:

> because the discourse of enterprise presupposes that no organisational context is immune from the effects of globalisation, it therefore assumes that ostensibly

different organisations – schools, charities, banks, government departments and so on – will have to adopt similar norms and techniques of conduct for without so doing they will lack the capacity to pursue their preferred projects ... The urgency with which such claims are deployed gives the impression that 'There is no alternative'. (1994a: 137)

The pressures towards organisational isomorphism that result from these globalising narratives have borne with considerable force on public service organisations in particular (see also Cutler and Waine, 1994: 3–5). The narrative descent from the global to the local constructs equivalences between different entities. In this globalised environment nations, corporate bodies and individuals are seen to face the same challenges and have the same objectives (survival or success). Global change has created the conditions in which nations must compete against each other, organisations must compete for markets and resources, and individuals must compete for jobs, income and security. These equivalences rest on a naturalising assumption about the universality of 'being enterprising'. Individuals, organisations and nations share common impulses or drives and these should not be blocked or repressed. As a consequence, change is not only an economic imperative but also socially, organisationally and psychologically desirable as the 'liberation' of previously repressed potential.

> The arrival of trust status ... marks a genuine watershed in the history of X's hospitals – and one that promises so much for our staff, both in terms of the opportunities for personal career development and the chance to help us to develop comprehensive patient services of the highest quality and reputation. (NHS hospital trust 'Agenda for Action', 1995)

Such specific narratives of change construct a unity of identities and interests – here between the organisation, its staff and its users. All can benefit from the promise of change.[1] The cascade of change from the global to the local accomplishes a range of narrative closures. The first is at the global level where change tends to read as uni-directional or non-contradictory and as such resulting in clear imperatives or directions for lower level changes. Such lower level changes are represented as the natural or logical reflection of global or universal tendencies. Global and national changes are then constituted as the necessary conditions of organisational projects for change. Choice – the exercise of discretionary power – tends to disappear from such narratives. For example, the Trust quotation above talks of 'the arrival of Trust status' – an apparently immaculate conception whose basis in political and organisational choices disappears. In practice, choice tends to be reduced to simple binary oppositions – 'change or die' – in which choices about the character or direction of change are repressed.

Being on the right side: dualities and oppositions

The narrative structures we have described are established partly through sets of dualities and oppositions in which the discontinuity between past and future is highlighted. These are usually expressed through a series of concepts or phrases in two columns, with 'past/undesirable' in the left hand column and 'future/desired' in the right. While the narratives claim to be descriptive of reality, however, the oppositions serve as prescriptions. That is, if we want to achieve the 'happy ending' of successful narrative closure, we have to ensure that a shift from the features of one column to those of the other takes place.

Such lists span both political and managerial discourse. For example, desired changes in the welfare state might be expressed in terms of movement:

From provider dominated	to user dominated;
from monopolistic	to market-driven;
from compulsion	to choice;
from uniformity	to diversity;
from a culture of dependency	to a culture of self reliance.

Prescriptions for change are set out through such structured sets of oppositions in which the 'bad' old days are contrasted with the new flexible, responsive and, above all, managerial future. What is interesting is the correspondence between the common structure of dualities and oppositions of both political and managerial discourses on change.

There are close correspondences between the oppositions of political ideology and those of the new managerialism, for example in the ways that the discourses of 're-engineering' and of 'reinvention' are constructed. The Hammer and Champy text on re-engineering (1993) identifies the implications of their approach through the following list:

Jobs:	from simple to multi-dimensional
Roles:	from controlled to empowered
Values:	from protective to productive
Managers:	from supervisors to coaches
Structures:	from hierarchies to flat
Performance management:	from activities to results
Job preparation:	from training to education

while Osborne and Gaebler's approach to 'Reinventing Government' (1992) constructs most of its ten 'principles' through oppositions:

Steering not Rowing
Empowering rather than serving communities
Funding outcomes, not inputs
Meeting the needs of the customer, not the Bureaucracy
Earning rather than spending
Prevention rather than cure
From hierarchy to participation and teamwork

These lists highlight the contrast between terms that represent a stereotyped and demonised past and those offering a visionary and idealised future. There are some difficulties with this discourse of change. One is that while the 'Froms' and 'Tos' are clearly set out, what happens in the middle – the process of change itself – is of less concern. At the same time, these contrasts recurrently conflate description and prescription in ways that disguise the normative construction of the new and mean that the rhetoric becomes deeply confused with reality. The process of change, encompassing many different dimensions and elements, is depicted as undifferentiated, as global, and part of a process which is inevitable. Such lists fail to tell us what the conditions of change are: all the terms look the same, so the change from 'bureaucratic' to 'flexible' appears to be equivalent to the change from 'producer-driven' to 'consumer-led'. Change is presented as homogeneous and unilinear, making things which are different in quality and in kind seem to be part of the same process. In the public sector context in particular, such representations over-ride the experience of change as intentional rather than inevitable – the result of political choices. The simplifying features of the change discourse mask the complexity of the ways in which change has been applied and experienced, and the deeper continuities of management and organisational practice. Rather than a shift from A to B, most change processes are characterised by uncertainty and ambiguity, uneven development, and incomplete closure (Nadler and Tushman, 1989) and tend to produce dilemmas for those living through them (Clarke and Newman, 1993b). Finally, and perhaps most importantly, the discourse suggests that change is all in one direction: all of the 'old' is to be discarded in favour of the 'new'.

Speaking the past: the problem of resistance

One of the achievements of the discourse of change has been to produce consent to the programmes of restructuring. By consent, we do not just mean its ability to recruit enthusiasts as committed 'change agents' or 'champions'. The discourse has a broader impact because of its capacity to draw on languages which connect to a diverse array of objectives, commitments and criticisms of the old regime. While the spartan language of efficiency had only a limited appeal (although it was difficult to resist), the visionary language of both the new managerialism and the New Right has tapped into much more potent vocabularies of motive. For example, the discourse appropriates the vocabularies of anti-paternalism, user-centredness and empowerment which were central features of challenges to the old welfare state and which were associated with 'progressive' movements both inside and outside the state. As a result, the discourse has been able to speak for and offer positions to a variety of individuals and groups who were critical of the old ways of doing things. Their consent may be partial and conditional, tempered by concerns over resources or how far the rhetorics are realised in practice, but they are positioned *within* the transformative project. Proponents of decentralisation and of greater choice and diversity in forms of service provision have found themselves co-opted to the discourse. Similarly, those committed to the necessity of modernising the machinery of government have been attached to the project while trying to disentangle themselves from its New Right specifics. It is precisely because the discourse is constituted out of different ideologies (managerialism and the New Right) that it is able to address and speak for these diverse constituencies and 'bring them on board'.

However, such conditional consent is also the source of attempts to inflect the discourse of change in particular ways – to attempt more of this (empowerment) and less of that (efficiency) within the field of possibilities that the discourse represents. Both generally and in particular organisational settings, it is possible to see attempts to adapt the discourse to make it fit other purposes and values. In Chapters 5 and 6, we explore some of these micro-political processes of adaptation within the discourse. But it is important to remember that the discourse and the ways in which it is embodied in specific organisational settings is not just a field of possibilities. It is also a framework of constraints which make some outcomes impossible or at least difficult to accomplish. For example, Flynn (1994) has traced the impact of public sector reform, especially the introduction of contractual relationships between organisations, on management processes. He suggests that such contractual relations are more likely to favour neo-Taylorist management processes rather than Human Resource Management approaches based on commitment building and staff development.

The discourse of change also demobilises potential opposition and alternative possibilities in a more systematic way. As we argued in Chapter 1, challenges to the old regime emerged from feminist critiques of the state's role in reproducing patriarchal relations; from black groups exposing the conditions and processes of institutionalised racism; and from the disability movement's concerns with the 'disabling' consequences of the ways in which social welfare was administered. At the same time, the developing consumer movement highlighted issues of the inadequacy of the relationship between providers and users of services; and community and voluntary organisations called for greater openness, access and accountability. Many of these critiques originated in the 'new social movements' of the 1960s and 1970s (Newman and Williams, 1995; Williams, 1996). They were also expressed in the development of radical branches of some state professions (social work, teaching, health) and, to a lesser extent, in some trade unions (Carpenter, 1994).

There were, then, a variety of demands for change. However the targets were fundamentally different. Where the new managerialism has been successful is in 'winning consent' to one kind of change agenda and in silencing others. It has given us a whole set of ideas about how change is to be deployed, and what are the appropriate targets of change (organisations, services, employees), and what are not appropriate (community power, responsiveness to feminist and other perspectives). The very word 'radical' now belongs to the New Right and the transformational discourse of change. It is aligned with concepts such as cultural change, business process re-engineering and other strands of the managerial armoury of change. In other words, the managerial conception of change has excluded other views of what could or should be changed. It has filled the discursive space in which change is conceived. It defines the terrain and direction of change. It expresses the imagined futures and the ways of getting there. It establishes the limits of the possible, the imaginable, and, above all, the sayable. Anyone who wishes to join this debate needs to find ways of accommodating themselves to the discursive terms of reference or risk being left on the margins – 'lost for words'.

There is a literal sense of loss of words. Terms which once appeared to belong to radical vocabularies and progressive ideologies have been re-articulated into competing ideologies. The trajectory of the term 'empowerment' is indicative of this process. Once it appeared to be an essential element in the vocabulary of the new social movements – expressing conceptions of inequality and forms of oppression which necessitated collective action. Subsequently, it has entered the political and organisational discourse of transformation – articulating the projects of empowering the consumer-citizen, front-line workers, and managers themselves. Similarly, the demands for greater diversity in social welfare provision (and employment) emerging from groups positioned outside of the universalist norms of post-war welfare have come to be spoken for by consumerist and managerial languages which claim to 'value', 'respect' and 'enable' diversity – albeit in limited and individualised forms (Newman and Williams, 1995). The colonisation of languages of opposition by the discourse of transformation creates an *apparent* unity of interests against the old ways. Change is thus represented as 'in everyone's interests', leaving a problem about how to articulate dissent from both the old and the new.

Other words which formed the vocabulary of past radicalisms now seem to give little purchase on contemporary political and organisational discourse. Concerns with inequalities and egalitarianism or with the construction of alternative social arrangements have proved difficult to articulate in debates dominated by the transformational discourse. It is no longer the case that they are dismissed as 'utopian'. Rather it is now the transformational discourse that possesses and disseminates utopian visions. Past radicalism fails to connect because it is represented as 'old fashioned', superseded by new possibilities and promises. When the world is constituted as divided between 'old' and 'new', there are difficulties associated with how to criticise the old (for example, for the ways in which it reproduced social inequalities) without being co-opted to the new. Equally, there are problems of how to criticise or resist the 'new' without being aligned with the vested interests of the old regime. These problems coalesce around the issue of how to articulate *alternative* directions and demands for change.

Because the radical ground has been occupied by this combination of managerialism and the New Right, many of those who used to be the locus of radical political agendas have increasingly found themselves in the position of seeking to conserve what used to be. This echoes the argument of Blackwell and Seabrook (1993), who debate the interaction between radicalism and conservatism in the broader politics of British society. They point to a paradox in which 'the only radical politics left to us should be based on resistance, recuperation and remembering. But in a social and economic system which requires a reversal of all those things, to oppose means to conserve' (1993: 4). In the context of the institutions we are discussing here, this means that to resist the managerial agenda for change means supporting the old regime. This exposes painful contradictions. For example, opposing the opening out of services through consumerist initiatives is untenable, because it implies simply seeking to conserve professional power. The difficulties of this position arise from the intersection of two processes. On the one hand, opposition to change implicates those who would have once been defined as 'progressives' in potential alliances with traditionalist professionals (who would once have been the 'opposition'). On the other, such opposition is already positioned within the change narratives themselves.

As we have seen, such narratives construct change as inevitable, necessary or desirable and the audiences of such narratives are positioned in ways which treat their assent to these logics as unproblematic. 'We' are spoken for as more or less enthusiastic participants in the process of change: 'our' survival, success or growth is aligned with that of the nation and the organisation. To refuse this identification is difficult, since the narratives do not permit positions of scepticism, uncertainty or doubt. What they construct is a further duality. On one side are the 'participants', the 'enthusiasts', the 'committed' – those who have learned to love. On the other are those who are 'Against Change'. As an effect of the narrative logics of the descending imperatives of change (from the global to the local), to be against any particular change is also to be against change itself. As Maile has noted, in local government ' "Change" is used to invite Officers to recreate their work identities and to move away from the negative images that have been directed at "bureaucrats". Anyone resisting such a "calling" is implied to have a traditional or subservient mentality, or to be unwilling to meet the exciting challenges offered by shifts in Local Authority administration' (Maile, 1995: 734–5). The discourse of change also identifies resistance as stemming from flawed personal, organisational or social motives, most often construed as the protection of 'vested interests'. Thus, the Audit Commission described the task of 'moving to a user-centred approach to social care' as meaning that 'a number of vested interests and established power structures will have to confront change' (1992: 26). While we would not wish to deny questions of power in organisational settings, what is important about the deployment of concepts of vested interests in such change narratives is the way they cast doubt on the motives of potential refusers or resisters while the change agents themselves are innocent of any taint of bad faith (not least because they are discursively aligned with global imperatives).

What is at stake here is the way in which the discursive space available for the debate about public services at both political and organisational levels has been occupied – or colonised – by the imperative discourse of change. In this colonising process, the discourse of change has (selectively) appropriated the dynamic and critical languages of past radicalism: speaking in the name of users (as customers), committed to the 'empowerment' of everyone, and promising to overthrow old power bases and their vested interests. Tom Peters's (1993) conception of 'Liberation Management' captures both this radicalism and its limited conception of agency – it is a discourse of and for management.

Dissent from the discourse is difficult to articulate – in the sense of having few pertinent vocabularies through which it can be spoken. This does not mean it is absent. On the contrary, it is clear that there continues to be a variety of sources and forms of dissent, ranging from defensive conservatism to marginalised radicalism both within and beyond the state. But the scope of the discourse of change has meant that much of this exists in the form of *passive dissent*. Familiar examples are the patterns of scepticism or cynicism that are a recurrent response to the inspirational language of organisational transformation. This treats the discourse of change as 'empty rhetoric' – a dazzling imagery that conceals a grim reality of declining services, shrinking resources, and gung-ho managers following the latest big idea while the front line struggles on.

Such passive dissent – as well as the more visible attempts to articulate resistance – pose problems about how to assess the effects of ideological or discursive strategies. Most statements of (post-Foucauldian) discourse theory have treated discourses as producing subjection: the creation of new subjects who enact the discourse. In this case, we would be looking for the production of 'change agents' or 'enterprising selves' as the effect of the discourse. We suggested in Chapter 2 that the outcomes of the discourse are more complex than this. While there are, indeed, change agents who have been empowered by this discourse, it is not uniform in its effects. Indeed, in some ways we are tempted to suggest that its impact on alternative or oppositional positions is as important as its success in producing the subjects of change. Its co-option of radical vocabularies, its demobilisation of dissent and its identification of resisters as either nostalgic or mere vested interests are potent elements in the discursive strategy. We would want to make a distinction between being subjected *by* a discourse and being subjected *to* it. 'Subjected by' points to what might be called the ideal effects of discourses – the production of new subjects who identify with it and enact it in their practices. By contrast, 'subjected to' suggests the experience of being regulated by and disciplined through a discourse, without it engaging beliefs, enthusiasms or identification. Rather than enacting it from commitment, such subjects enact the discourse of change conditionally, because 'there is no alternative'. It is recognised, more or less enthusiastically, as the new rules of the game which produce compliance rather than commitment (although compliance may be ingeniously inventive, as we shall see in Chapter 5).

We think that these are the conditions that make it possible to speak of the discourse of change as *hegemonic*. It has colonised the ideological or discursive field in which change can be imagined or articulated. It is not that it is the only vocabulary or perspective, but it has established the dominance that allows it to position the others – to co-opt some, to ally with others and to render oppositional vocabularies irrelevant. The creation of immobilised, inarticulate and above all *passive* dissent is the accomplishment of a hegemonic position in an ideological field. It is important to insist on treating ideological or discursive fields in this way because it is too tempting to see them as simple either/or formations. Either 'discursive subjection' or 'hegemony' has been accomplished, and there is no opposition, or there is resistance and so it has failed. We have tried to indicate that it is *how* particular discursive or ideological strategies manage to configure the relationships between contesting and overlapping perspectives that needs to be the focus of attention. It is this configuration, indicating the capacity of a particular discourse to organise the positions of others in a field, that identifies a hegemonic position.

Our analysis of the discourse of change has concentrated on the accomplishment of a hegemonic status through the articulation between New Right radicalism and transformational managerialism. This discourse has set the agenda of change, defining its meaning, its direction and the means of its accomplishment. It is the core discourse that other contending positions must negotiate in attempting to articulate their projects. In particular, it has established the need to remake organisational forms of the state around the managerial prerogative: the 'right to manage'.

Note

[1] Corporate missions often create a confusion about modes of address to staff, with tensions between an inclusive 'we' (the whole organisation) and a differentiated 'we' and 'you' (where the 'we' designates corporate management and 'you' the staff). The Trust document quoted above goes on: 'The single most important factor in determining this Trust's success is its staff. I hope *you* will recognise *our* efforts to deliver excellent hospital services to the people *we* serve and know that *you* will work with *us* to build an organisation proud of its services, its expertise and its reputation' (emphasis added).

4
The Making of Management: Regimes of Power

In the previous chapter we examined the way in which managerial ideology and New Right politics coalesced in the discourse of change that directed and legitimated the reconstruction of the public sector. In this chapter we focus on the impact of managerialism on the welfare state using the concept of *organisational regimes*. This focus on regimes highlights the issues of power and relationships involved in managerialism, rather than – as in the previous chapter – managerialism as ideology and discourse. The changing organisational regime of public services has not involved a simple displacement of older bureau-professional regimes by managerial ones. Rather, the new patterns are uncomfortable and contradictory combinations of old and new regimes within the overarching logics of managerialism.

Establishing the 'right to manage'

As Pollitt has argued (1993: 3), managerialism has its centre in the idea that managers must be given the 'right to manage' – the freedom to make decisions about the use of organisational resources to achieve desired outcomes. This is both an ideological demand and a practical issue of organisational power. It also ensures that managerialism is a continually contested regime. The 'freedom' or 'right' of managers to manage necessarily involves them in conflicts of power over organisational resources, decision making, labour processes and so on. As a result, the scope and effectiveness of the 'right to manage' has been historically and culturally variable.

The place of managerialism in restructuring the state was associated with a wider context of a reassertion and extension of the right to manage in the private sector. As a consequence, the arrival of managerialism in public services needs to be treated as something more than a simple transfer of long standing private sector practices into the public sector. The forms and relations of management in the business world were themselves undergoing significant changes during the late 1970s and 1980s. This 'new managerialism' appeared in the context of processes of economic restructuring that changed the social composition, place and shape of labour forces (Clarke and Newman, 1993b). This took a variety of forms: de-unionisation and the loss of collective negotiating rights; the 'greening', 'feminisation' and casualisation of labour in the search to reduce labour costs; and the greater mobility of the enterprise in national and international terms (see, for example, Bluestone and Harrison, 1982; du Gay, 1996; Hudson, 1988; Sayer and Walker, 1992). These restructurings of labour are both more and less than is represented in the concepts of 'flexible specialisation' or 'post-Fordism'. Such concepts over-estimate the significance of the particular forms of coordination which they describe, and under-estimate the use of other strategies in the remaking of both capital and labour in the 1970s and 1980s (Rustin, 1989; Sayer and Walker, 1992). Finding ways of becoming 'lean and mean' was an organisational imperative of the new managerialism and an economic requirement of capital recomposition in face of declining profitability. It was most forcefully expressed in the constant concern with overmanning and the need to shed excess capacity and excess labour.

Moody (1987) has argued that, in the late 1970s and 1980s, corporate capital elaborated a set of demands about the conditions that needed to be established by both local and national governments in order to attract capital investment and to ensure the success of such investment. These demands focused on the need to liberate capital from the shackles of the post-war political and economic settlements. This 'business agenda' sought capital's release from the state in the form of over-taxation and over-regulation; and from the unions whose restrictive practices and organisational power represented an inhibition on the 'right to manage'. The business agenda highlighted the problem of organised labour and its place in the post-war settlements. Although there were significant transatlantic differences, in both Britain and the USA the position of unionised labour was seen as a major blockage to the proper workings of the free market and effective corporate management. Organised labour prevented the efficient operation of 'free' labour markets through disrupting pricing mechanisms and labour mobility (the *extra-organisational* dimensions of union power). Unions also inter-fered with managerial discretion *within the organisation*, especially getting in the way of managerial control of labour processes through demarcation agreements and other forms of shop floor power (MacInnes, 1987). As well as being left stranded by capital flight (the shift of investment overseas), organised labour was subjected to an elaborate battery of attacks: new industrial relations legislation; displacement from national corporatist insti-tutions; single or non-union workplace deals; the surrender of workplace negotiating rights; 'give-back' deals and so on.

The growing flexibility of some forms of capital also exposed the vulnerability of ossified corporations to both external competition and predatory stock markets. The 1980s saw the rise of takeover mania, or what Reich (1984) termed 'paper entrepreneurship', in the activities of the corporate raiders. The heightened competition and the insecurity which came in its wake was seen as breaking the complacency of corporations made comfortable by their monopolistic or near monopolistic trading positions and bolstered by a view of management as a stabilising rather than dynamic process. For example, Tom Peters argued that 'on balance, the raiders are, along with the Japanese, the most effective force now terrorising inert corporate managements into making at least some of the moves, such as downsizing, that should have been made years ago' (1987: 32).

This business agenda was articulated in the name of the market, the customer, the nation and the spirit of enterprise. However, its primary objective was to remove the shackles from the processes of capital accumulation. It sought to change both the extra-organisational and intra-organisational constraints on those processes. In this way, it constructed a particular affinity between the 'free market' and the 'free manager' as the practical embodiment of capital within the enterprise. Consequently one central goal was that of re-establishing the right of managers to manage freed from unreasonable restrictions and impediments:

> Managers for twenty years have had a buffeting and beating from government and unions and we have been put in a can't win situation. We have an opportunity now that will last for two or three years. Then the unions will get themselves together again; and the government, like all governments will run out of steam. So grab it now. We have had a pounding and we are all fed up with it. I think it would be fair to say that it's almost vengeance. (Collinson, *The Financial Times*, 5 January 1981, quoted in MacInnes, 1987: 92)

The new managerialism has been both a source and beneficiary of these wider economic and political transformations. It promised a management equipped to take advantage of the changing internal and external environments of organisations, ready to match the pace of external change with internal dynamism. Its prescriptions for management style and strategy emphasised dynamism, flexibility and innovation. The stress on building corporate cultures and commitments provided strategies through which the loyalty of workforces could be engaged in the enterprise of national and organisational success (du Gay, 1996: ch. 3).

Becoming businesslike – managerialism and welfare organisations

During the 1980s and 1990s there was a growing proximity between the New Right agenda for changing public services and the new managerialist arguments about organisational transformation. This emergent alliance started at a relatively low level. Conservative prescriptions for change during the 1980s tended to refer to a relatively generalised conception of business management as providing the model for public service organisations (Cutler and Waine, 1994: ch. 1). This conception stressed the need for public organisations to 'become businesslike' and its major reference points were those of financial and performance management. At this point, management was identified as the organisational force through which the predominant objectives of tighter financial control and increased productivity could be obtained. This narrow conception of management – identified by Pollitt (1993) as 'neo-Taylorism' – centred on subordinating public sector organisations to the principles of what might be described as good financial housekeeping. Financial management took an increasingly significant role both at the initiative of central government (as in the Financial Management Initiative) and because financial calculations and principles became the dominant 'rules of the game' for local government and other sectors. Financial expertise became the most prized organisational knowledge both as a means of control and as a means of manoeuvring within these new controls. This was also the period of 'creative accounting' in local government as authorities tried to find new means of both managing and accounting for scarce financial resources (Cochrane and Clarke, 1993). Humphrey and Scapens have argued that:

> The accounting ideology of the private sector, with its emphasis on individual financial responsibility and its apparently systematic and ordered approach to management ... had considerable appeal. By offering to bring intangible, intractable matters under managerial control and giving contentious issues a technical appearance, any opposition seemed illogical and irrational. (1992: 142–3)

Allied to this concern with financial management (itself the institutional parallel of the macroeconomic objective of reducing the Public Sector Borrowing Requirement) was the objective of improving public sector productivity. These objectives were inscribed in the expanding role of the Audit Commission (dealing with local government and the NHS) with its agenda of scrutinising and promoting 'value for money' services which addressed the three Es of economy, efficiency and effectiveness. The Commission produced a steady stream of reports detailing the room for improvement in the management of a range of public services from the NHS to the police. The Commission was one of the bearers of the central government initiatives concerned to improve performance management through the setting of targets and the more rigorous monitoring of achievements. The twin concerns with financial and performance management had as their objective the promotion of public services which were more 'transparent' and more 'accountable'. Cochrane has suggested that in the context of local government, at least, these reforms were less than wholly successful:

> It is not clear ... that an increased role for central structures of financial management necessarily implies a greater 'rationality' for the organization as a whole. On the contrary, the experience of the 1980s suggests that it may serve to mask a rather more confused and uncertain set of responses. The attempts to impose a new rationality from above, through the departments of central government and the development of increasingly complex financial rules, do not seem to have been very successful – and since current spending by local authorities actually rose across the decade it is clear that more modest ambitions to reduce levels of public spending in this sphere were not achieved either. (1994: 149)

By the late 1990s, however, it is clear that 'becoming businesslike' meant more than the adoption of good business practices within the setting of public service organisations. The shifts towards mixed economies, market relations, the separation of purchaser and provider functions, the creation of Agencies and more or less autonomous trading units meant an increasing number of functions were being operated through organisations which were asked to imagine themselves as 'businesses'. The strategy of dispersal created a variety of mechanisms through which new forms of organisational autonomy were devolved within the limits established by central government. Within the frameworks of policy, finance and inspection created by central government, these semi-autonomous organisations were increasingly exhorted to manage themselves.

In the process, such organisations developed the apparatus of contemporary business management. They produced visions, missions and business plans. They surveyed the competitive environment and looked for their 'niches' and their 'competitive edge'. They developed human resource strategies, planned culture shifts or blueprints for re-engineering. They prioritised quality and customer-centred front-line people processing systems. Many developed performance related pay systems allied to performance measurement and staff appraisal. Some engaged in local pay and conditions bargaining. Across the range of public services, organisations settled to the task of 're-inventing' themselves as quasi-businesses. The remaking of the state towards a more dispersed form enlarged the space for management and provided new legitimations for increasing managerial discretion. Since public sector organisations (and their 'partners' in the voluntary sector) were increasingly expected to behave as if they were businesses, they were also expected to be managed in appropriate ways. Managerialism thus developed a tighter 'fit' with the changing organisational structures and fields of relationships that characterised the dispersed systems of the new state form. Managerialism both provided the appropriate forms of internal discipline and discretion and constituted the conduits of implementation, control and performance audit that were identified as the conditions of accountability to central government.

There are, of course, issues about how deep such processes have penetrated into organisational life. It has been argued that organisations have developed this array of plans, strategies and visions as a matter of symbolic compliance or legitimation – that is, producing the symbols that organisations ought to have. These arguments about the depth and consequence of change are important and complex ones which we explore more fully in the next chapter. But it is difficult to find any reform in the last decade which has not drawn on and contributed to the installation of a managerial mode of coordination – from the creation of Civil Service Agencies to the reorganisation of health and social care around market relations.

Changing regimes: the powers of managerialism

In Chapter 1, we discussed the ways in which the welfare state was organisationally constructed around the twin principles of bureaucratic administration and professionalism to produce 'bureau-professional' regimes. Of course there was a wide diversity of organisational cultures and forms of social relations within this regime. But we have used the idea of organisational regime to concentrate attention on how power is organised within and between organisations. We use 'regime' here in a rather different way from the concept which is emerging to theorise the political economy of urban development (Collinge and Hall, 1996; Peterson, 1981; Stoker and Mossberger, 1994). But it shares a focus on the underlying relations of power in a number of ways. It allows us to go beyond the interplay of multiple interests (professional, administrators, managers) and the actions of individuals to explore the underlying structures and logics of a specific mode of coordination. It also involves a view of power as productive (through its modes of attachment, normative power and structures of legitimation) as well as more instrumental concepts of power over specific groups. Stone suggests that 'What is at issue is not so much domination and subordination as a capacity to act and accomplish goals. The power struggle concerns, not control and resistance, but gaining and fusing a capacity to act – power to, not power over' (Stone, 1989: 229). Regimes represent a point of sedimentation of economic and political interests: the managerialisation of welfare both provides the means through which the interests of capital are pursued (through the containment of public sector spending) and the legitimating framework for a politically driven project of state transformation. Finally, the concept of regimes is focused on both intra- and inter-organisational dimensions of power. That is, it does not just concern the way in which managers control decision making and resource allocation within a particular organisation, but concerns the way in which the flow of power across and between organisations (for example between statutory and voluntary bodies, between national and local bodies) is realigned.

We can identify a number of dimensions of power associated with organisational regimes:

- *Modes of attachment*: what cultural attachments provide the sources of identity or belonging to organisations and occupations.
- *Decision making, agenda setting and normative power*: who makes decisions about what issues; the capacity to define what decisions are available to be taken; and the frameworks of criteria or principles that should govern decision making.
- *Sources of legitimacy*: the underpinnings of the legitimate deployment of these various forms of power.
- *Relational power*: how particular agents or groups of agents are positioned in structured relationships within and beyond organisations.

We explore each of these dimensions of power more fully in what follows, contrasting the characteristic formations associated with bureau-professional regimes with those of managerial ones. In doing so, we are concerned with bureau-professionalism and managerialism as 'ideal types'. The ways in which they are enacted and overlaid in practice will be explored in Chapter 5. At this point we are concerned with setting out their differences in order to illuminate the shifts in modes of power in the dynamics of change, giving attention to different forms these might take in emerging managerial cultures.

Modes of attachment

In the old regimes, identifications were structured by the complex of bureau-professionalism itself and to the wider conceptions of public service embedded within it. In the process, there were a number of cross-cutting attachments: 'local' ones to the employing organisation and sections or departments within it; more 'cosmopolitan' ones to an occupational or professional grouping that transcended the specific site of employment; and often unarticulated notions of 'public service' were overlaid on these. Bureau-professional regimes placed people in relatively clearly defined positions and in predictable trajectories of career development and movement (with advancing administrative or professional seniority). In this regime, then, identification was multi-dimensional and, at times, uneasy (with tensions between professional attachments and administrative or organisational loyalties). By contrast, the new managerialism promised a corporate culture of mutual commitment to the overriding values and mission of the organisation. Its mission was to create a homogeneous and shared culture which would bind all workers to the pursuit of corporate objectives.

The new managerialism placed great stress on giving up traditional modes of attachment and sought to bridge the motivation gap by combining culture management (the creation of purposes and meanings) with performance management (measuring what really matters). It stressed reduced supervisory control to achieve enhanced integration, moving from compliance to commitment (see Hopfl, 1992). The aim was to create the transparent organisation where everyone is responsible for achieving corporate objectives and everyone is enterprising in pursuit of them:

> The new vocabulary of teamwork, quality consciousness, flexibility and quality circles thus reconciles the autonomous aspirations of the employee with the collective entrepreneurialism of the corporate culture. (Rose, 1989: 117)

However, the practice is considerably more complex than the inspirational rhetoric of the new managerialism might suggest. 'Old' attachments and control systems do not just simply wither away. At the same time, new approaches to performance measurement, the use of 'invisible' monitoring systems through information technology (Garson, 1989) and the use of customer surveys to discipline front line workers (Fuller and Smith, 1991) point to attempts to regulate labour processes. They also reflect the importance of neo-Taylorist modes of control alongside new strategies of building corporate identification and commitment. Despite this complexity, there was a sustained attempt to displace forms of extra-organisational loyalty and attachment (to a profession, to the 'civil service' or to 'public service' in general, or to the clients and communities served).

The attempt to elaborate corporate cultures reflects the fragmenting effects of dispersal in which individual fortunes are seen as increasingly tied to the success – or at least survival – of a particular organisation. Whatever other flaws it might have had, welfare professionalism always contained threads of collegiality and cosmopolitanism which ran counter to local organisational regimes. These threads evoked a sense of belonging to something other than a particular organisation, department or unit. Such trans-organisational connections have been a fertile ground for engagement with the politics of social welfare over the past two decades. As such they have been identified as the source of disruptive or dislocatory symbols which undermine the promises of managerialism and corporate success. The *Guardian* printed an extract from the University of Humberside's 'Strategic Plan to 2000' that emphasised the problem of multiple loyalties: 'Academic staff often display loyalty to their subject and discipline and also to their students and school. Such loyalties are often separate from, and may conflict with, loyalty to the university' (*Education Guardian*, 30 May 1995: 4). Other loyalties thus form a difficult terrain for managerial regimes. They undercut attempts to build corporate identities and attachments and manifest themselves as a further problem to be *managed*. But they also offer alternative frameworks and rationales for decision making.

Decision making, agenda setting and normative power

It is possible to trace particular formations of power embedded in the bureau-professional regimes of the 'old' welfare state. *Decision making power* operated in two organisational spaces: the implementation of bureaucratic rules (their application to specific cases) and the exercise of professional discretion involving the application of specialised knowledge to complex cases or processes (ranging from diagnosing medical conditions to how to teach children). *Agenda setting power* refers to the capacity to define what decisions need to be made and in bureau-professional regimes these centred on connecting formalised categories of 'need' to the assessment of individual cases. The 'agenda' for bureau-professional regimes was structured around the identification and assessment of need and organising the application of expertise to the problem of meeting legitimated needs. These concerns defined the sorts of decisions that were 'the business of' bureau-professional regimes. *Normative power* was organised through bureau-professional discourses of 'needs' and 'rights' through which access to benefits and services was negotiated. It was this normative power which also provided the legitimating discourse (that of bureau-professional expertise and discretion) for this organisation of power through the claim that 'professionals know best' (and the implicit requirement that they should be trusted as a consequence).

Bureau-professional relationships were characterised by the power of such staff to categorise, define and treat service users. That is, they were able to deploy decision making, agenda setting and normative power within the scope of individual client/worker interactions, as well as in the administrative processes of service planning. In bureau-professional interactions, the power of service users was based on limited entitlements to certain universal services, with the fall-back possibility of expressing their interests or concerns to their MP or local councillor. They had little power to influence the ways in which services were delivered or the processes through which bureau-professional power was enacted.

Managerial regimes articulate rather different conditions and distributions of power. *Decision making power* is the prerogative of managers (at different levels of the organisation) since the capacity to make decisions is what embodies 'the right to manage'. This is what rhetorically distinguishes management from administration: managers are *active* decision-makers, while administrators merely implement or interpret decisions made else-where. There are, of course, significant tensions between the rhetoric of managerial freedoms, or the 'empowerment' of managers to take local decisions, and the constraints within which these operate in a public sector where limits are set both by legislation and by centrally set cost controls and performance targets. However, the rhetorical significance of decision making power reflects the emphasis on devolution of managerial respons-ibility down to and within organisations, and the limiting of upward accountability to a narrow range of performance measures. The logic of managerialism is that managers are accountable for what they deliver, but not for how they deliver it. It is results, not methods, that count, and to achieve good results managers must have the maximum room for manoeuvre in the decision making process.

Agenda setting power in managerial regimes centres on making decisions that address the framework of organisational objectives and the deployment of resources. Decisions about activities or interventions cannot be taken in isolation from their implications for costs or contribution to organisational performance. *Normative power* in managerial regimes foregrounds the calculus of 'efficiency' and 'performance' as the frame of reference for organisational action. This is not just the narrow sense of cost efficiency but denotes the wider set of concerns with how best to achieve, measure and control organisational performance. As such, the normative power of mana-gerialism defines the dominant terms of reference from controlling costs through to the production of quality. Appeals to intangible benefits, values or other goals which are not formulated as part of the corporate objectives are thus disempowered. Normative power is deployed in the setting of rationing criteria and the establishment of priorities between different services and different groups of users, rather than in individual face-to-face interactions. These take place within a managerial, rather than a pro-fessional, calculus. Even if it is 'professionals' doing it, they are operating within a different regime of power enforced through the twin constraints of budgetary restrictions and devolved managerial accountability.

Managerialism challenges the bureaucratic and often paternalistic basis of the normative power of bureau-professional regimes, but offers a different set of logics and constraints. At first sight the user has more power. He or she has the power to complain, to express their choice about a 'service package', school or tenant management scheme, and in many cases to express a view about the way in which services should be offered through consultation or 'user involvement' exercises. Some can also deploy market power through choosing private, rather than public, health or insurance provision. But for those using public services, the areas of choice and involvement are very limited. They are exercised in the area of decision making power, but users rarely have the opportunity to be involved in the arenas of calculative or normative power. That is, what services are to be provided, to whom, and according to what order of priorities, become part of the business decisions of managers subject to the logics of strategic positioning and financial survival.

Sources of legitimacy

As with the bureau-professional regime, it is the field of normative power that also provides the legitimating discourse. It empowers managers as the primary agents in organisations because managers 'do the right thing': they are the people who know about organisational efficiency and performance.

The legitimacy of managerialism draws on a starkly articulated juxtaposition of the failings of other means of coordinating and controlling social welfare. The qualities of management were contrasted with the problems of the old regime and its dominant forms of organisational power: bureaucracy, professionalism and political representation (see Figure 1).

Like the binary divisions of past and future that we discussed in the previous chapter, it is possible to see the vilification of the old and the idealisation of the new in these contrasts. Nevertheless, it provides a useful starting point for thinking about the reconstruction of power associated with processes of managerialisation.

BUREAUCRACY is:	*MANAGEMENT is:*
rule bound	innovative
inward looking	externally oriented
compliance centred	performance centred
ossified	dynamic
PROFESSIONALISM is:	*MANAGEMENT is:*
paternalist	customer centred
mystique ridden	transparent
standard oriented	results oriented
self-regulating	market tested
POLITICIANS are:	*MANAGERS are:*
dogmatic	pragmatic
interfering	enabling
unstable	strategic

Figure 1   *Legitimating managerialism*

The legitimacy of managerialism is partly based on the view that it brings greater transparency. The decisional power of managers, linked to devolution and decentralisation, demonstrates (at least in principle) who is responsible for what decisions. It also positions managers as accountable – either upwards to policy makers (through performance measurement, audit and evaluation systems), or downwards to customers and users. But whereas political accountability in bureau-professional regimes was institutionalised through its hierarchical structures which provided for direct upward accountability to Ministers or local politicians, the dispersal of power in managerial regimes makes direct political control of decision making more problematic, leading to what some have termed a 'democratic deficit' (Stewart, 1993). In its place, managerial regimes seem to offer more direct accountability to users. Bureau-professional regimes stress accountability to politicians, and promise the best 'treatment' for those in need, legitimated by professional criteria of judgement. By contrast, managerial regimes stress accountability to users, and promise the best service to customers, tested by customer satisfaction ratings and performance on league tables.

The legitimacy of managerialism, like that of bureau-professionalism, also depends on its internal knowledge base and the sciences/technologies from which these are derived. Bureau-professionalism offers the pursuit of the 'public good' based on the application of forms of expert power which are service specific. These are substantive forms of knowledge about particular sorts of needs and interventions. By contrast, managerialism promises the best use of public resources based on the deployment of calculative power. The knowledge of managerialism is 'universalist', applicable to all organisations rather than substantive and specific. It is presented as a rationality which transcends the differences of services or sectors.

The rationalism of managerialism provides a non-partisan (and de-politicised) framework within which choices can be made. Competing values are reduced to alternative sets of options and costs and assessed against their contribution to the organisation's performance. They are subjected to a rational analysis which claims to stand outside and beyond partisan claims of different 'interest groups'. While different professional or occupational groups may pursue their parochial interests, management represents the organisation's best interests (for example, see Green and Armstrong's discussion of 'bed management', 1995). The calculative technologies of managerialism thus provide a foundation for enacting the new logics of rationing, targeting and priority setting. Its quantitative and evaluative technologies form the basis for the new roles of contracting, audit and regulation. The scientific knowledges which they deploy position managers as neutral and impersonal. Managers can be trusted: they are not part of the war between different political and occupational interests.

The rational/technical character of managerial knowledge offers the promise of resolving two different forms of 'chaos'. The first is the chaos of the old regime – the irrationality of unmanaged systems in which the decision making of 'street level bureaucrats' cannot be controlled, and in which bureaucratic control mechanisms proliferate seemingly stupid and irrational systems of rules which get in the way of effectiveness (Peters, 1987). Managerialism represents a way of imposing a rationalised order on this chaos. The second promise of managerialism is that of coping with the complexities and uncertainties of the modern world – the 'chaos of the new' – through the quasi-scientific techniques of strategic management and the delivery of fast paced change and innovation. Where bureaucracies adapt slowly and in a rather ramshackle fashion, creating new rules and functions to cope with new situations within a framework of getting by and making do, managerialism promises to organise the irrational within a rational framework.

While the decision making and normative power of managerialism provides the basis for the legitimation of the managerial regime at a macro-level, there are difficulties in talking about managerialism as a set of knowledges and powers abstracted from the organisational forms in which they are deployed. The next section explores some of the variabilities within the managerial regime in order to identify the dynamics of power within organisations.

We have chosen to discuss these shifting relationships of power by sketching three different organisational orders: the 'traditional', the 'competitive' and the 'transformational' or 'excellence' (Newman, 1994, 1995). The traditional order is based on what we have earlier described as the bureau-professional regime. The competitive order is characterised by its primary orientation to the market, its modelling of organisations as businesses and by the dominance of the discourses of entrepreneurialism and competitive success. The transformational order is characterised by the modelling of organisations as dynamic, progressive and customer oriented, and by the pre-eminence of the discourses of culture, HRM, quality and values. Each has rather different sets of sources of internal power and legitimacy through which the social relations of organisations are structured. None of these exists in a pure form, but we treat them as typified formations in order to unlock the different forms of hierarchies, relationships and subject positions through which they order their internal and external worlds.

Changing relations: orders of place and power

Regimes of power are not just about who gets to exercise particular sorts of power over aspects of organisational life. They also involve relational power – fields of relations between different social groups within and beyond organisations. Some dimensions of this are well established in the study of public services and their organisational forms. So, it is possible to trace the shifting balances of power between bureaucrats and professionals, or between bureau-professionals and managers, or workers and managers. Such terms form the dominant classification of studies of organisational relations of power (for example see Ackroyd et al., 1989; Cutler and Waine, 1994;

Harrison and Pollitt, 1994). However, they often seem strangely dis-
connected from the wider world of social relations – in particular the
complex and intersecting formations of class, 'race' and gender. More
accurately, we should say that they have been more readily linked to the
concerns of the sociology of class, but have limited connections to gendered
and racialised social divisions. Although we cannot hope to resolve all these
issues about changing relations of power within the confines of this chapter,
we do want to indicate some of the connections between organisational and
social relations in the processes of managerialisation. The changing relations
of power do not just involve organisational or occupational groups, they also
shape – and are shaped by – the social formation of such groups.

The traditional order: bureau-professional relations

The traditional order is based on the interaction of professional and
administrative power, each delivering its own language, imagery, relationships and ways of doing things. Each produces particular places and subject
positions within a hierarchical pattern of relationships. Professionalism
offers a range of identities tied to the (externally derived) orderings and
hierarchies of specific professions. There are both hierarchies of status
within each profession (consultant/registrar/junior doctor, social worker/
senior practitioner/team leader, etc.) and hierarchies between professions
(nurses, para-professionals, doctors). These external orderings are translated
into hierarchies of expertise and experience within organisational settings.
Administrative discourses offer functionally specific identities (finance,
personnel) and a hierarchy of clearly defined grades and status positions, as
elaborated within the traditional Civil Service. Distinct organisational structures produce boundaries between administrative and professional work,
clerical and 'support' roles, and service tasks such as cleaning, catering,
building maintenance and so on.

   In the traditional order, these divisions both follow and reinforce class
relations. These class relations operate around the distinction between
professional and higher grades of administrative roles, and the panoply of
male and female support work ('blue collar' and 'clerical'). Such distinctions were the focus of different organisational and occupational attempts at
'closure' – regulating access to status, power and privilege. They were also
embedded in multiple forms of potentially antagonistic distinctions between
'us and them': between blue and white collar workers; between workers and
bosses; between professionals and administrators. These distinctions were
usually embodied in strong collective identities and formalised in local and
national collective bargaining processes and agreements, resulting in differentiated conditions of service. Conflicts across such distinctions were both
frequent and highly formalised – if not ritualised.

   Such relations allocated subordinate roles to workers from black and
ethnic minority groups, typically in support rather than professionalised
occupations (if they are employed at all). The combination of exclusion and

subordinated inclusion in the relations of bureau-professionalism suggest why 'race' became such a contested focus of employment policy in public services through the 1970s and 1980s. Characteristically, such challenges were addressed by the formation of new rules and regulatory processes – in the form of bureaucratised equal opportunity policies governing recruitment and staff development. As we argued in Chapter 1, such accommodations were accompanied by attempts to recruit staff selectively from minority ethnic groups to create processes of service provision where staff would 'match' the social composition of the specific communities being served (Lewis, 1997).

The traditional order also followed and reinforced conventional gender roles and divisions, both in its employment practices and in the familialised imagery around which the 'support' or 'adjunct' work of women was structured (Davies, 1995a; Newman, 1994). Bureau-professionalism was based on strong gender divisions, with very clear boundary distinctions operating horizontally, with some professions and occupations being seen as men's work, and some – typically the 'semi' or 'para' professions – being identified as women's work. This traditional order was also structured vertically, with women predominating in low level support and front line service delivery roles, and rarely present at higher levels of the hierarchy.

The dislocation of bureau-professional regimes in the restructuring of the welfare state has been accompanied by a blurring of some of these boundaries. 'Management' is no longer the sole province of the most senior organisational tiers where men are generally to be found, but has cascaded down organisations to relatively low paid, low status service delivery functions, drawing more women into jobs with managerial titles and responsibilities. At the same time the gender typifications of some jobs have become weaker, with more men prepared to enter traditional female domains as a result of the erosion of opportunities in male occupations. The hierarchies of expertise are also shifting, leading to the regendering of some occupations (e.g., personnel management being replaced by human resource directors, hospital matrons by directors of nursing). As well as men entering female spaces, some women have entered the male preserves of management, but within a highly gendered regime of managerial power. For example, Charlotte Williamson argues that the corporate governance model of boards in the NHS is 'essentially male' and is therefore a source of tensions:

> In essence, it [the corporate governance model] is a command structure for controlling the distribution of power in hierarchical organisations. . . . Although there is now much discussion about implementing corporate governance, the model itself is regarded as unproblematic. It is not. It is a masculine model which has developed from men's work in commerce, industry, the church and the military. It reflects men's assumptions, values and preferred ways of working. These are not wrong; indeed the model is attractive and convincing. But it has consequences for women trying to work within its prescriptions, when it can seem inadequate to the task of governance in today's health service. (1995: 27)

The traditional order of bureau-professional power has been brought increasingly into question as organisations attempt to respond to the imperatives of competition and change. Some of the consequences are examined in our analyses of the emergence of competitive and transformational organisational orders.

The competitive order: the relations of macho management

While most public service organisations have now been exposed to competition in one form or another, their responses have differed. 'Being competitive' is not an objective set of attributes, but depends on interpretations and myths about how the business world operates, as well as how closely different organisations are involved in marketised or competitive processes. But many public sector organisations have taken on images of competitive behaviour as requiring hard, macho or 'cowboy' styles of working. It is as if the unshackling of bureaucratic constraints has at last allowed public sector managers to become 'real men', released from the second class status of public functionaries by their exposure to the 'real world' of the marketplace. 'It's a case of growing up. Whereas [before privatisation] we were kiddies playing with the thing, it is now a man's game' (Whittington et al., 1994: 840).

Such responses to competition have consequences for the reordering of workforce relationships in a number of ways. One of the defining features of the competitive order is the weakening of trade unions and the decline of collective bargaining, particularly at a national level. In these conditions, staff are primarily conceived of as a cost, whose impact on organisational performance needs to be minimised. At the same time, the productivity of labour has to be increased, often through simple intensification. A variety of strategies have been visible for managing labour costs: contracting out; renegotiating terms and conditions of service; 'downsizing' through redundancies; creating more flexible forms of labour and so on (see, for example, Cousins, 1988; Pinch, 1994). The traditional divisions between management and workforce are eroded, to be replaced with a new set of 'us' and 'them' typifications based on distinctions between core and periphery. Contracting out (through compulsory competitive tendering (CCT), market testing and the new drive to define and concentrate on the 'core business') means that divisions are emerging between different labour force groups as organisations seek greater workforce flexibility.

These strategies have implications for gender, 'race' and class relations. The formation of these 'flexible labour forces' tilts employability towards low cost labour, while at the same time worsening the conditions of employment. Thus, employment chances for women have increased, but these opportunities are simultaneously concentrated in part-time, low paid and insecure work. Those parts of the public sector most susceptible to being contracted out were initially support and service roles such as cleaning or catering. Such contracting out tended to be accompanied by a sharpening of concern over costs and a downward spiral of pay and conditions. Its impact was unevenly distributed, affecting working class occupations in the public sector, where workers from minority ethnic groups were most concentrated and where there was a high proportion of women. These changes intensified trends in the composition of welfare work around 'race' and gender by making the most vulnerable groups of employees more vulnerable through casualisation and sub-contracting. But research on the impact of CCT shows that these processes have a differential impact on men and women. One major study concludes that:

> The differential between male, usually full time, and female, usually part time, manual workers has been exacerbated under CCT. The low status of the work of cleaning and catering staff remains. This is in spite of the fact that CCT means that the services are no longer invisible in the council structures. Moreover, many of the 'savings' made under CCT of manual services have been achieved through the flexible use of the lowest paid, part time manual workers. (Escott and Whitfield, 1995: 165)

The same study shows how the move to a competitive order tends to involve a weakening of equal opportunity issues and procedures. Such regulatory processes are seen as the legacy of the old, bureaucratic order – more 'red tape' which gets in the way of 'doing business'. The competitive order is usually highly inventive in its efforts to demonstrate why such issues are 'not our business' or 'do not apply here'. Even the limited equal opportunities agenda developed in public service organisations is viewed as an unwarrantable intrusion on the freedom of managers to go about their business.

In the 'core' of the competitive order, women may retain their old employment rights and statuses, but are removed from the paternalist protectiveness of the traditional order and exposed to the full rigours of a macho, competitive style of working (Newman, 1995). One analyst, exploring both the under-representation of women at senior levels and the hardening of management style within the NHS, talks of the rise of 'macho managers' who 'are reluctant to engage in real partnership and prefer conflict to collaboration', which she argues results in demoralised staff and poorer services (Maddock, 1995). Celia Davies points to the emergence of new languages that reference the shift towards a management approach that is 'aggressive, harsh and confrontational':

> There is now a form of 'gender talk' in the National Health Service (NHS) that was quite unknown a decade ago. It refers disparagingly to the 'men in suits', and questions the relevance of a 'grey suit' mentality that brings to bear an economic calculus that is devoid of human warmth or sympathy and that distances itself from the suffering that those in the frontline of health care must face on a daily basis. (1995a: 27)

Hostility to the 'men in suits' is by no means limited to the NHS. Concerns about the impact of the competitive order on public sector and voluntary organisations have centred on the emergence of a 'business culture' that embodies an apparent insensibility to the processes and relationships. However, other forms of management culture, especially those drawing on the 'excellence' literature and new HRM strategies, view such processes and relationships as central to organisational success. While competitive success may remain the ultimate goal, notions of 'transformational management' differ in important symbolic respects from the management strategies of the competitive order.

The transformational order: partners in change?

This order is oriented towards the ethos of radical transformation which we examined in Chapter 3, based strongly on the prescriptions of the 'excellence' school of management set out by Peters and Waterman (1982); Peters (1987) and others. It focuses not on short term competitiveness, but on building long term capacity through transforming relations with customers and staff. The capacity to be quality oriented, flexible and responsive to customers is seen to depend on the 'empowerment' of staff and their commitment to service values and to the success of the enterprise as a whole. The emphasis, then, is on commitment building through the deployment of 'affective' management practices (for example, through visionary and inspiring leadership and through culture change programmes stressing values and mission) and through an emphasis on workforce participation and involvement. This means that, although 'hard' Human Resource Management strategies such as workforce flexibility and downsizing are deployed, the emphasis for workers in the core is on the 'soft' aspects of HRM, based on the building of a partnership between managers and employees, the flattening of hierarchies and the eradication of (visible) status divisions.

Such a partnership model appears to displace the patterns of power and control through which relationships in the other two regimes are structured. However, power does not disappear by being made less visible. The ideology emphasises corporate consensus, and promulgates the view that old lines of conflict are no longer relevant in the new world of change. This is most significant around class relations, involving the further weakening of trade union power. Workforce/management relations become individualised (through individual targets and appraisal systems, sometimes likened to performance related pay), and the stress is on establishing direct channels of communication between managers and workers (through team briefing and a panoply of internal communications strategies, from newsletters to corporate videos) rather than being conducted through trade union representatives.

The partnership model also has implications for 'race' and gender (Newman, 1995). In particular it suggests that, now the worst excesses of discrimination have been overcome, opportunities are genuinely open to all – anyone can rise to the top. And indeed there are now some visible symbols of the 'success' of this in the appointment of women and, to a lesser extent, members of black and ethnic minority groups to senior positions (though what happens to the individuals concerned is another matter – visibility often comes with a high price tag). The ethos is that people are to be valued for their contribution rather than their social or organisational status: all have something to contribute to the mission of corporate success. The effect of this ethos, however, is to repress the possibility of internal conflict within the organisation. Any challenge about continued inequality, or about racial or sexual harassment, is potentially seen as disturbing the harmonious equilibrium and dividing teams of inter-dependent co-workers.

There are particular issues about the gender dynamics of this regime, based on contradictory images of management style. The practice of becoming leaner, fitter and faster organisations has a tendency to produce the worst excesses of 'macho' management (whether practised by men or by women). On the other hand, the drive towards being more people oriented, linked to the creation of new modes of attachment, requires the partial 'feminisation' of management. By this we mean the partial shift away from the dominance of 'male' skills at the core of a *technology* of management towards a greater emphasis on the skills of communication and culture building, network and partnership management, providing good relationships with customers and workforce, and managing the complex processes of change and transition. These form the core of a *relational* view of management. The former deals with the masculine-typified domains of structures, systems, plans and technologies, and engages with a world of strong boundaries (between different organisations, different roles, different tasks) through rationality, calculation and linear thought. The latter deals with feminine typified domains of people, processes, relationships, style and image, and engages with a world of weak boundaries, interconnectedness, complexity and uncertainty. It works by 'feel': sensing interrelationships and shaping emergent patterns. It emphasises the importance of dealing with the affective domains of human interactions and relationships. While management must encompass both domains – it is necessary to be able to count as well as communicate, to enforce as well as empower – the 'feminine' typified skills have undergone a profound, though unacknowledged, revaluation from the work of Tom Peters onwards. Nevertheless, the imagery is not all about revaluing the feminine. It also evokes many of the 'heroic' features of the transformational discourse we described in Chapter 3, whose inspirational, visionary and 'championing' qualities are derived from masculine images of leadership.

Mixed messages: the problem of knowing one's place

These three different organisational orders do not exist in isolation; they co-exist and interact. Such processes produce conflicting messages and injunctions for employees as older and newer sets of messages are overlaid on each other in complex ways. For example, workers with a grievance may become trapped between the procedural mechanisms of redress enshrined as points of continuity with traditional orders, and the 'macho' styles or 'partnership' expectations of emerging regimes. Female or black male workers who have fulfilled the expectations of total commitment in the transformational order, leading project teams and taking on responsibility for corporate success, may be short-changed in the promotion stakes because of continuities with the gendered and racialised typifications of the traditional order.

More subtly, the competitive and the transformational orders serve to rework the shifting boundary between 'public' and 'private', which interacts with the traditional expectations of male and female work roles and domains. In Chapter 2 we argued that the restructuring of the state involved a complex reworking of the boundary between public and private in the provision of social welfare. These contradictory shifts are also visible in the changes in the internal orders of welfare organisations. Bureau-professional regimes and their traditional order placed a low valuation on the 'intimate' and 'personal' dimensions of interactions with both senior staff and service users. Such tasks – what Davies (1995b) has called 'adjunct work' – tended to be predominantly female and were viewed as 'feminine' (whether 'caring for' clients and patients or 'supporting' male professionals). The dominant imagery of bureau-professional regimes was masculine – the depersonalised application of expertise and rules (Witz, 1992).

The competitive order takes this further. Its economic calculus depersonalises the provision of services in a different way – by insisting on the commodification of labour like any other resource. This de-differentiation of public services underpins the description of competitive managers as 'grey suits' – they are viewed as unable to see what it is that makes public services different. By contrast, the transformational order attempts to make the organisation more 'personal': it asks for enthusiasm and commitment and it attempts to link personal and organisational values. In the process, it undercuts the distinction between the 'public' world of work and the 'private' feelings of workers by insisting that work is more than contractual compliance – it is a process of simultaneous corporate achievement and self-realisation (du Gay, 1996).

We also want to highlight the interaction between, on the one hand, the re-designation of major areas of social and health care to the 'private' world of family and community (that is, to the sphere of mainly female labour), and on the other the intensification of managerial labour at the 'core' of organisational labour forces in a public sector under pressure. To compete in the managerial career stakes now means demonstrating commitment through long (often excessive) hours of work and being able to cope with high stress. Staying on to be present at the crucial meeting to deal with the latest crisis has to take precedence over familial, relationship or community commitments. Whether the meeting is effective or not is sometimes less significant than being seen to have the commitment to be there. Such intensification, linked to career uncertainty and occupational fragility, has a profound impact on both men and women, with implications for their children, partners and parents as well as their own quality of life. These pressures may, however, impact differently on men and women in a social climate in which male identity remains more closely tied to the workplace than that of women, and in which many of the 'female' responsibilities of caring for the young, the sick and the elderly are being returned to the private domains of women's labour in home and community. These pressures are sharpened as women as mothers have become the targets of blame for a range of social ills, from crime and delinquency in the young to the more general social ills produced through what has been termed the 'parenting deficit' (Etzioni, 1993). At the same time, many women themselves are having doubts about the value of 'career success' in these emerging forms of managerial regime (Marshall, 1995). If second-wave feminism fought for greater access to the male bastions of power in the workplace, women in the 1990s are beginning to find this something of a poisoned chalice. Just as women have been allowed to become managers, management itself has been transformed into the containment of the uncertainties, pressures, stresses and discontents of public sector restructuring, organisational downsizing and cuts in services to users and communities. Whether in managing these tensions within organisations or in interactions with service users, there has been an intensification of the 'emotional labour' involved in providing public services.

Despite the fact that the two variants of managerialism we have described rework the boundary between the public and the private in different ways, they both seek a similar outcome – the intensification of labour. The competitive order seeks this through contractual compliance while the transformational order seeks it through affective commitment (Flynn, 1994). Both, however, have consequences for the relationship between the worlds of organisational life and 'private life' beyond the organisation. The realignments of this relationship are played out within a complex process of regime change in which external and internal shifts of power intersect with the social relations of gender, 'race' and class.

Thriving on chaos: the dominance of managerialism

Our analysis of the different forms and relations of power provides a starting point for thinking about the place of managerialism in state restructuring. Change has been uncomfortable and uneasy, involving resistances, compromises and shifting alliances which have taken different forms, reflecting different organisational histories, different locations in the welfare state and different policy reforms. Some of these differences are explored further in the next chapter. What is clear, however, is that the process of managerialisation has not resulted in simple patterns of institutional change, but complex and uneven alignments of managerialism and bureau-professionalism. At one level this is not surprising. The extensive people processing of social welfare requires skills and competences other than those of managing. NHS Trusts require staff who know about medicine and illnesses as well as those who know about 'bed management'. Social services need people to conduct assessments of needs as well as those who know how to purchase 'care services'. Nevertheless, managerialisation has left nothing untouched in the way bureau-professional regimes have been transformed. We want to suggest three ways in which managerialism has reshaped the place and power of bureau-professionalism: displacement, subordination and co-option.

Displacement refers to the process by which management has superseded bureau-professionalism in the way public services are organised as regimes. Here organisations are reshaped around a command structure which privileges the calculative framework of managerialism: how to improve efficiency and organisational performance. Complete displacement is relatively rare: the dominant relationship between bureau-professionalism and management has been one of *subordination*. This takes the form of framing the exercise of professional judgement by the requirement that it takes account of the 'realities and responsibilities' of budgetary management. Increasingly, professional assessment encounters budgetary implications at an earlier stage, such that the assessment of need no longer takes place prior to – and separate from – the resourcing of intervention but alongside it. This is most clearly visible in the fields of health and social care. The combination of devolved budgets and care assessment and planning in community care was an attempt to discipline the 'irresponsible' exercise of professional judgement about needs by making it coterminous with the allocation of resources. Where 'need' was once the product of the intersection of bureaucratic categorisation and professional judgement, it is now increasingly articulated with and *disciplined by* a managerial calculus of resources and priorities.

But many areas of professional service are characterised by a rather different strategy: that of *co-option*. This refers to managerial attempts to colonise the terrain of professional discourse, constructing articulations between professional concerns and languages and those of management. Thus, corporate missions and strategies have increasingly moved from the bare pursuit of efficiency to a concern with standards of service, the pursuit of excellence and the achievement of continuous improvement. Perhaps the most obvious example is the epidemic of quality. Quality appeared to be the 'home ground' of professionals, committed as they were to the maintenance of standards, and dissemination of good practice. Nevertheless, as a number of authors have demonstrated, 'quality' is also a central mechanism for disciplining professional autonomy (Jackson, 1994; Pollitt, 1993). The systematisation of quality through the production of indicators, comparable information and evaluation seeks, in Peter Jackson's delightful phrase, to 'curb the promiscuity' of quality. But the growing managerial attention to service matters reflects a simultaneous concern with how to control bureau-professional practice and to 'bring professionals on board', building their attachment to corporate cultures and directions.

These are strategies in the struggle between regimes. They produce new focal points of resistance, compromise and accommodation and we will examine these aspects in more detail in the next two chapters. However, we want to suggest that managerialisation has shifted the terms of reference on which conflicts and tensions around social welfare are fought out both within and beyond organisations. If managerialism is not yet 'hegemonic' in the sense of having established itself as the uncontested regime of social welfare, it is nevertheless the dominant force in the field. The most obvious indicator of the impact of managerialism is the rapid growth in the number of people who have the title of managers (e.g., in the NHS).[1] These are either imports or converts – the former brought in from the 'real world' of business; the latter produced through management training or development programmes. Dramatic though this growth has been, it does not provide an adequate measure of the shift to managerial regimes. The pressures towards devolution and decentralisation have produced organisational regimes in which both managerial tasks and the calculative or normative framework of managerialism are dispersed throughout organisations. These processes create both 'hybrid' formations (through which bureau-professionals become managers) and a more widely dispersed managerial consciousness.

The 'hybrid' form is now widespread in what were formerly bureau-professional services and we use the phrase to denote the incorporation of professional workers, characteristically through processes of devolution and delegation, into the new structures of corporate coordination. Clinical directors, ward managers and fund-holding practices in the NHS; head teachers under LMS; care management in social services; devolved operational management in policing and so on rest on the construction of articulations between professional and managerial modes of coordination (see also Fitzgerald et al., 1995). We have argued elsewhere (Clarke and Newman, 1993b) that such 'hybrids' evoke a complex of motivations and commitments. Such positions are often an uncomfortable place to be because they are subject to conflicting demands and expectations in a field of tensions between service and corporate concerns. Such hybrid formations are also the focal point for 'devolved stress' as significant organisational tensions and conflicts come to be embodied in single individuals. One might suggest that the incipient revolt of governors and head teachers in the 1995 round of education budget management indicated the potential structural as well as personal instability of the hybrid form.

Devolution and decentralisation also have the effect of creating a 'dispersed managerial consciousness', the embedding of the calculative frameworks of managerialism throughout organisations. By this, we mean to refer to the processes by which all employees come to find their decisions, actions and possibilities framed by the imperatives of managerial coordination: competitive positioning, budgetary control, performance management and efficiency gains. The use of the word 'consciousness' is not meant to imply that people think of themselves as managers (although the rhetorical devices of 'we are all responsible now' clearly seek such an effect), but that people are increasingly conscious that managerial agendas and the corporate calculus condition their working relationships, conditions and processes and have to be negotiated.

Internalising managerial regimes

The capacity of managerialism to permeate organisational life, to define the organisational environment within which people act and to establish its calculative framework as the dominant one is not simply a product of change within organisations. It also derives from the changing 'external environment' (see Harrison and Pollitt, 1994: ch. 5). The restructuring of the state form through delegation, decentralisation and contracting has created a field of inter-organisational relations that necessitate competitive positioning. So, even though staff in public service organisations might not welcome the shift to 'business cultures', this is tempered by a recognition that organisations are positioned in this new field of forces. This is the most potent underpinning of managerialism – the perception that, for any particular organisation, there is no alternative. This internalisation of managerialism as the necessary internal corollary of the changing external environment can be exemplified in three core managerial ideas: 'core business', 'ownership' and 'audit'.

The conception of *core business* is the effect of processes of service fragmentation (between providers) and forms of quasi-market competitiveness. It mimics the business idea of 'being focused', shedding activities that do not contribute to the primary goal. In the public sector it represents a shift away from the idea of complex organisations serving multiple constituencies, responding to a diversity of needs, and attempting to find a balance between potentially conflicting interests and goals. This has always been one of the defining features of the public, rather than private, sector, bringing with it particular problems of applying business techniques such as strategic planning or performance measurement (Moss Kanter, 1989). The idea of core business represents an attempt to define the focus of attention of the organisation in terms of a narrow definition of service and/or customer group. Definitions of core business are formed in the field of possibilities constructed by external or statutory requirements and internal organisational politics.

Definitions of core business legitimate withdrawal from previously undertaken activities which become redefined as inessential. Recent examples might include schools withdrawing from extra-curricular provision, or decisions by police forces not to respond to burglar alarms. Notions of core business order the priorities of claims on organisational resources, and create distinctions between 'core' and 'non-core' activities, the latter becoming vulnerable to either contracting out or, if there are no providers interested, being curtailed. Pre-existing forms of public service are thus reshaped, and services become fragmented, with gaps between the fragments that survive. One example highlighted by the Audit Commission concerns foot patrolling (the 'bobby on the beat') by police forces. Beat patrols do not contribute much to the attainment of current performance and efficiency targets for police forces. On the contrary, they are a relatively wasteful use of resources and, on such indicators, do not fall within the core business. On the other hand, the Audit Commission's study reflects others in showing very high levels of public demand for more beat patrols as an essential precondition of feelings of public safety and order (Foster, 1996). An even more striking example was provided by a radio discussion about problems of access to public transport. A woman with small children had to travel beyond her local station because of the impossibility of getting a pushchair across to the station exit. The manager interviewed defined this as a problem for the 'mobility impaired'. This, he suggested, was not part of their business, but a matter which might be addressed in 'partnership' with the local social services department (*You and Yours*, BBC Radio 4, 20 May 1996). Such examples suggest that definitions of core and non-core are not a simple matter, and if the lines are drawn too narrowly there are likely to be 'perverse effects' in terms of unanticipated problems or a decline in public legitimacy.

The attempts to build corporate cultures around the specification of core business embody a retreat from the older expansive conceptions of public service or even of generic fields of public provision (such as education or health). The identification of 'core businesses', allied to corporate organisational cultures, makes the external environment into one mapped by strategic plans, bifurcated into threats and opportunities and peopled by cut-throat competitors. It has the effect of narrowing frameworks for the evaluation of public services to assessments of their 'performance' and 'efficiency' as a business. To paraphrase the emerging common sense on performance measurement: what doesn't get measured, doesn't get done. Although this is usually applied within organisations, it is equally, if not more, relevant to what happens in the fields of provision which span organisational boundaries.

The effects of defining core business overlap with the issue of *ownership*. The creation of a sense of ownership – of missions and targets, budgets and responsibility for results – has been one of the most sought after effects of the managerial revolution, constructing commitment and motivation among staff in the pursuit of corporate objectives (Clarke and Newman, 1993a). Nevertheless, there is a conception of ownership which is a less discussed effect of such initiatives: ownership as proprietorialism or possessive individualism. Owners tend to stake out property rights – the rights to the exclusive use of what they own. It is, therefore, not surprising to find the new field of service provision being characterised by ownership conflicts. Such conflicts centre on issues of who owns customers (and their needs and the resources that might accompany them); who owns service responsibilities and the resource implications that they bring; and who owns those practices that take place in the interstices between organisations or departments. The current shunting of provision for the frail elderly between health and social service organisations, or of 'difficult' pupils between schools, demonstrates some of the consequences of such boundary management strategies. Following the pre-privatisation break-up of British Rail, we were privileged to hear a conductor apologise for a delayed train with the comment that '*They* were having trouble with *their* track, and that has made *us* late'.

Ownership, then, strengthens the possibilities of internal and external conflict, and tends to prioritise local (managerial) priorities over wider service loyalties and commitments. So, the 'boundary disputes' between health and social care raise questions about who owns types of needs as well as who has the definitional power over how needs are to be categorised (Charlesworth et al., 1996; Vickridge, 1995). There are intra-organisational tensions about internal markets or re-charging policies, particularly exposing the overhead costs of central services. There is also the commodification of inter-agency or inter-professional goodwill, with attempts to re-charge the cost of contributing to joint initiatives, for example in child protection work (Charlesworth et al., 1996). In the present conditions, promoting ownership of a budget may create a new sense of fiscal discipline and responsibility but it is also likely to create competitive manoeuvring to maximise income and reduce expenditure.

Thirdly, what Michael Power (1994) has referred to as the *audit explosion* indicates the growth in both internal and external evaluations of performance and compliance. The term audit points to the origins of this process in the 1980s concern with financial control and scrutiny, but it now refers to the more extensive apparatuses of evaluating organisational performance. In part, such processes may reflect the increasing impossibility of trust between citizens and service providers, between government and its agencies, or between clients and contractors. But they are also strategic responses from the centre aimed at both extending the disciplines available to regulate the periphery and overcoming the dislocating relationships of an increasingly dispersed form of the state. The growth of audit, in its many forms, contributes to isomorphic tendencies in the current system, pressing organisations towards the idea that there is one best way of running things. In part, this tendency is the effect of demands for organisations to possess systems that will generate comparable information to facilitate the process of evaluation. But it is also the result of some degree of blurring between the evaluative functions of audit and the concerns of organisational design. Some of this is visible in the trajectory of the Audit Commission which has increasingly developed a prescriptive agenda about organisational and management structures for public service organisations (Gray and Jenkins, 1993: 20).

The growth of audit may have perverse effects on welfare services by transferring scarce organisational resources from service production or delivery to information and monitoring systems (Hoggett, 1996: 22–4). In the public sector context, they have increasingly become enmeshed in the intensification of competitiveness (rankings, league tables) despite the acknowledged problems of both comparability and the identification of appropriate indicators (Cutler and Waine, 1994: ch. 2). It may be that no one believes them – either the supposed beneficiaries of the information or the service providers subjected to them – but they are taken seriously in practice, since failing to do so has resource consequences. As a result, organisations, units and individuals are likely to find themselves pursuing objectives and targets in which they may have little confidence (whether they be waiting list reductions or telephone answering rates) and which may withdraw attention and resources from activities perceived as more significant.

These changes in the field of relations between organisations and between the state and its agencies place managerial regimes at the centre of restructuring. As we argued in Chapter 2, managerialism provides the 'cement' that links the component parts of this dispersed field and lays claim to the new freedoms that have accompanied delegation and decentralisation. While the processes of managerialisation are contested, such challenges increasingly take the form of how other sources and forms of power are coming to terms with managerialism as the dominant regime.

The combination of dispersal plus managerialism has dramatically changed the structure of social welfare in Britain. This is not just a matter of new organisational forms or approaches to welfare delivery. These changes have rearranged the forms and relations of power that order social welfare. Most strikingly, the devolution of responsibility to semi-autonomous organisations has created the 'freedom to manage' at an organisational level, subject to the increasingly centralised control of policy, resources and evaluation. This has important political implications in that it allows central government to adopt two roles in relation to the provision of services. First, it represents the public by performing evaluation, playing an 'honest broker' role in collecting and disseminating information about comparative perform-ance among service providing organisations. Second, it is able to separate itself from responsibility for delivery by insisting that this is a matter for 'local management'. The fact that such representations have not always been successful – recently in relation to the NHS and the Prison Service – should not distract attention from the way in which the shift to a managerial regime enables this positioning.

Making performance an organisational responsibility through dispersal has other consequences, too. It means that questions of efficiency and effectiveness have become increasingly defined at the level of specific organisations. As we saw with issues of core business and ownership, this results in parochial conceptions of services, needs and resources with multiplying possibilities of 'boundary disputes'. In particular, it implies organisationally based strategies of pursuing efficiency and controlling costs that aim to transfer them elsewhere. Some of these strategies involve the transfer of costs to other organisations insisting that these needs are 'not our business'; some transfer costs to labour forces (through externalisation and changes in terms, conditions and levels of employment) and some involve the transfer of costs to users and carers (through earlier discharge, care in the community, etc.). Such organisation based strategies are both inter-organisational and inter-sectoral – for example moving costs to the voluntary and 'informal' sectors where labour costs may be lower – or even not charged at all.

Finally, these changes have had consequences for the internal orders of organisational life. They have installed management as a new command system which features business managers, chief executives, quality coordinators and internal audit staff. They have also installed *managerialism* in the sense of new regimes of power structured through the domination of decision making, agenda setting and normative power. As we have argued, this is not a simple matter of dissolving the old regime of bureau-professional and replacing it with managerialism but a process of realigning bureau-professionalism into a more subordinated place in the new order. We explore some of the instabilities associated with this realignment in the following chapters.

This chapter has focused on a particular level of analysis – that of changing regimes of power – in order to identify the dominant tendencies associated with the shift to managerialism. This analysis has enabled us to trace the reconfiguration around new forms and relations of power within and between organisations. We have also traced some of the main strategies by which managerialism has displaced, subordinated and coopted bureau-professionalism and the implications for the reshaping of organisational orders around the different managerial formations (competitive and trans-formational). However, there are limitations to dealing with these changes at the level of 'regimes'. This focus is not very attentive to the differences between fields of welfare – education, health, social care, housing, and income maintenance. In each of these, the policy and regime changes have proceeded through different means and at different paces. Equally, how managerial regimes are installed and their relations with the old regime of bureau-professionalism are issues that are played out in specific institutional and organisational settings. In one sense, this would have always been true – NHS hospitals were always different from local authority social service departments – but the processes of dispersal and the proliferation of semi-autonomous organisations have multiplied the number of sites in which these tendencies are enacted in practice. This is one reason why the next chapter moves to explore the level of institutional formations of manage-rialism. But this proliferation of institutional and organisational settings also means that dealing with regimes at a general level is particularly important. As the delivery of policy disappears into this multiplicity of organisations, it is necessary to keep hold of a level of analysis which looks for the common threads.

Note

¹ The public debate about 'management' in the NHS has been interesting for the way the competing designations of 'managers' and 'bureaucrats' have been deployed, in which a growth in the number of managers is a good thing but a growth in bureaucrats/bureaucracy is a bad thing. This indicates both a 'politics of representation' and underlying issues about the tendencies to the systematisation (if not bureaucratisation) of innovation in welfare organisations.

5

Incentives, Institutions and Identities: Shaping the Managerial State

So far, we have dealt with the place of managerialism in the restructuring of the state in relatively general terms, focusing on the political and ideological changes that have taken place. However, the consequences for particular organisations, groups and individuals cannot simply be read off from these general trends. In this chapter, we examine some of the conditions which shape the differential and uneven effects of the 'managerial revolution'. In doing so, we take as our starting point the dangers of determinism in accounts of state restructuring (see also Mohan, 1995: ch. 1). The primary danger of determinism is that of seeing change as the inevitable product of economic and political forces. The process of constructing managerial regimes has been contested, and the dynamics of change are partly conditioned by the differential power bases of professions and unions across different sectors. For example, some parts of the medical profession and related occupations have consistently contested NHS reforms. Within central government, the process of change has been influenced by the power of individual government Departments *vis-à-vis* the Treasury, not to mention that of individual ministers within the Cabinet (Deakin and Parry, 1993). As a result, we argue that it is necessary to treat the process of change as shaped by the interplay of power and interests rather than the inevitable product of macro economic and political processes.

We also want to question assumptions about the degree of closure of managerial ideology and the effectiveness of discourses in producing new managerial subjects. We have witnessed not a smooth and unproblematic change of attitudes and ideas, but a struggle for consent. In this struggle, all parties have deployed language, stories, symbols and myths in the attempt to define the meaning of events, to establish the nature of the problems to be addressed and to link them with preferred solutions, and to establish the legitimacy of particular sets of ideas and practices. These struggles have taken place both in the arena of national politics and within organisations, where the proliferation of visions and missions, the intense activity to produce symbolic change (from corporate logos to customer care charters) and the efforts to improve communication can be seen as part of the process of installing managerialism as the legitimate mode of organisational coordination.

At the core of the arguments about the outcome of these changes lie competing views about the relationship between 'structure' and 'agency'.

These raise questions about how far people are coerced or constrained, and how far they can determine their own actions, shape their own agendas, form their own definitions of reality, and identify and pursue their own interests. This has become a particularly sharp debate in the context of this book, because of the tension between the emphasis in managerial ideology on individual managerial freedom, on the right to manage, and on the empowerment of staff, all of which stress human agency, and the deterministic tendencies of relatively abstract theorisations of post-Fordism, the new public management and other analyses which foreground the structural dimensions of change.

This chapter is concerned with managers as both the objects of change strategies and as the subjects through whose agency change is delivered. It explores the dynamics of the institutional terrains which they are shaped by, and which they shape. The chapter addresses the question of how managerialism is interpreted, adapted and resisted by managers and others, within the pattern of structural change outlined in the earlier chapters. It argues that managerialism is not a unified set of discourses and practices, and that it is enacted by social actors who make sense of their world in a diversity of ways. The dynamics of this process are beginning to emerge from empirical studies of the impact of restructuring and the interaction of different regimes, some of which we explore below. An understanding of these dynamics is important to an understanding of how managers as agents influence the practice of the emerging 'managerial state'.

Institutionalising managerialism

In this chapter we explore models derived from public choice theory, a number of variants of new institutional theory, and discourse theories which address the production of subjects. We then go on to assess how far each can help to conceptualise the processes of uneven development, resistance and contestation within the managerialisation of public services.

Managerialism as incentives and constraints

Public choice theory, on which the New Right has drawn extensively, is based on critiques of the incentives embedded in the monopolistic bureaucracies of the past. These, it is argued, resulted in a less than optimal use of public resources due to a range of factors: the self interest of politicians, the vested interests of bureaucrats, and the inefficiencies of distribution systems not based on price mechanisms (Walsh, 1995). The pattern of state restructuring which we discussed in Chapter 2 has attempted to unlock these old patterns of incentives and to destabilise old power bases (especially those of professionals and of local politicians). New structures of market based incentives have been introduced through externalisation, contracting, internal markets and privatisation. Restructuring has also been based on the principle of separating policy from delivery (or 'steering' from 'rowing') so that provider organisations can be run on a quasi-business footing. These changes aim to subject public sector organisations to the pattern of incentives found within the private sector marketplace, even where there is no direct exposure to market pressures. The remaking of many public organisations as quasi businesses has been based on an attempt to structure incentives around outputs, measured through performance indicators and publicised through league tables tied to financial or market rewards. Political and professional structures of incentives have been squeezed by new funding arrangements, resource constraints and the requirement that organisations pursue efficiency savings.

These measures have been accompanied by a range of new incentives for schools, hospitals, civil service departments and local authorities to shift their structural positioning through opting out, seeking trust status or voluntary externalisation. They also seek to promote a sharper business awareness. Incentives have been designed to encourage public organisations to develop closer links with the private sector through a panoply of 'partnership' arrangements. Underpinning many of these attempts to bring about change has been a belief that public organisations must be exposed to some variant of market forces in order to bring about any fundamental cultural shift:

> What was called for was not structural change to the ways in which public sector workers operate, but institutional change in the governing norms, values and beliefs with which they operate. The new market based institutional framework will, it is hoped, lead to changes in values and attitudes, to new ways of thinking and acting. (Walsh, 1995: 30)

This pattern of quasi-business incentives has been mirrored *within* organisations. Many have been restructured around internal markets and business units, with devolved budgets and tight efficiency and performance goals. The external climate of resource constraints has been accompanied by a sharpening of internal competition for resources. These all deliver new internal patterns of incentives and seek to ensure that managerial forms of calculation permeate the organisation and inform the choices of individuals. The analysis of changing patterns of incentives and controls gives a useful focus on the interplay of power and interests (government–organisational, centre–periphery, management–worker) and suggest the interaction of economic and organisational change (e.g., the ways in which organisations 'mirror' external restructuring processes). But there are problems in assuming that people follow these new incentives directly and unambiguously.

> The 'rational actor' model at the heart of all public choice accounts assumes that: people have sets of well-formed preferences which they can perceive, rank and compare easily; . . . people are 'maximisers' who always seek the biggest possible benefits and the least costs in their decisions; . . . people are basically egoistic, self regarding and instrumental in their behaviour, choosing how to act on the basis of the consequences for their personal welfare (or that of their immediate family). (Dunleavy, 1991: 3)

Such assumptions neglect the ways in which change involves social and cultural processes that shape how people make sense of their worlds. There is a danger of assuming a direct correspondence between macro level change (a new structure of incentives) and micro level change (individual or collective behaviour). As a result, public choice theory is rather limited in its capacity to explain processes of change and their uneven impact. It thus reflects the *under-socialised* model of the person, in which actions (outcomes) are seen as a direct response to motivational pressures (incentives), that dominate economic theory.

Managerialism as a set of institutions

One developing body of theory which attempts to overcome some of these difficulties is new institutional theory, which studies the development of norms, rules and patterns of behaviour and extends the analysis beyond assumptions of the effectivity of incentives in producing new motivations. Lane comments that '[i]n order to understand the logic of public management, we need both institutions and interests, motivation and rules' (1993: 73). In this perspective, managerialism can be viewed as an institution: a set of rules of action, shared typifications of the world, shared cognitions, which produce regularities of thought and action. 'Institution' is what Lowndes (1996a) terms a 'meso level' concept between the macro level of structure and the micro level of individual action, in that institutions are both made by individuals and constrain their actions. These institutional constraints comprise both formal rules and norms (e.g., those embodied in government legislation and regulations) and informal norms and customs which shape actions and relationships within organisations and across organisational boundaries. Managerialism as an institution is embedded in organisational structures (e.g., business units and internal purchaser/provider divisions) and in organisational processes (e.g., internal charging), but it also transcends organisational boundaries. It has a legitimacy which goes beyond the preferences of individual actors and organisations. The process of managerialisation, then, can be understood as a shift in the 'rules of the game' for those working in public services. But it is also a social process in which actors make meanings and establish norms, conventions and habitual practices.

Variants of institutional theory offer rather different understandings of these processes of rule making and rule following (DiMaggio and Powell, 1991; Lowndes, 1996a). Some focus on the ways in which institutions are formed by rational actors pursuing their interests; others explore the social processes through which shared understandings are shaped and conventions formed. Economic and public choice variants explore the ways in which patterns of incentives shape social action, but within an institutional framework in which economic norms and conventions are shaped to respond to the problems of developing markets in the public sector. Such perspectives acknowledge and seek to theorise the 'imperfections' of the workings of market and of political incentives, highlighting the effects of 'bounded rationality' implying that actors must develop adaptive solutions to imperfect knowledge. They also highlight the opportunistic behaviour of other actors, and the difficulties of monitoring and enforcing contracts for complex services. New institutional economics, then, takes account of the social and political factors which may distort rationality as actors create new institutionalised patterns of behaviour to minimise the uncertainties they face (North, 1990). The focus on links between incentives, interests and actions remains paramount, but the outcomes are not always those which would be defined as optimal in terms of efficiency criteria.

From this point of view, managerialism can be understood as patterns of rules and norms which shape the way in which incentives and constraints are translated into action. It suggests that the managerial imperatives stemming from the introduction of markets and contracting are mediated by social processes. But the model of change remains one in which environmental forces and other 'exogenous' factors determine outcomes, even if the outcomes are not necessarily optimal.

Managerialism as a logic of appropriateness

In contrast, some strands of institutional theory see action as being shaped through taken-for-granted expectations and a shared logic of appropriateness. Change, then, requires a shift in what is considered to be appropriate. March and Olsen define rules as 'routines, procedures, conventions, roles, strategies, organisational forms and technologies' around which activity is constructed (1989: 22). These rules change incrementally as a result of historical experience, or more radically by the de-stabilising of older sets of rules and norms. They may be imposed by direct coercion, or may be part of a code of appropriate behaviour that is learned and internalised through socialisation or education. March and Olsen argue that 'Action is often based on identifying the normatively appropriate behaviour than on calculating the return expected from alternative choices' (p. 22). Indeed, institutional routines may be followed even when it is not in an individual's interests to do so. They distinguish between a 'logic of appropriateness associated with obligatory action' and a 'logic of consequentiality associated with anticipatory choice' (p. 23). Their preference for the former implicitly challenges the 'rational actor' model at the heart of much economic theory.

March and Olsen use these frameworks to highlight the difficulties of producing deliberate, controlled change. 'Institutions change, but the idea that they can be transformed to any arbitrary form is rare' (p. 56). This is especially the case with attempts at transformative change as it is 'easier to produce change through shock than it is to control what new combinations of institutions and practices will evolve from the shock' (p. 65). March and Olsen's view of change has been criticised as flawed, because of the focus on stability, and functionalist in its view of change as an evolutionary response to a changing environment (Lowndes, 1996a). Nevertheless, it does highlight how rational theories of choice cannot adequately explain the progression of change. Change has unintended consequences: innovations are transformed during the process of change, through social actors shaping them to make them more consistent with existing procedures and practices in order to maintain stability in the face of pressure for change. Changes are resisted or corrupted, but also adapted as new institutions are 'spontaneously elaborated' (March and Olsen, 1989: 65). March and Olsen go on to argue that: 'The political system seems unable to digest comprehensive reforms in one single operation, and the development of meaning becomes a more significant aspect of the reform than the structural changes achieve' (1989: 95). This suggests that both governmental and internal organisational *processes of legitimation* are central to the struggles over meaning that pervade the process of institutional change.

Managerialism as a process of legitimation

One variant of institutional theory stresses the way organisations seek to legitimate themselves by incorporating institutional features valued in the external environment. Meyer and Rowan (1991) term these features 'myths' because they perform a ceremonial or symbolic role through which the organisation gains legitimacy:

> [O]rganisations are driven to incorporate the practices and procedures defined by prevailing rationalised concepts of organisational work and institutionalised in society. Organizations that do so increase their legitimacy and survival prospects, independent of the immediate efficacy of the acquired practices and procedures. (1991: 41)

Such rationalised elements might include personnel functions, modern accounting practices, advertising departments and other organisational templates which reflect the current myths of the institutional environment rather than specific organisational needs. Organisations adopt the features of what a 'good organisation' is currently supposed to possess. This model has primarily been used to explain the ways in which organisations came to adopt the institutional features of bureaucracy. Meyer and Rowan suggest a continuum of organisational forms. At one extreme lie organisations whose success depends on the confidence and stability achieved by incorporating the institutional rules of bureaucracy, and which are therefore 'loosely coupled', with significant gaps between the ceremonial and mythic aspects of their policies and their implementation and practice. At the other end of the continuum lie organisations with strong output controls (production and business focus) in which efficiency is more important than legitimacy. Ceremonial and mythic activities are, then, counterposed to the pursuit of efficiency and a focus on performance outputs.

Basing this continuum on a contrast between the ceremonial based and the performance oriented organisation is, however, a problem, since 'performance' itself is a socially constructed and mythic concept. It is itself something to be performed in the search for legitimation (Corvellec, 1995). We want to suggest that the development of the managerial state has actually produced more, not less, search for such symbolic organisational legitimacy. A raft of new institutional practices – league tables, forms of audit, charter marks, performance indicators and so on – have been introduced which require a good deal of attention and resources to be spent on legitimating activity, whether this produces increased organisational efficiency or not. As organisations compete for government funding and for contracts for the delivery of services, not to mention customers for their services, their reputation becomes of critical importance. Being seen to be 'well managed' and 'businesslike' is clearly an advantage. This leads to the institutionalisation of features of the business world as legitimating practices: for example, the production of strategic plans; the restructuring of organisations into business units; the development of marketing and business development functions; or the attainment of Investor in People status. As the characteristics of the 'successful' organisation are refined and redefined, so all organisations face the pressure to comply: 'we can't not have one . . .'.

DiMaggio and Powell talk about this process in terms of 'isomorphism':

> Organisations compete not just for resources and customers but for political power and institutional legitimacy, for social as well as economic fitness. The concept of institutional isomorphism is a useful tool for understanding the politics and ceremony that pervade much modern organisational life. (1991: 66)

They identify three varieties of isomorphism: coercive, mimetic and normative. Coercive forms are those institutionalised and legitimated by the state, or those based on relationships of power and dependence which arise from contracting. So, government rules linked to such processes as compulsory competitive tendering (CCT) have led to new organisational shapes and procedures across the public sector, while funding constraints have driven the search for 'partnership' arrangements with non-public sector agencies. Equally, there are isomorphic pressures developing on the voluntary sector to 'become businesslike' as a result of the development of contracting arrangements with statutory bodies. Harris (1996) has described how 'not for profit' organisations felt driven to change organisational objectives, management and monitoring processes as a result of the contracting process (see also Charlesworth et al., 1996).

Mimetic processes of isomorphism arise where organisations model themselves on each other as a response to uncertainty: for example where technologies are imperfectly understood, goals are ambiguous, or there is general environmental uncertainty. DiMaggio and Powell highlight factors such as the role of consultants, the transfer of individuals between organisations, and 'ritualistic behaviour' adopted to increase legitimacy, suggesting that: 'The ubiquity of certain kinds of structural arrangements can more likely be credited to the universality of mimetic processes than to any concrete evidence that the adopted models enhance efficiency' (1991: 70). Such mimetic processes have been visible in public sector restructuring, for example in the importing of 'real managers' from the private sector and the extensive use made of management consultants to advise on organisational development. Agencies such as the Local Government Management Board have acted as disseminators of 'good practice' and principles of the 'well managed authority'. Somewhere between the coercive and the mimetic, it is also possible to see such governmental agencies as the Audit Commission, the Inspectorates and the funding and management agencies. These have increasingly linked 'evaluative' and 'advisory' roles in a tendency to establish templates for organisational structures, cultures and processes.

Finally, 'normative' sources of isomorphism are seen by DiMaggio and Powell as linked to professional and occupational socialisation. Here we might point to the explosion of management journals and conferences, and the development of training courses and certification programmes in the public sector during the late 1980s and 1990s. Both management education in general and 'public sector management' as a specific variant have provided important routes through which such normative isomorphism could circulate.

At the heart of the process of legitimation is the work of myth making. We are currently witnessing the forging of a number of 'managerial myths', each of which is accompanied by its own logic of appropriateness. For example, there is the myth that business units can and should act as if they were real businesses, which is symbolised in the production of the 'business plan' as an organisational ritual. There is the myth of financial delegation, in which such units are supposed to believe they gain real control over their 'own' resources. It is also possible to identify mythic features of strategic management, based on the notion that top teams are 'in control' and able to form a coherent and unifying sense of direction and purpose for organisations struggling to reconcile conflicting goals. Each operates as a pervasive template that informs how managerial change is to be enacted. They also serve as powerful legitimating structures of meaning in the process of constituting managerial actors ('I'm a strategic manager, so I don't have to bother with the mess of day to day operational decisions'; 'you are a business manager, so must ignore anything that isn't part of your core business'; 'he has delegated financial responsibility, so must keep the ''bottom line'' constantly in mind'; 'they have become purchasers rather than providers, so must forget about providing any form of social care themselves').

Both old and new models of how the public sector should work are built on legitimating myths. The 'old' public sector institutionalised a mythic set of images about the uniqueness and difference of public and private which limited the transfer of ideas and practices between them. New models incorporate myths about how the commercial world behaves which may themselves be partial, distorted or outdated. Writing about the way in which service complexity produces perceived difficulties for the writing and monitoring of contracts for public services, Walsh notes that these issues have also arisen in the private sector, leading to transformations in market practices and contract forms: 'It is increasingly common, for example, for companies to cooperate as well as compete, and to move away from rigid contracting processes. If care is not taken, the public sector, not for the first time, will find itself adopting approaches to management precisely at the same time that they are being abandoned as ineffective in the private sector' (Walsh, 1995: 30).

Each pattern of myths produces its own 'logic of appropriateness' which underpins decision making. Douglas (1987) argues that myths are legitimated by naturalising analogies, which are linked to hierarchies of authority. Drawing on this view, Mackintosh suggests that: 'For a social convention to develop as an institution, it needs a naturalising principle, which appears to confer a natural status on social relations, and a grounding in reason' (Mackintosh, 1995b: 6). In the context of public sector restructuring both management and the market have carried exactly such 'naturalising' legitimations. Management has been legitimated by reference to its status in the real world of business. Markets are naturalised as the primary way of conducting human business – partly because they are a widespread phenomenon and partly because the model of the market and its economic actors has been generalised as a template for describing human conduct. Such myths conceal the ways in which markets are themselves socially constructed institutions: 'The social construction of business structures and practices means that not only are they the product of collective beliefs, conventions and moral codes which vary between societies, but also the nature of economic success and ways of achieving it are dependent on dominant conceptions of economic practices and rationalities' (Whitley, 1992: 123).

One of the strengths of new institutional theory is that it draws attention to the political and social processes which shape the operation of both the market and bureaucracies. But we can readily see how such myths legitimate certain political solutions to the problems of public services, and how each is 'functional' in sustaining particular institutions. What is more difficult, from the perspective of institutional theory, is to understand how, and by whom, these myths are themselves created and sustained. It is here that we need to conceptualise managerialism not just as a set of institutions forged by social actors as they respond to collective problems in the new environments they face. Such institutions are also *carriers* of managerial ideologies through which the struggle to win consent to new social and political arrangements is conducted, and a set of discourses through which managerial subjects may be produced. Both perspectives involve the need to bring questions of *power* back into the analysis.

Managerialism as ideology and discourse

Myths are an important dimension of ideology in that they help win consent to particular structures of meaning and forms of action. In Chapter 3, we talked of how managerial ideology helped to unlock old structures of meaning through the discourses of change and transformation. Meyer and Rowan argue that the adoption of appropriate language is crucial to external processes of legitimation:

From an institutional perspective, a most important aspect of isomorphism with environmental institutions is the evolution of organisational language. The labels of the organisation chart as well as the vocabulary used to delineate organisational goals, procedures and policies are analogous to the vocabularies of motive used to account for the actions of individuals. (1991: 50)

They go on to argue that this has internal consequences too: 'Affixing the right labels to activities (e.g., personnel) can change them into valuable activities and mobilise the commitments of internal participants and external constituents' (1991: 51). We want to argue that the adoption of managerial and business language both serves to legitimate organisations and to change roles and goals within them. As such, it is an important resource in the struggle for consent. New language can be used to symbolise change and to mobilise new identifications and commitments. But language also provides the tools with which individuals make sense of who they are within the changing fields of knowledge that pervade their environments. Discourse theory views discourses – sets of languages and practices linked to a particular regime (such as professionalism, bureaucracy, managerialism) – as embodying *productive* power rather than merely controlling power. That is, discourses offer particular kinds of subject position and identity through which people come to view their relationships with different loci of power. Du Gay suggests that during the twentieth century a range of management discourses have appeared (scientific management, human relations and so on) 'which have offered novel ways of imagining "organisation" and have played an active role in "making up" new ways for people to conduct themselves at work' (du Gay, 1994b: 657).

The discourse of managerialism, linked to the new regimes of organisational power which have displaced bureau-professionalism, is part of the process through which new subject positions are created, through which 'administrators', 'public servants' and 'practitioners' come to see themselves as 'business managers', 'purchasers', 'contractors', 'strategists', 'leaders' and so on (see also Maile, 1995). These new ways for managers to conceive of and conduct themselves can be very different. As we suggested in Chapter 4, some of the new discourses can be seen as proposing essentially *rational/ calculative* representations of managerial roles and practices: the discourses of efficiency and of some variants of strategy and marketing. By contrast, others propose *affective* modes of engagement and interrelationships: leadership, cultural change, customer care. Some are *hard*, involving clear definitions, roles and actions (delegated budgets), while others can be seen as *soft*, implying a weakening of boundaries (teamwork, flexibility, partnership). Some appear to be overtly *value driven* (serving the customer) while others appear to be *value neutral* or technical (workforce planning).

These discourses offer new subject positions and patterns of identification – those of management as opposed to professionalism; of Human Resource Management (HRM) as opposed to personnel management; of strategy as opposed to planning; of leadership as opposed to administration; of innovation and entrepreneurship as opposed to the conservative stewardship of public resources. Managerial discourses create the possibilities within which individuals construct new roles and identities, and from which they derive ideas about the logic of institutional change. As Chapter 3 argued, one of the key characteristics of managerial discourse is the way in which it constitutes managers as active agents – as change mobilisers, dynamic entrepreneurs, shapers of their own destinies and controllers of their own environments. This suggests that the 'mastery of management' is not just a process of responding to new market incentives (as in public choice theory), nor of learning of managerial norms and rules (as in some versions of institutional theory). Rather, it is accomplished through the constitution or production of new social actors (subjects) through whose agency new state institutions and organisations are shaped.

Disciplining managerial subjects

The processes of creating 'managerial subjects' involve specific relations of power. Du Gay contrasts the instrumental rationality of bureaucracy with the engagement of emotions and the private domains of the individual into the workplace inherent in the discourse of excellence: 'governing organisational life to ensure "excellence" was deemed to necessitate the production of certain types of work-based subject: "enterprising", autonomous, productive, self regulating, responsible individuals' (du Gay, 1994a: 131).

The discourse of excellence places a premium on engaging the imaginations of staff, winning their commitment, and supporting a process of identification with the aims of the organisation, rather than simply directing them. This process of engagement and identification is seen to take place through symbols and ceremonies, through the production of 'inspiring' visions, and through the personal style and power of a leader. All of these invoke the need for self regulation, rather than compliance. These productive processes of control operate with, rather than displace, formal, rule based control devices. This is the basis of the 'directed autonomy' implicit in notions of empowerment (Hopfl, 1994). While managerial ideology alters the balance between 'roles' and 'rules' in favour of the former, the dissonances between them have to be managed.

> Self regulation by apparent consensus is the norm of professional management. In accepting the challenge put forward by Peters and Waterman to manage directed autonomy, the manager becomes the locus of the implicit contradictions in the term. Managers are required not only to manage the meanings of others, but their own embodiment of meaning, of conflict and variable commitment. (Hopfl, 1994: 40)

The processes of producing a range of self regulating patterns of identification are buttressed by disciplinary and surveillance strategies. Managerial discourses can be viewed as hierarchies of knowledge and expertise which legitimate the reordering of roles and relationships within organisations and the labour force as a whole. The discourses of 'quality management' and of 'HRM' serve as different kinds of example. Reed (1995) explores quality management practices in terms of a form of organisational control and surveillance – as 'intellectual technologies' which (albeit imperfectly) link central government change programmes to organisational practices. Kirkpatrick and Martinez-Lucio (1995) identify ways in which the external representation of customer interests is used to legitimate intervention and change in public organisations, such as decentralisation, cultural change, changes in employment practices and bargaining relations.

Similarly, the discourse of Human Resource Management, which is increasingly displacing the personnel function as bureaucratic organisations seek external legitimacy and internal transformation, can be viewed both as a hierarchy of knowledge and as a legitimation of structural changes which realign internal relationships between employer and employee. Townley (1994) argues that HRM can be seen not just as a possible new managerial role and identity, but as a range of techniques and strategies through which new managerial subjects are constituted. The development of HRM has meant that individuals have become subject to new forms of knowledge and control. It deploys a range of techniques designed to reconstitute individual identity: staff development, training, mentoring and so on. These can be understood as strategies through which organisations aim to create new managerial subjects with rather different sets of loyalties and identities from professionals and bureaucrats. Townley argues that HRM practices constitute individuals as objects whose traits, skills, attitudes and values can be defined and measured: 'to be manageable, workers must be known; to be known they must be rendered visible' (1994: 83). At the same time, HRM is concerned with creating and embedding new attachments between individuals and organisations through what might be termed 'commitment management'. Leadership, vision, communication, cultural change and the 'empowerment' of staff are the supposed means of delivery, and the aim is to bring about fundamental change in the motivations, identifications and allegiances of individuals. It is part of the panoply of the human sciences through which more and more aspects of an individual come to be revealed – not just the performance of tasks, but self esteem, relationships and motivations, and emotional capacities (Hollway, 1991).

The discursive perspective illuminates some of the complex issues of identity and the process of transition involved in 'becoming' a manager. It views the person as fragmented, subject to multiple and overlapping discourses, each of which invokes rather different subject positions and identifications. It foregrounds the emerging 'hierarchies of knowledge' on which managerialism is based, and so draws attention to the micro politics of power within managerial regimes. Despite this, we want to register some reservations about discourse theory. It is not directed to explaining the conjunctural conditions in which specific discourses rise or fall. Indeed some would see this as an inappropriate question, implying a model of causation that is inconsistent with discursive analysis. As we argued earlier, it is also important not to assume that new subjects can simply be read off from new discourses. There are dangers in assuming that the disciplinary and surveil- lance processes which subject individuals to new forms of power and control are effective. We would want to emphasise that subjects are caught up in the play of different, and sometimes conflicting, discourses.

Enacting managerialism

The previous section examined a number of ways of conceptualising the processes through which managerial regimes are institutionalised. These represented the dynamics of change with different emphases on the *imperatives* or the *freedoms* of managerialism, allowing individuals and organisations a more or less active role in shaping the institutions and practices of management. Each carries with it a danger of assuming the effectiveness of change: that is, that new economic incentives will produce appropriate responses; that managerial institutions will develop optimal solutions; that myths and legitimating practices will be functional for organisational survival; that discourses will be effective in producing managerial subjects; and that disciplinary practices will produce compliance. When we explore how managerialism is enacted in practice, however, what we find is a picture of uneven development, variability and complex articulations of old and new regimes. This section explores a number of recent studies of restructuring that highlight these unevennesses. Although they are focused on different services and draw on different theoretical resources, they share a common concern with how new institutional arrangements are formed *in practice*. Together they suggest that neither the grand plans of state reform nor grand theories of state restructuring adequately capture the specific organisational practices and outcomes that result from change.

Professionals and markets: responding to incentives?

Whittington et al.'s analysis (1994) of market driven change in two professional service sectors, Research and Development and NHS hospital trusts, highlights the complex and multi-level nature of the process. The introduction of market incentives, they argue, produced significant changes in roles at different organisational levels, with top managers becoming more strategic, line managers more business oriented, and professionals developing a role as 'part time marketeers' as well as practitioners. Support services changed in character, with commercial support (finance and marketing staff) growing in importance, and professional support staff reduced in numbers and tending to be absorbed into professional hierarchies. This, then, suggests ways in which market incentives impact on organisations and different groups within them.

However, the authors argue that there is a danger in 'totalising' accounts of change and a need for more nuanced understanding of managerial control. In particular, issues of consent, compromise and contradiction are important in theorising the process of change. They identify 'enthusiasts' in recently privatised research laboratories, principally among the scientists and engineers, who actively seemed to revel in the new conditions partly because of their legitimacy in the prevailing 'enterprise culture' of the time. 'Macho' imagery was used by some enthusiasts for the new culture of the marketplace. Whittington et al. also describe the appropriation of the discourse of the market and the language of customer needs by professionals. One respondent (an NHS consultant) saw such language as a useful defence in the continuing politics of a large hospital: 'artfully assembled figures on "market demand" and rhetorical appeals to "service quality" provided him with new ammunition in bargaining for resources' (1994: 841). Their study also suggests some of the contradictions inherent in change. Decentralisation, while enhancing the market responsiveness of departments or units, can tend to erode rather than enhance the power of the centre and the strategic coherence of the organisation as a whole. It can also produce high levels of internal competition. 'Thus for top management, the shift to a market-driven regime actually entails some risk to control' (1994: 841).

Rather than managerial change 'filtering down' from the strategic centre of an organisation, the multi-level model they use suggests that change may be unevenly developed at different levels, and indeed that the top management level may lag behind. They conclude:

> In dealing with skilled and service sector employment, at least, many recent academic accounts have been too one sided, emphasising only the control advantages for management of market-based forms of control. Quite clearly there are advantages to be had, but our analysis of the process of change suggests that these are not easily won. Decentralisation offers professionals new areas of opportunity and discretion, new ways of playing political games or exercising their skill. Professionals may even revel in the competitive excitements of the market, while top management strives to rein them in. In sum, market forms of control are no more a panacea than the strict controls of Taylorism. At least in professional services, resort to market pressures is a strategy laden with compromise and contradiction . . . theorization of new managerial strategies needs to be sensitive to difficulties of implementation, to workforce initiative and to unintended consequences. (1994: 843).

This study underlines the problems of assuming linear effects of change. It points to the instability of new 'incentives' in the way that they are appropriated for divergent, and unintended, purposes within the micro-politics of specific organisations. But it also tempers claims that these changes install or enhance managerial control by suggesting that such strategies are played out in struggles to enforce and resist centralised control of professional work.

Shaping economic institutions

Whittington et al.'s study also suggests that market processes constitute a language that can be taken up and used in different ways within organisations. This approach de-naturalises the 'market' by treating it as something other than a pre-given set of external facts and conditions. Recent work by Mackintosh (1995b) has taken this further in analysing the development of *economic culture* in local government, based on research in social services departments responding to the introduction of markets for social care. This work attempts to understand the economic behaviour of purchasers and providers within the new structures. However, it seeks to go beyond conventional economic models which assume that the efficacy of change will depend on how well individuals learn the new patterns of 'businesslike' behaviour required by the new incentives. She draws on institutional theory, but argues that:

> The new institutional structure provided by the legal framework and regulations offers an incomplete set of instructions and incentives to those supposed to implement them, leaving considerable room for judgement and discretion. Furthermore, the incentives offered are in some ways contradictory, not providing the possibility of a wholly consistent response, and threatening to undermine some of the outcomes – such as high quality and falling costs – which they are supposed to promote. (1995b: 3)

The incompleteness and contradictory nature of incentives means that emerging patterns of behaviour are evolutionary, and reflect the ideas and rules that people develop to cope with the demands and dilemmas of their situation. As Mackintosh wryly suggests, 'Even economists therefore have to take into account that those who work in the public sector do not merely learn, they think' (1995b: 4). She also develops a rather different view of the economic concepts which have proliferated within the discourse of managerialism:

> The economic framework of the reforms has not only generated a new organisational model of public services, it has also offered a new vocabulary with which to think about it. There has indeed rarely been such a startling case study of attempted transfer of a new vocabulary into an existing set of organisations. From markets and competition, through business units and contracts, to prices and customers, economists and management consultants have quite literally sought to put words into people's mouths. (1995b: 4)

Rather than emphasising the ways in which such new discourses construct new kinds of managerial subjects, however, Mackintosh explores the ways in which the meaning of the new economic concepts is actively shaped by practitioners: 'people (not just managers) within public services have been forced to try to give this terminology meanings they can live with: meanings that make their worlds manageable' (1995b: 5). The diversity of meanings that are produced result in variations in the shaping of quasi-markets in practice. Mackintosh draws attention to the different ways in which being in the market is understood at different levels of the organisation, expressed in both perceptions and practices. She also emphasises how purchasers of care services view 'playing the market' as enhancing their power to get a 'good deal' for their clients. Here, both the new arrangements and the languages through which they are represented are resources to be deployed in brokering power within and between organisations.

Enacting the 'right to manage'

Markets have been only one of the forms of restructuring. The decentralisation of operational autonomy in the form of the 'right to manage' has been
an equally significant process. Birchall et al. (1995) explore these issues in
three services: health, education and housing. Their central interest is in how
far greater managerial freedom can act as a 'galvanising force' (1995: 10) to
bring about greater efficiency, accountability and improved standards of
service. Reviewing a series of government pronouncements which underpinned the development of the new public management, they suggest that:
'From this perspective, the manager, rather than the professional, the
administrator or the politician, is seen as bearing the central dynamic of
progressive social and economic change' (p. 13). They highlight the dis-
juncture between this rhetoric and the experience of managers. In the case of
the NHS trusts they studied, they comment that 'what is perhaps most
striking is the shortfall between the projected gains from trust status set out
in the government's original policy documents and the actual experiences at
all our fieldwork sites' (p. 14).

The extent of the freedom to manage was limited by financial and other
forms of regulation. In particular, financial regimes were perceived as
restricting the business ethos that underpinned the rhetoric of trust status.
However the trusts welcomed their new ability to resist interventions from
the District and Regional Health Authorities under whose control they had
operated in the past. Senior managers in grant maintained (GM) schools
similarly welcomed their freedom from Local Education Authority control,
citing increased responsibilities and satisfactions as a result of greater power
and flexibility.

The research illustrates the impact of different forms of political control
and institutional constraints (financial rules, personnel freedoms, etc.) in
different services. Managerial freedoms were greatest in housing associations, because of their closeness to the market and their distinct service
characteristics. There were also differences between schools and hospitals
relating to dimensions of size and degree of internal differentiation. It is
clear that the 'right to manage' takes different forms. The nature and extent
of cultural change also varied. In the NHS, Trust status was perceived to
have led, in some cases, to increased identification with the hospital on the
part of staff. GM schools had been more able to develop a sense of 'purpose
and mission'. Opt outs to housing associations through large scale voluntary
transfers brought significant changes in both organisational structures and
cultures, with a stronger sense of identification with the housing association
by front line staff than had been the case under local authority control. But
these developments were not necessarily accompanied by the deeper cultural
change intended by the reforms, in the sense of staff becoming more goal
oriented and conscious of performance issues.

> First, most of our respondents were able to specify a number of variables that
> could serve as performance indicators. We suspect, but cannot prove, that the

general level of sophistication in this regard has increased considerably over the last decade or so. Second, however, few of the people we have interviewed seem themselves primarily to think in this context. When asked, they can name some possible indicators, but unless they *are* specifically asked they do not talk much in these terms at all . . .

Furthermore, the larger notion of developing a strategic response to changing the performance of their organisations was evidently quite opaque to the great majority of the managers and professionals to whom we spoke. They preferred the traditional language of inputs, processes and relationships to the new language of visions, strategies and goals. (1995: 46)

They also appeared much more comfortable with 'mission' goals, related to professional activity, than with 'system' goals related to efficiency or profit. 'There was certainly a degree of organisational identification, but this was of a traditional kind – "our school", "our hospital" – rather than being fashioned into a vision of a competitive, goal oriented corporate entity' (1995: 47). The researchers conclude that there was little evidence of deep seated cultural change. Staff welcomed greater autonomy for their organisations since this enabled them to 'get on with the job' – but the job was still conceived predominantly in professional-producer terms. 'Opting out was, in some cases, a form of dynamic conservatism: autonomy was desired so that professionals could go on doing the things they traditionally valued and trained for' (1995: 47). The authors suggest that while managerial ideology has shaped the government agenda and rhetoric of change substantially, it has not necessarily formed the central consciousness of managers. They experience the desire for freedom from political control but are more likely to be oriented round 'service' missions than effectiveness. We need, then, to be cautious in assessing the effectiveness of manageralism in producing managerial subjects and identities in a direct and consistent way.

Uneven development: change as complex and contradictory

Although they draw on different methods and theories, these studies highlight the ways in which individuals and groups actively construct the meanings of the changes they experience, and create new institutional norms and patterns, new logics of appropriateness, within a nexus of social relationships. The creation of managerial subjects and the institutionalisation of managerialism are both dynamic processes. Managerialism is enacted in different ways in different sites and settings. These processes are played out in contexts that shape the outcomes. In drawing out issues about the uneven development of the managerial state, we focus on three particular dimensions: variations between and within organisations, contradictions in the process of change and the intersection of different regimes.

Variability between and within organisations

Birchall et al. point to variations between services, related to their closeness to the market, the size of organisation and degree of internal differentiation, the degree of closeness to the customer, the type of professional base and the strength of 'mission' as opposed to 'system' goals. While external changes have undoubtedly produced some kind of overall shift towards greater managerial consciousness within public sector organisations, there is a great deal of unevenness *between* services (see also Ackroyd et al., 1989). The outcomes depend on the power base of its professions, differences in nature of political constraints and controls, and the symbolic importance of the institutions to public consciousness. Local government, with relatively weak 'welfare state' professions, but with a political power base which constituted an oppositional force to central government through the 1980s, was an early target for reform in contrast to the health service, with its strong professional power bases and tradition of public loyalty. There is also, however, variation *within* services, with some local authorities approaching managerialisation as a progressive and transforming force, and others resisting change; some health trusts developing aggressive business cultures and others adapting only at the margins.

There are also variations within particular organisations. Whittington et al.'s study of market driven change in 'professional' organisations shows that the introduction of markets has led to change at all levels of the organisations studied. However, there has often been a 'lag' with senior managers slower to develop their strategic role than line managers and practitioners were in developing business and marketing roles. Mackintosh shows how different discourses are found at different levels of the social services departments studied, with staff involved in care assessments and spot purchasing developing a strong business orientation with a sharper market model (based on cost competition) and senior managers more likely to speak the language of partnerships and collaboration. So managerialism does not necessarily 'filter down' an organisation. The formation of managerial regimes in organisations distributes both forms of power and forms of constraint to different levels. Thus senior managers may be given greater discretion but also be made more 'responsible' (through tighter performance specifications and targets, linked to performance related pay, for example). At the same time, they may find it more difficult to control the discretion of their subordinates because of the decisional autonomy which has been devolved to front line or first level management roles.

These points about sector and organisational variability are perhaps most explicitly developed in a recent study of change in local government (Lowndes et al., 1996). This uses institutional theory to highlight the lack of coherence of New Public Management. Three variants are identified: an efficiency oriented element (stressing productivity and managerial control), a market oriented element (stressing competition and contracting), and a user oriented element (stressing service quality and responsiveness).[1] These variants may all be present in a single organisation, and are potentially contradictory. Such contradictions, we suggest, produce tensions and dilemmas for those living and working through change.

Tensions in the process of change

While some economic and political versions of institutional theory see change as constant progress towards the 'best solution', social and organisational variants see institutions as less malleable. They adapt slowly and in unanticipated ways. Meyer and Rowan (1991) recognise that there are tensions between institutions whose rules conflict with each other: institutional environments are pluralistic and societies promulgate sharply inconsistent myths. The various studies we have cited show that some of these inconsistencies arise from the processes of structural change, in which incentives and constraints do not all work in the same direction. For example, Whittington et al.'s study points to the inherent tensions between internal decentralisation and the possibilities of a coherent strategic role at the centre. Others arise in the gap between legitimating myths and organisational practice. Birchall et al. highlight tensions between the imagery of the market and market practices in different sectors, and Mackintosh, from a different standpoint, reveals tensions between models of the market and market practice across purchaser and provider roles. Some of these tensions are played out in lines of fracture within organisations, for example between the 'centre' of a local authority and its service oriented departments. Some tasks may require bureaucratic modes of regulation; others high levels of flexibility and innovation. These tensions may arise from the coexistence of multiple institutions in the process of change (Lowndes, 1996b; Lowndes et al., 1996). Multiple institutions give rise to multiple rules. For example, the institutions of audit (performance measures, standards, inspection) are in potential – and often actual – conflict with the institutions of entrepreneurship and the market (flexibility, responsiveness and dynamism). In contracting, the institutions of tight specification and close monitoring may be in conflict with the institutions and norms of partnership and collaboration.

The discourses of business entrepreneurship, efficiency and customer centredness all work in different ways and offer different kinds of subject position. Whittington et al.'s study, while not drawing on discourse theory, suggests possible tensions between the discourses of strategic management and business management; and Mackintosh points to tensions between the discourses of competition and collaboration in the shaping of economic culture in public institutions. But there may also be increasing internal conflict *within* individuals, invoked by the spread of 'managerial subjects' through and down organisations, and the tensions between multiple allegiances and goals that have to be resolved as a consequence. Changes of role – from administrators to managers, from controllers to leaders, from client identified 'carers' to resource controllers, from 'professional expert' to a provider of services to customers – are likely to lead to a number of dilemmas and tensions, rather than a simple displacement of one role by another (Clarke and Newman, 1993b). For example, Stewart (1996) traces some of the emerging conflicts of loyalty for NHS managers:

> In any organisation there can be a potential clash between loyalty to clients or customers, to colleagues and to the organisation as a whole. A dilemma may arise from a clash of personal loyalties, from wanting to do the right thing, from concern for the good opinion of colleagues, or from fears about the threat to one's career if one is judged disloyal to the organisation. (1996: 30)

These potential conflicts, she suggests, operate differently at different levels of management, with trust managers' loyalties invoked both to the NHS and to a specific organisation, and regional managers being subject to tensions between the 'field' and the 'centre'. Managers here and elsewhere are likely to both experience and reproduce mixed messages resulting from the overlay of old and new patterns of authority, loyalty and identification. These tensions are the effect of the intersection of old and new regimes in the institutionalisation of the managerial state.

The intersection of different regimes

All of the studies we have discussed illustrate the ways in which professionalism intersects with, rather than being displaced by, managerialism. Whittington et al. show how professionals learn to 'work' the market, for example by inserting enough time or funding into contracts to allow the pursuit of a pet project, or appropriating the discourse of the market in the struggle for resources. Birchall et al. highlight the interaction of different regimes more sharply, by showing the way in which professionals pursued decentralisation to gain more managerial freedoms, but were more likely to be oriented round 'service' goals than managerial criteria of organisational effectiveness. Mackintosh similarly suggests the continuity of professional values and motivations on the part of both 'purchasers' and 'providers' in the developing market for social care. She also indicates how emerging market practices were cross-cut by a continuing reliance on professional knowledge, relationships and trust.

Tensions may also exist between beliefs, language and practices. That is, people may adopt new behaviours but retain old values – as in the care managers cited by Mackintosh who were avidly 'playing the market' in the interests of their clients. They retained a self image as advocates for the client rather than as purchasers seeking the best deal for their organisation. New goals, identities and allegiances are likely to exist alongside old formations rather than displacing them. So, clinical directors, social services managers and school head teachers manage the tensions between their 'business' goals (involving rationing services to keep within cost limits, attracting purchasers or customers in competition with other providers) and their professional goals (securing the health of patients, the care of the elderly, the education of children). Older discourses and the subject positions and identities associated with them have not gone away – they linger on not just out of nostalgia, but because *specific* practices continue to require them. Generic managerialism has to be enacted in the context of producing or delivering particular public goods and services. Its own 'mission' (the pursuit of greater productivity of efficiency) cannot effectively substitute for specific service goals and the forms of expertise needed to achieve them. As a consequence, both occupational knowledges and identities (being doctors, social workers, teachers) continue to occupy discursive space within the new institutions in tension with new occupational knowledges and identities (being managers). What has been constructed is a field of tensions within which people manoeuvre, form alliances and make choices. These tensions are often dramatised in simple but potent competing representations: being business-like versus public service; managers versus professionals; competition versus collaboration; customers versus patients and so on. In practice, though, organisational regimes are enacted both between and within these representations as they are made meaningful in particular settings.

Beyond fluidity: shaping the managerial state

The different theoretical approaches we highlighted in the first part of this chapter vary in their capacity to illuminate the complex and contradictory nature of the process of change, and the variations and tensions in emerging managerial practice. Some forms of institutional theory tend to see change in terms of the diffusion of standard norms and rules across organisations. We would expect the rules and structures of managerialism to be much more uniform and universal than they are. To some extent this might be explained in terms of the variety of institutional frameworks created within different services, and at different stages of government rule making. But even within specific organisations, or specific groups within them, people 'play the game' in a different way with different priorities and with different orientations. Some adopt managerial frameworks avidly. Some hold on to older loyalties and identities (while often learning to play the new games with great success), and some attempt to bend or shape the rules to pursue a range of personal, organisational or social agendas.

Such tensions and variations are acknowledged within institutional theory. DiMaggio and Powell argue, albeit in passing, that 'although we stress that rules and routines bring order and minimise uncertainty, we must add that the creation and implementation of institutional arrangements are rife with conflict, contradiction and ambiguity' (1991: 28). These produce a diversity of ways in which managerialism is enacted: what Lowndes (1996b) terms multiple managerial regimes, each based on a cluster or nexus of institutions. Despite such developments, the focus in much institutional theory is on institutional stability rather than change, since institutions are viewed as functional for the continuity and efficiency of economic activity. The functionalist implications of the dominant focus on institutions as a source of social order (to which Mackintosh and Lowndes are exceptions) means that these tensions are under-theorised. While institutional theory can offer a

more subtle analysis of the managerial norms and informal rules that follow
from restructuring processes, especially the introduction of market mechanisms, it cannot adequately explain their interaction with other sets of formal
and informal rules – for example, those derived from the political context
such as rules of probity and accountability.

This chapter has explored the ways in which the processes through which
managerialism is enacted are complex, contradictory and dynamic. It has
dealt not just with the spread of the new managerialism but its interactions
with older regimes, each of which gives rise to different patterns of
subjectivity, frameworks for action and criteria for success. The process of
change is both more open and less deterministic than is imagined within
totalising explanations based on the logics of post-Fordism, or post-
bureaucratic organisation, or the wholesale shift from 'old' to 'new' forms
of public management. Lowndes et al. argue that the value of new institutional theory is its capacity to move beyond such totalising explanations.

> The focus on component institutions avoids reifying the 'new public management'
> as a more or less coherent entity existing in opposition to 'old' public manage-
> ment; [and] the understanding of change in terms of many and disparate processes
> of institutionalisation and de-institutionalisation avoids a 'once and for all'
> perspective which sees 'change' as an event with a prescribed outcome (which
> can either succeed or fail). (Lowndes et al., 1996: 10)

Nevertheless, all is not fluidity and indeterminacy. The processes of state
restructuring have involved a change in the *hierarchy of legitimation* of
different regimes, through which managerialism and business discourse have
become dominant over professional, administrative and political discourses.
This change in the power of different regimes forms the conditions of
institutional adaptation and enactment that we have examined in this chapter.
The restructuring of the state and the centrality of managerialism to that
process has radically shifted the terrain on which these institutional processes are played out. For us, this is the central issue about moving to an
institutional *level of analysis*. It is at the same time both a necessary, but
insufficient, level. It is necessary because it opens up questions about how
structural shifts are enacted in practice – and in ways that are not the direct
outcomes of the 'grand plans' of policy makers and politicians. The
contradictions, inconsistencies and incompletenesses of the macro-level
changes create the conditions for and resources with which individuals turn
managerialism into lived practice. On the other hand, the 'meso level' of
institutional theory cannot be abstracted from the wider structural transformations and treated as an *independent* level of analysis. It is precisely the
structural and ideological shifts that create the fields of tensions, constraints
and possibilities within which the processes of institutional elaboration take
place.

This poses the problem of how to treat the institutional level as the site
of both constraint and creativity. The structural changes have produced a
new organisational settlement that is simultaneously a field of constraints
and a field of possibilities. Formally, this is captured in conceptions of

decentralised authority, conditional empowerment, or structured autonomy. However, such concepts are primarily addressed to the conditions under which organisations pursue the 'operational management' of policy. What they focus on are the formal structures and mechanisms by which de-centralised power is conditioned and disciplined by the 'centre'. So the autonomy of service organisations is constrained by the concentration of policy making power at the centre, by the growing apparatus of performance evaluation, and by the sets of contractual or quasi-competitive relationships in which individual organisations are embedded (Hoggett, 1996). These clearly constrain the room for manoeuvre of specific organisations in decisive ways. But structural decentralisation and the 'right to manage' also create a power base from which managers can act in ways not always intended by politicians. Managers carry a range of commitments and objectives which are invoked as old and new regimes interact, as in the case of hospital trust and regional NHS managers. Lowndes et al. (1996) show how managers prioritised ideas of accountability to the public and listening to users as well as efficiency and professionalism in service delivery. Managers enact a range of goals, loyalties and identifications in the processes of creatively shaping and adapting new institutional arrange-ments.

Nevertheless, these constraints and possibilities are not all that is involved in the making of managerial regimes. This process also engages the norms, rules, discourses and identities through which organisations work. What we have seen in this chapter are the complex ways in which institutional change involves struggles over meaning: the *inflection* of new patterns in the pursuit of diverse occupational, organisational and social purposes. From this standpoint, managerialism is itself a field of possibilities, open to local processes of resistance, appropriation and compromise. But it also con-stitutes a field of normative and discursive constraints. It is the dominant formation in the field of contending positions that shape institutionalised outcomes. It forms the terrain that other positions have to negotiate, accommodate to or inflect with in practice. The processes of creative adaptation that we have traced in this chapter are adaptations to the rise of managerialism. They are not abstract struggles to make organisations, rather they deal with the problems of how to make managerialised organisations meaningful, habitable and workable in divergent ways. Managerialism has set the 'rules of engagement' – the field of constraints – without having the capacity to determine the outcomes.

Such issues indicate why the institutional level of analysis is important in understanding the development of the managerial state. It is not simply a way of tracing the complexities of implementation nor grasping the vari-ations in how managerial regimes are enacted. This level is also important because it has consequences for the process of structural reform. Rather than a smooth, coherent and linear process, the restructuring of the state has been characterised by successive change initiatives, some of which have been designed to correct 'failures' of implementation in earlier reforms. The oscillation between hands-on and hands-off control, noted by Harrison et al. (1992) in the NHS but also visible in other areas, reflects the problems of controlling the process of institutional adaptation. The institutional level is not merely the end point in a chain of determinations, but also has consequences which act back on the larger scale process of change. The 'under-determination' of institutional change produces adaptations, whose effects have consequences for the political project of restructuring. Many studies of public sector management point to the interplay of multiple and competing objectives – or different 'stakeholder' interests. Local variants of these are framed by what remain contested views about the nature and proper role of the public sector and about the balance of power between organisations and politicians. Similarly, there are tensions in the relationship between 'efficiency' goals and the delivery of professional or political agendas. Many of these involve not just competing views of management, but concern the contested nature of the boundary between management and politics. They also mean that questions about the proper relationship between public service organisations and the 'public' are continually revived. We turn to these issues in the following chapters.

Note

[1] Elsewhere Lowndes has identified these as different managerial 'regimes' (Lowndes, 1996b).

6

Capturing the Customer:
the Politics of Representation

In Chapter 1, we pointed to the way in which the restructuring of the welfare state was undertaken in the name of the consumers of services, while in Chapter 4 we considered the claims of different organisational regimes to be able to represent the best interests of the users of services. Here we examine the ways in which service users are caught up in the organisational politics of the emerging managerial regimes, as the subjects of competing attempts to speak for and 'capture' them as a focus of organisational power and legitimacy.

The rise of the customer

> In a world in which cable television systems have fifty channels, banks let their customers do business by phone, and even department stores have begun to customise their services for the individual, bureaucratic, unresponsive, one-size-fits-all government cannot last. (Osborne and Gaebler, 1992: 194)

The consumer has been a central reference point in the drive for public sector reform from the mid 1980s onwards. Notions of transforming organisations around concepts of customer centredness were emerging from the private sector and the 'excellence' literature. Peters and Waterman's 'Back to Basics' messages for US companies included the injunction to become close to the customer: 'in observing excellent companies, and specifically the way they interact with customers, what we found most striking was the consistent presence of obsession. This characteristically occurred as a seemingly unjustified over commitment to some form of quality, reliability or service' (1982: 157). This injunction was subsequently formalised into the need to 'Launch a customer revolution', which involved turning organisations and management asssumptions upside down (Peters, 1987). This argument is inextricably linked to the other injunctions of the new managerialism: autonomy, entrepreneurship, and the need for continuous innovation. The application of these ideas to public services demanded the subjection of professionals to new logics of appropriateness and required them to reinvent themselves as 'entrepreneurs' competing for the consumer's business (du Gay and Salaman, 1992). Neither bureaucratic inertia nor professional arrogance had any place in this bright new world.

This form of new managerialism, coupled with the public choice theories emerging in political think tanks, formed a double rationale for the emergence of the customer in the British public services. This twin rationale embedded notions of the customer at the centre of attempts to build new organisational and management arrangements in the public sector. But consumerism has not just been the property of the New Right. To understand the politics flowing around notions of 'the customer', and the way in which they can be appropriated for a range of purposes, we need to examine some of the underpinning assumptions of consumerism.

> Consumerist theorists argue that there is an imbalance of power between those who provide goods and services, and those for whom they are provided. The former possess all the advantages of corporate power and organisation, resources, and political influence. The latter, in the marketplace at least, have the choice of buying or not buying a product or service, and – where competitive markets exist – of choosing according to their own preferences. (Potter, 1994: 250)

Potter traces five key factors which provide a structural underpinning of consumerism: those of access, choice, information, redress and representation. Examining the application of these principles to the delivery of public services, she identifies a range of tensions and limits to the application of 'pure' consumerist principles in a public service context. She concludes that:

> consumerism has a lot to offer public services. If one accepts that an imbalance of power exists between those who provide public services, and those for whom they are provided, and if one also accepts that the primary purpose of public services is to serve the public, then a careful application of the five principles can be enormously helpful in suggesting how public services can do their job better. (1994: 256)

But Potter and others (Flynn, 1990; Rhodes, 1987) have pointed to a number of critical issues which present limits to consumerism as the primary model for public services. One is the limitations of the principles themselves (rather than just problems in applying them). For example, consumerism is primarily focused on modes of delivery rather than on decisions about what services should be provided. Consumerism is also inadequate to express the range of relationships between the public and welfare organisations – as users, potential users, as individuals or groups affected directly or indirectly by the activities of state organisations (as regulators, resource allocators, funders and so on), and, critically, as citizens. This leads to a third problem: the focus of consumerism on individual rather than collective choice. Potter argues for a 'public service orientation' that addresses a broader perspective than that of service delivery, in order that it can embrace issues of citizenship, but goes on to comment that:

> Consumerism can help authorities to advance from considering individual members of the public as passive clients or recipients of services ... to thinking of them as customers with legitimate rights and preferences as well as respon-

sibilities. But it will rarely be enough to turn members of the public into partners, actively involved in shaping public services. . . . consumerism is fine as far as it goes, but it does not go far enough to effect a radical shift in the distribution of power. (1994: 257)

This analysis is helpful in identifying the importance of issues of *power* in consumerism. It is no surprise, then, that it is a set of ideas which have been deployed in different ways, for different purposes, in reshaping public service organisations. The politics of consumerism operate at both the level of state restructuring and the micro-level of organisational politics. The first sections of the chapter explore the contradictory ways in which consumerism has informed state restructuring and identifies issues about the changing representations of the consumer in the new regimes. We then move to the level of the 'micro-politics' of consumerism and the struggles to 'capture' the customer.

Consumerism and the challenge to the old regime

Consumerism has been deployed in the orchestration of critiques, from both Left and Right, of the bureaucratic paternalism and professional self interest operating in the old welfare state. These critiques have taken different kinds of inflections. At one level, they have been articulated to neo-liberal concerns, supported by public choice theory, to open up state organisations to market pressures. The New Right attack on state welfare identified monopoly provision by public sector organisations as an inhibition on consumer choice and much of the restructuring project was legitimated by reference to enabling the welfare user to exercise such choice. Although the early phases of reform were driven by the search for financial control, embodied in efficiency savings and the quest for 'value for money', the consumer emerged as the reference point for the later wave of service-specific reforms, in *Working for Patients* and *Caring for People*, for example. There, the introduction of marketised relationships into health and social care were identified as both promoting efficiency and creating choice:

> Stimulating the development of non-statutory service providers will result in a range of benefits for the consumer . . . a wider range of choice of services; services which meet individual needs in a more flexible and innovative way . . . competition between providers, resulting in better value for money and a more cost-effective service. (Secretaries of State, 1989: para. 3.4.3)

This commitment to reshaping welfare services around consumer choice has been visible in specific welfare reforms (for example, in public housing, education, health and community care). It has also figured centrally in the overall vision of public services articulated by the Major administrations of the 1990s, particularly in the idea of the Citizen's Charter and its subsequent derivatives (Pollitt, 1994). Barnes and Prior have noted that:

The commitment to furthering choice as an objective of public policy is spelled out in the Citizen's Charter. Four means of increasing choice are specified:

- Privatisation of public services – 'in a way which promotes direct competition between providers as far as possible'.
- The introduction of contracting with the private sector for services which remain a public sector responsibility.
- Developing choices within public services 'by introducing alternative forms of provision and creating a wider range of options wherever that is cost effective'.
- By consultation with the people who are affected by services – 'their views about the services they use should be sought regularly and systematically to inform decisions about what services should be provided' (Prime Minister, 1991: 4–5). (Barnes and Prior, 1995: 53)

The Citizen's Charter simultaneously opened up state organisations to greater scrutiny and control, and enabled a degree of centralisation of power, for example the power to enforce priorities through the operation of performance targets and league tables. As with other reforms, the Charter and its derivatives have had complex effects on the balances of power around the state. Drawing on the example of the impact of charters on the police and elsewhere, Wilson has argued that 'given the hostile environment within which public services have been operating . . . managers can hardly be blamed if they fear that performance indicators will be exploited for political purposes and simplistic conclusions may be drawn from them' (1995: 99). By contrast, Pollitt has suggested that 'like so many other developments forced through in the name of the consumer, the Charter is in many ways a charter for managers as much as for users. The standards which are crucial to the whole enterprise are to be set by managers, who are advised to consult consumers but are in no way obliged to comply with their wishes' (1994: 11). These different perceptions of the consequences of the Charter initiative for power flows indicate the problems of establishing the impact of consumerist initiatives.

At another level, the language and approaches of consumerism have cross cut the arguments deployed by proponents of the 'empowerment' of users, the decentralisation of power, and a greater recognition of issues of diversity in the delivery of public services. For example, in 'Beyond Bureaucratic Paternalism', Hambleton and Hoggett (1988) draw on the language and techniques of consumerism to support their call for a shift of power to users and a greater democratisation through the decentralisation of local authority services. Beresford and Croft (1993) attempt to develop and extend consumerist frameworks in their review of methods of securing greater 'citizen involvement' and the empowerment of community, rights, disability and service users' organisations in public services. Barnes (1997) has traced the growth of self-organisation by welfare users and its implications for the politics of welfare. The 'user movement' has addressed a complex range of issues in welfare services – not just issues of consumer 'choice' but also questions of rights, power and accountability.

Fiona Williams has identified three conceptions of difference and diversity in welfare services: 'The first is an individualist notion of diversity which operates through choice. The second is managerialist and focuses upon the management of differentiated needs. The third is anti-discriminatory and mobilises difference as political identity' (1994: 73). Although each draws on very different views of services and their users, their common attention to issues of 'difference' make the consumer/user a central, if ambiguous, figure in the politics of state restructuring. These ambiguities underpin Skelcher's comments on the possibilities and problems of consumerist developments in public services:

> At one level the greater priority now accorded to consumer-led services is to be welcomed. It offers the prospect of public services becoming more sensitive and relevant to the needs of the community, and in some cases may contribute towards an increased level of local democratic control and accountability. However, there are also dangers: of a populist consumerism which ignores and reinforces the inequalities to be found in society; of a focus on surface changes designed to make a poor service acceptable; and of public services being squeezed between reducing budgets and an increasingly articulate and demanding public. There are, therefore, a range of political questions raised by the current climate of public service consumerism. (1996: 66)

Managerial regimes, professional power and the welfare consumer

Consumerism, then, has occupied an ambiguous position in the remaking of the 'old regime' of the welfare state. Although driven by and through the New Right reforms, it has connected with wider impulses for change in at least three ways. First, it offers the possibility of services being more attentive to the issues of social diversity in the challenge that it makes to 'service led' structures of provision (see, for example, Audit Commission, 1992). The argument that services should be more focused on the specific needs of their users is one which has commanded widespread support, not least among professional groups who have historically claimed to be 'client' or 'user' centred. Second, consumerism focuses organisational attention on service delivery and the interaction with users. Coming after the experience of both resource and cultural impoverishment of the neo-Taylorist search for more and more efficiency savings, renewed attention to the content and process of services offered an opportunity to concentrate on what 'really mattered'. Finally, consumerism embodied a more active view of the service user – not a passive recipient of bureau-professional decisions but an active participant in the process of defining needs and wants. This, too, echoed long standing internal and external criticisms of the old regime from diverse sources.

In sum, consumerism – despite reservations about applying the idea of the 'consumer' to social welfare – connected with a range of concerns within the welfare state about ways in which users deserved better than what they received. In the process, it fed into a range of pre-existing initiatives designed to improve services and relationships with users. 'Customer centredness' has been welcomed by many working in public services. The excellence literature and its focus on flexibility, responsiveness, user centredness, and even the 'empowerment' of service users formed a platform for those dissatisfied with the paternalism of the old regime to press for change in the way services were delivered. Customer centredness thus provided a potential point of alliance between many 'old' professionals and 'new' managers against bureaucracy and paternalism. Both sought to disarticulate bureaucracy from its coupling with professionalism in reforms of the old regime.

Such concerns also led to a range of initiatives in local authorities which involved the decentralisation of services to increase either local accessibility or local control (Burns et al., 1994). Other innovations included experiments with 'one stop shops' intended to provide a unified point of contact between users and the range of local services, and the development – long before the Citizen's Charter and its variants – of service standard specifications, guarantees and charters. The extent to which such initiatives transformed the organisational structures is arguable, since many were limited to remaking only the user interface and had few structural consequences beyond that point. Nevertheless, they are indicative of ways in which consumerism was not simply a top-down imposition of new ways of thinking on a recalcitrant and unchanging world of public services. They also suggest some of the conditions under which consumerism would emerge as a contested formation within managerialised regimes, not least the capacity of aspects of the old regime to claim that they were *already* 'customer centred'. As a result, the customer has emerged as a new focal point of conflicting interests and interpretations:

> The attempt to replace professional judgement with a more accountable and rationalised managerial system was always going to be more difficult in some public services than others. It is likely that the attempt to bring professionals under stronger managerial discretion will not disappear as the power of professionals is weakened; the problem will be displaced to reappear in a different guise at the heart of the customer focus. (Ling, 1994: 38)

One of the ways in which consumerist initiatives have been installed in the new welfare arrangements is through the introduction of marketised relationships which served to dislocate the old regimes and subject them to new competitive, organisational and managerial disciplines (Taylor-Gooby and Lawson, 1993a; Walsh, 1995). We trace some of the implications of these changes for Ling's argument about the centrality of the 'customer focus' in the next section.

Markets and the rise of the discriminating customer

At the heart of the discourse of consumerism lies the notion that the best way of ensuring greater user choice and user power is through the marketplace. A range of market mechanisms have been introduced into public services, including competitive tendering and market testing, the separation of purchaser and provider roles in quasi-markets and internal markets, 'voucher' schemes and other customer based funding arrangements, and the direct charging of customers. While the introduction of marketised relationships has generally been motivated by the desire to secure efficiency gains, it has tended to be legitimated through reference to the broadening of choice and accountability and the improvement of quality (see, for example, the title 'Competing for Quality' given to the report introducing further civil service reforms, H.M. Treasury, 1991).

The creation of markets, contracting and customers in social welfare has attracted increasing critical attention. Much of this has focused on whether or not such models are appropriate for the organisation of public services and on whether there is really a 'customer' role which empowers individual users to make choices (Barnes and Prior, 1995; Walker, 1993). Many studies have emphasised the artificial and imperfect conditions of markets in social welfare (e.g., Hudson, 1994; Le Grand and Bartlett, 1993). There are a range of arguments that the necessary conditions for being a consumer do not exist in public services. For example, there are limits set by the availability of competing providers (both nationally and locally) which do not permit 'exit' by the customer dissatisfied with a particular provider. Some public services (highways, sanitation, etc.) may only be consumed collectively, while there are mismatches – both social and geographical – between those who pay for public services and those who consume them. Thus, the council tax payers of one borough may be funding services which are primarily consumed by those who pass through or visit (roads or Tourist Information services, for example).

More structurally, there are very few services in which the 'cash nexus' – the direct exchange of money for services received – functions in a way equivalent to most commercial transactions. Payment – through taxation – is separated from the consumption of services. Even where payment for services is increasing (for example, in the field of social care), this is characteristically mediated by other principles such as means testing. Such conditional problems about the appropriateness of the customer model have been extensively discussed in a growing literature about consumerism and citizenship in relation to public services (see, for example, Keat et al., 1994; Prior et al., 1995). At the heart of these is the resourcing, policy making and regulatory role played by central government, which determines the parameters and forms of competitive behaviour within particular markets. One distinctive result is that rather than trying to attract customers many public service organisations are engaged in trying to limit entry to services. The management of demand thus takes priority over attracting business, reflected in a growing concern with issues of priority setting, targeting and rationing of services through various means. For example, Mark and Brennan (1995) have explored the idea of 'demarketing' in relation to health care, suggesting that the purposive and systematic reduction of demand needs to be addressed.

Studies of markets have also pointed to the 'perverse incentives' that they contain which may run counter to other proclaimed goals of public provision (such as equity). Thus, organisations may be encouraged to engage in 'cream-skimming' in various ways or to off-load customers with high cost needs on to other organisations (Le Grand and Bartlett, 1993). Many of these studies have also highlighted the centrality of the 'proxy customer' in the purchasing of welfare services, and the implications for limitations of welfare consumerism. In fields such as health and social care, decisions about which services to purchase are taken by an intermediary agent rather than directly by the consumer. Thus, district health authorities and fund holding GPs are those who exercise choice within the NHS internal market, while care managers are responsible for putting together the 'packages of care' for those receiving care in the community (Langan and Clarke, 1994; Salter, 1993).

Less discussed but equally significant is the way in which markets were constructed as an alternative to the flawed processes of professional representation of need in social welfare. Professionals took the user's 'presenting symptoms' as the basis for interpretation that was a precondition for treatment. Professional power rested on an argument that needs were not transparent but required the application of expert knowledge in order to identify them accurately and respond to them appropriately. The marketised model of social welfare represented a direct challenge to such professional paternalism, offering a view of needs as wants, transparent to their owner. 'Choice' presumes such transparency – the consumer is an essentially knowledgeable figure, both about his or her own wants and how they may best be satisfied. However, in health care, patient need continues to be mediated by the medical profession at the point of contact (GPs), although professional representation is now more complexly articulated with managerial calculations. In fund holding practices and District Health Authorities engaged in contracting with hospitals, managerial and financial considerations discipline – even if they do not override – medical assessment. 'Clinical judgement' is now framed by the calculative rationality of financially matching demand and organisational capacity. There are occasional well-publicised moments at which the two different systems of representation of need are in conflict. But it is also clearly possible for managerial concerns to constrain the field of choice by professionals, such that professional power operates within a narrowed field whose boundaries are established by the normative and agenda setting power of managerialism. It is also possible for the two frameworks of representing need to be uncontroversially aligned (e.g., when a poor medical risk is also a high cost/ low return managerial assessment).

In social care, the purchasing function of social services departments is the proxy customer, embodied in the care manager and based on the assessment of user and carer needs. Again, professional and managerial calculations intersect in needs assessment, connected to the (more or less nominal) 'purchasing' of packages of care. At points, the twin discretions may be compounded in the same person – the fund holding GP or the care manager – who has both to represent the needs of the user and represent managerial calculations. The advocacy role of the professional is undercut in such circumstances, since the hybrid professional-manager is both the advocate and the decision maker. Langan and Clarke have argued that the care manager role in community care exemplifies this process:

> In community care, there is a potential conflict between the customer, asserting her entitlement, by right as a citizen, to a particular service, and the care manager acting as the custodian of scarce public resources . . . Care managers, on the other hand, emphasize needs rather than rights, and have a wider responsibility to stay within a budget while ensuring the efficient delivery of services. Such an approach may prove particularly insensitive to the demands of disabled people and minority ethnic groups. Despite the 'user-led' language which has accompanied the introduction of community care, the pre-eminent tests of managerial efficiency are likely to remain resource centred and there is a clear danger that user pressure towards diversity of needs will not fit easily with cost-effective managerial concerns. (1994: 86)

Nor is there any reason to think that the representation of user need is likely to be more transparent than under the old regime. Needs are still the subject of 'expert' transformation through the processes of diagnosis/assessment, even if customers are encouraged to articulate their wishes and users are drawn into the process of decision making through user panels, and 'partnerships' between users and assessors. The conflation of managerial, consumerist and professional codes of representation may even mean that the process of judgement becomes *less* transparent, in that it will become more difficult to disentangle need assessment/diagnosis from processes of resource calculation. Nocon has argued that in both social and health care, the managerial concern with resource and cost control has taken an increasingly dominant role: 'Just as care managers may find themselves guided more by the availability of resources than by identified needs, there are indications that purchasing authorities, for their part, may be more concerned with low prices rather than appropriate services' (1994: 78–9).

This situation corresponds to what Williams (1996: 74) has called the 'managerialist notion of diversity'. She argues that while this view of diversity breaks with some aspects of past welfare practice by giving greater emphasis to individualised conceptions of need, 'the approach to the definition of difference still lies firmly rooted in professional or managerially defined categories – old, sick, at risk, disabled, people who are dangerous to themselves and others, vulnerable and so on. Even the category "ethnic minorities", having eventually achieved recognition, has found itself wedged uncomfortably into a rather discrete, essentialist and managed client group' (1996: 74). This managerialist conception of need may be more attentive to the customer and his or her social circumstances and may recognise the implications of social difference for welfare needs, but it does not shift the balance of power from welfare organisations to users. They are provided with little additional leverage on the process of enforcing their own definitions of need and how they are to be met. Instead, they encounter normative frameworks of professional discretion overlaid – or compounded – with the calculus of managerial discretion.

Representing the customer: the politics of information and the politics of quality

Although the restructuring of the welfare state has increased the possibilities of individuals buying themselves out from public services through paying for private provision, the introduction of markets and charters has created something less than a 'sovereign consumer' of public services. In the absence of direct consumer power – the possibility of choice and exit being exercised by service users – the customer has become the focus of competing claims by different interests within and between organisations. These focus around who can best 'represent' what the customer wants or needs. Ling has argued that 'the customer focus is sufficiently diverse and contested to allow it to be linked to a variety of political positions. As much as being ''agents'' of the New Right, public sector managers are constrained by a variety of often incompatible expectations' (1994: 58). This variety of positions and expectations is also part of the internal life of public service organisations and manifests itself in different ways of speaking for the customer. These competing claims are visible in two emerging sites of organisational politics. The first concerns ways of representing the customer's needs: what we have called the politics of information. The second concerns competing claims about how to reflect what the customer wants in evaluations of organisational performance: the politics of quality.

The politics of information

The arrival of consumerism in public services challenges the taken for granted orders of knowledge and information in the old regime. In particular, it undermines the complacent claims of professionalism to 'know what the user needs'. This claim was central to professional authority and underpinned the exercise of professional judgement. By contrast, the imagery of the customer articulates more directly with the business discourse of managerialism. The customer belongs to the discourse of managerialism in the same way that the client or patient belongs to the discourse of professionalism. The managerial claim to be able to act on behalf of customers is manifested in its ethos: being customer centred is one of the foundations of organisational dynamism. The claim is also embodied in the technologies of contemporary managerialism – the use of customer surveys, market research, focus groups and other marketing techniques. These are the technical means by which managerialism legitimates its claim to knowledge about customers and what they want. As a consequence, customers do not arrive as a free floating representation in the changing organisational regimes – they are already constructed and attached to one of the contending regimes and its forms of representation. This ability to speak for the customer has underpinned the capacity of managerialism to drive through other organisational transformations (quality initiatives, audit and performance review, decentralised structures, etc.). These may have other legitimating conditions, since they embody ways of 'being businesslike' or of achieving efficiency, but they command extra legitimacy by virtue of their capacity to speak in the name of the customer.

What is at stake here is the transformation of what forms of representation are valued currency in welfare organisations. Knowledge of the customer has come to be more highly valued than bureau-professional knowledge of the client, not least because the technologies of customer research generate what appear to be reliable and extensive quantitative data about preferences, expectations and levels of satisfaction. Such data form a sharp contrast with the informal and qualitative knowledges of the client which is typically the basis of professional claims. These are part of professional 'common sense' and acquired through experience and professional socialisation. One consequence of these pressures on professional knowledge can be found in defensive attempts to 'hold the line' and resist the introduction of the customer discourse in favour of the languages of patients, users, students, etc. The continuing insistence that this 'is not a business', that 'social care is different', or that 'we teach students' rather than 'service customers' is, of course, always about more than the words. It is about the changing conditions of, and balances of power within, welfare organisations. At the same time (and sometimes in tension with) such defensive strategies, there are more assertive attempts to translate bureau-professionalism into a competing representational system by struggles to 'capture the customer'. As Walby and Greenwell (1994) have shown, much of the organisational politics of the new NHS involve attempts to control the high moral ground demarcated by the phrase 'in the best interests of the patient' over which shifting alliances contend. Professionalism counters the claims of managerialism by asserting its capacity to be 'close to the customer' at the 'front line' in ways that management cannot accomplish.

These attempts to speak in the name of the customer, and thus achieve legitimacy within organisational politics, are not processes that necessarily change the status or power of the customer. Ian Harden has argued that this shift towards valuing knowledge of the customer does not imply a movement towards individual rights in public services. Rather it involves the internal redefinition of what counts as valued information within the organisation.

> There are also other ways of getting information, applicable to services of all types, such as surveys and feedback from individual complaints into the policy-making process. . . Whatever may be thought about the desirability of such developments, their implementation is not a matter of individual rights, but of re-organisation of the service concerned to make it responsive to whatever indicator of preferences is to be used. Individual rights in relation to public services and input from individual preferences into decisions about the demand for public services are different things, with different purposes. (1992: 12)

Although Harden is primarily concerned here with the relationship between user preferences and user rights, his arguments point to the shifting valuations of different types of knowledge and information within public services. The 'indicators of preference' to be used in service design and delivery are the end results of these micro-political processes. The establishment of organisational goals, objectives and success criteria – and their cascading down to the level of individual appraisal or evaluation – involve conflicts over what objectives are to be set, and whose interests they are intended to represent. In this process, different groups in organisations try to mobilise their knowledge of the user/customer's needs to legitimate a particular set of objectives and the allocation of resources that may follow from them. Walby and Greenwell have argued that, in the context of the NHS:

> There is competition for the status of the best representative of the user of health services ... Traditionally, this role has been successfully claimed by the doctor, either as a general practitioner, or the hospital consultant to whom the patient is referred. Nurses are increasingly seeking a portion of this role, especially those influenced by the new nursing philosophy and by the increasing weight such nursing projects place on the care of the whole person. (1994: 68)

They also point to other claims to this status – in the form of Community Health Councils, pressure groups and user organisations – while noting that the NHS reforms turned to DHAs and GPs (as fund holders) as the most effective 'purchasing agents': those best equipped to represent the needs of consumers. Such arguments were also at stake in the claim by Roy Lilley, Chairman of the Homewood NHS Trust, in 1995 that 'doctors' first loyalty should be to the trust' because the Trust itself represented the best interests of the patients. The same types of issues are visible in other settings. Competing definitions of what the customer really wants and who is best able to represent those wants are central to the definition of organisational purposes and objectives and to the allocation of resources that follow from them. The ensuing politics of information involve overlapping struggles: about what words are used to define the user of a service; about who has the information that best represents their needs/wants; and about what those needs 'really' are. In the process, the customer becomes an organisational resource to be captured by contending interests. At the same time, customers also become an issue to be managed by the organisation, raising questions about how they are to be consulted, informed and involved in decision making. Each of these decisions has implications for who collects and owns what sorts of knowledge about users and the power that flows from it.

The politics of quality

These conflicts over knowledge about the customer form part of a wider politics of information within the restructuring of public services in which the 'knowledge base' of professions, which legitimated their organisational authority, has been subjected to a variety of attacks. Alongside customer surveys, there is the expansion of audit and evaluation systems which expose the practices of bureau-professional work to external scrutiny and comparison – both about costs and performance. Such systems demand that the objectives of the organisation are made explicit and measurable, despite defensive professional claims about the irreducible complexity or unquantifiable character of their work. In each field of public service there have been heated debates about the collection and publication of data from performance evaluation systems: for example, over mortality rates as a basis for comparing hospitals; clear up rates for police forces; examination pass rates for schools and so on. In part, such evaluative systems have been justified by reference to their role in ensuring accountability for the spending of taxpayers' money but also as providing the information that will empower customers to make better informed choices.

Evaluation has, in many cases, moved beyond the perceived crudeness of simple performance measures in the explosion of quality in public services, with new commitments to quality assurance, quality control, the setting and attainment of standards (such as BS5750 or local variants) and enthusiasms for initiatives such as Total Quality Management systems. What Kirkpatrick and Martinez-Lucio (1995) have called 'the politics of quality' in public services are complex, not least because of the variety of contending and overlapping definitions of what quality might mean in practice. Although quality initiatives have tended to be 'top-down' (either nationally from central government or from senior management in specific organisations), the detailed specification of quality has proved to be a fertile ground for complex local politics of negotiation, conflict and alliance building. By contrast with the 'stunted' managerial culture associated with neo-Taylorist forms of control and their association with crude resource constraint (the language of efficiency savings and the like), quality represents the possibilities of more expansive views of public services and ones which might be more sensitive to the concerns of both users and providers.

Many professionals have seen quality as a site in which professional practices and values may be defended and where they may be able to reassert a claim to both represent and advance user interests. At the same time, quality is central to the managerialist agenda of disciplining professional autonomy in the search for greater organisational efficiency. At the micro-level of individual organisations, quality has contributed to the installation of managerial modes of coordination. It has played a part in expanding and legitimating new organisational systems which regulate the old professional bureaucracies, from processes of defining the core business, specifying objectives and standards and developing individual performance appraisal systems. In practice, of course, these integrative systems are tempered by and even subverted by other concerns (e.g., the role of peer review in some sectors). Managerialism has proved unable to fix or stabilise the practical meaning of quality in ways which disengage it from other definitions, not least because of a recognition that the effective regulation of professional work through quality control or assurance systems needs to take account of professional conceptions.

Pfeffer and Coote (1991) note the disparate assumptions and orientations of different models of quality. Much of the internal politics of quality takes place around which model or definition should prevail. For example, senior managers (not surprisingly) often favour managerial models, prioritising the development of uniform standards across a whole organisation (which acts as a control device) while professionals favour 'expert' views. Service delivery staff are more likely to favour consumerist models in which 'responsiveness' rather than standardisation is paramount (thus placing greater value on the skills and judgements of front line staff). Democratic models of quality usually remain marginal because of the multiple organisational power bases they challenge.

Ling has suggested that, in the Benefits Agency, there are competing interests reflected in the different criteria identified as relevant to service quality: 'it might mean the cost-effectiveness of the service, it might mean "quality" in the particular sense of a professional-client relationship with power remaining with a paternalistic agency, or it might mean the clear articulation of legally binding rights and ready forms of redress where these rights are not met' (1994: 50). He goes on to suggest that these conflicting interests have been prioritised or ranked in favour of administrative savings, while 'quality of service' was given a narrow meaning. The practice of quality management is, then, characterised by tensions between different definitions of quality, diverse attempts to 'speak for' the user/customer and uneasy compromises between professional attempts to define quality and the creation of bureaucratic systems (and empires) which regulate quality. As a result, quality remains a highly charged and unstable focus of attention through which a variety of social, organisational and occupational conflicts are played out. The concern to manage quality thus keeps alive contending views of the public and their relations to public services through the continuing arguments about how to 'represent' their interests, needs and experiences.

Viewed more widely, the coming of quality has played into trends in the restructuring of services at the level of the state. Like direct competition for customers, it has contributed to creating and sustaining a field of quasi-competitive relationships between providers in specific areas of welfare: between schools, hospitals, social care providers and so on. Quality is now one of the indicators of competitive performance and must therefore be addressed by each provider in search of customers or contracts. This may have perverse consequences. As each provider claims to be delivering quality and have their claims audited or evaluated, so it becomes more difficult to demand resources for the service as a whole. Claims for additional resources can be countered by the claim that organisations are already achieving quality standards, or that the 'best performing' organisations indicate what can be done within existing levels of resourcing. Such manoeuvrings are a reminder that there are both macro- and micro-level politics associated with quality, information and consumerism.

Consumerised welfare?

Not all of the struggles around consumerism have accepted its formulations of how to remake the relationships between services and their users. There have been continuing arguments about whether the customer model is the best way to achieve more responsive services. In part, these have centred on the relative merits of 'exit' (consumer choice) and 'voice' (user or citizen participation in the planning and delivery of services). For example, Barnes and Prior (1995) have presented a cogent critique of choice as the basis for a relationship between the public and welfare services, arguing that consumer choice may well have 'disempowering' consequences for service users:

> public services can be used in conditions which are likely to be experienced as risky, confusing and uncertain. This implies that, at the point of consumption, values such as confidence, security and trust may be more appreciated by users than the opportunity for choice ... Describing someone as a user of services is a description of a complex and shifting relationship ... A simplistic notion of choice as selecting between options cannot stand up to systematic analysis of the processes through which people come to receive and make use of welfare services. (1995: 58)

They go on to argue that empowerment needs to be pursued by extending opportunities for 'voice', understood as influence over the 'whole public service process ... policy-making, resource allocation, planning, organization and management, as well as consumption' (1995: 58). They suggest that such empowerment needs to address at least three types of social relations – individual users, 'collective' empowerment of groups or communities organised around common interests and the more general empowerment of 'citizens' in ways which recognise the wider public purposes of welfare provision.

These arguments, which reflect and develop those of many user groups about the limitations of consumerism, aim to redefine the relationships between users and public services. Consumerism externalises these relationships in the form of demands which are to be measured, assessed and prioritised by organisations who then perform the task of meeting them – or at least those that are identified as priorities. Although this is overlaid by attention to the 'people processing' skills and competence at the front line of organisations, the consumer is outside the organisational processes through which services are designed and delivered. Barnes and Prior argue for a more complex interleaving of internalised relationships where both users and citizens influence the organisation rather than consume its output.

By contrast, others have argued that the challenge to the 'old regime' that consumerism and quality have embodied could be taken further to empower customers and citizens (e.g., Bouckaert, 1995; Gaster, 1996). Such arguments insist that quality initiatives cannot be matters of organisational or technical implementation, but raise questions about the relationship between the consumer-as-citizen and government. They attempt to redress the limits of consumerism while building on its 'progressive' and transformational possibilities and suggest that the technologies of quality might be extended to create channels to citizens as well as to consumers. But this raises the question of how far citizens become drawn into such activities without becoming subjected to (and disciplined by) the discourse and practices of management. There is a danger that the state-citizen relationship itself becomes managerialised through becoming subject to a whole panoply of new 'technologies' of citizen-agency interaction.

Such attempts to fill the policy vacuums and political deficits of the managerial state by an extension, however progressive, of consumerist models can be seen as an example of what we have termed the managerialisation of politics, a theme to which we return in the final chapter. Here we have traced some of the consequences of the 'consumerist' strand of public sector restructuring. Despite its political character as part of the New Right assault on the old welfare state, the consumerist challenge to the dominance of the professional-bureaucracies has drawn on sources of support based in a variety of oppositions to the institutionalised power which they represented. Views of the user as more than a passive (and supposedly grateful) recipient of the services granted by a benevolent state have been championed by a range of different groups – in particular, disaffected professionals and user groups themselves. Consumerist innovations – both locally and nationally – were thus able to mobilise support because of their capacity to address issues of 'needs led services' and greater responsiveness to the diversity of users.

However, the introduction of consumerism into social welfare has effected only a limited change in power relations, in part because 'choice' has primarily been exercised by proxy consumers on behalf of service users in the marketised provision of public services. As a result, it is possible to see a micro-politics of competing representations of the customer involving conflicts between and within organisations. These conflicts have come to centre on the 'politics of information' – the prioritising of different sorts of knowledge within organisations – and the 'politics of quality' – the struggles to define the objectives and standards of services. Through these conflicts, the figure of the customer has been inflected in different ways – as a legitimation of managerial power, as a defence of professional practice and as a basis for demanding extensions of user rights and entitlements. The dominant tendencies have been towards constructing a new organisational settlement in which users are conceived of as individualised consumers, and in which social difference is framed within a managerialist conception of diversity. These tendencies are still contested – both within organisations and from outside – by more activist conceptions of users, citizens and differentiated social needs. But the micro-politics of information and quality through which these struggles are conducted tend to be structured within the calculative frameworks of managerialism and the individualised frameworks of consumerism. In the following chapter, we turn to the consequences of the 'consumer revolution' for political conceptions of the public.

7

Reinventing the Public

The New Right attack on the welfare state involved a fundamental hostility to the institutional forms in which social democratic representations of the public were materialised and sedimented. The changes that followed can be seen in terms of an attempt to reconstruct the relationship between the public and the state around the individualised and familialised figure of the consumer. These neo-liberal conceptions were embodied in the public choice critiques of producer monopolies, in the Thatcher claim that 'there is no such thing as society', and in her governments' efforts to make this claim come true. Consumerism addressed a nation of private interests through the rhetoric of choice, counterposed individual freedoms to collectivist social provision, and framed social differentiation within a language of the diversity of individual needs and wants. Reconstructions of the state form towards more minimalist direct provision and the dispersal of welfare services to other agencies have been undertaken in the name of this conception of the public. These processes of dispersal have broken up the old institutional representations of a social democratic public, diminishing the role of local government and other elected bodies, and promoting forms of market relations in housing, health and education. Such reforms aimed not only to break up the old institutional attachments but also to create new forms of articulation between the citizen-as-consumer and the state.

These changes aimed to dislocate collectivist notions of the public and the public interest, challenging the legitimacy of any claims (other than those of national government) to be able to speak for the people. Although distrust of such claims was not the invention of the New Right, it has certainly woven them into compelling narratives about the suspect, or even venal, motives of those who make such claims. In their place, the legitimate forms of representing the public are now dominated by the mandate of the national government at the centre and the technologies of customer surveys at the periphery. In place of the presumptions of trust associated with old public service ethics, the relationships of public service have been increasingly formalised through contractual mechanisms, monitoring and both financial and performance audits. The inescapable logic of economic individualism is that actors (either individuals or corporate entities) will pursue their own interests and seek competitive advantage. The widely perceived crisis of standards in public life and the range of inquiries and investigations which have resulted are not simply the effect of the 'elective dictatorship' of Conservative government, but also the consequence of a political ideology which has consistently insisted that 'public servants' are not to be trusted by the public.

This impoverished conception of the public – of both the 'people' and public institutions – has not achieved an ideological resolution of the crisis of the social settlement. If anything, there has been a growing sense of multiple dislocations being caused or intensified by this strategy. Such dislocations are perceived at the level of service organisation and provision (recurrent crises in the NHS), at the level of organisational governance (fraud, corruption, chief executive salaries and perks), and in the 'social fabric' (in terms of disorder, disaffection and marginalisation). Issues of social diversity have remained unresolved. The disability movement has clashed regularly with government over policy and legislation while racism, sexism and homophobia are continuing focal points of conflict both in the wider society and in the organisation and provision of services. If anything, diversity has been an increasing point of tension, exposing instabilities between neo-liberal and neo-conservative strands in New Right ideology and politics. While neo-liberalism has informed an individualist and consumerist view of difference (Williams, 1996), neo-conservatism has tended to revert to an increasingly narrow conception of an 'English way of life', reviving a traditionalist, mono-cultural, view of the people and their culture. Neo-conservatism sees this culture as being at risk from a range of corrosive influences – from working mothers to Europe and other 'aliens'. The neo-conservative mission has been to rescue Englishness as a moral order from such threats. As a consequence the New Right needs to be seen as oscillating between a neo-liberal conception of a 'nation of consumers' and a neo-conservative vision of 'little Englanderism'. Neither looks capable of resolving the continuing crisis of the social settlement. But their inability to do so has created the possibility of other attempts to reinvent the public.

Reinventing the public in the new public management

To move out of the terrain dominated by managerial and consumerist discourse has meant reconstituting notions of the public in various ways (Newman, 1996a). The idea of the public – the public sector, public service management, public service orientation, the public interest – serves as a symbolic marker of a terrain beyond the individualism of the consumer identity. It represents something 'other', expressing an alternative set of values which are cherished. This otherness tends to be expressed in terms of a series of oppositions or dualities in which, for example, 'public service' values are constituted by their very difference from 'business' values. Common oppositions are:

Private sector	Public sector
Management	Public administration
Business values	Public service values

| Consumers | Citizens |
| Individuals | Communities |

There are many problems in attempting to define the terms of the right hand column. For example, the public sector might be defined in terms of funding source, a particular form of relationship with the public, the extent of democratic control, the form in which accountability is inscribed, the nature and extent of competition, or the extent and nature of consumer choice (Prior, 1993). Many state institutions now operate across this boundary in complex ways, not only through partnerships, contracting and other patterns implicated in welfare pluralism, but also through an internalisation of many of the dimensions of the left hand column above. References to 'public service values' can easily slide into little more than a nostalgic reference to a past golden era in which there was a mythical consensus around what these values were. Notions of citizenship raise a host of questions concerning national, racialised and gendered identities, and the shifting boundaries of inclusions and exclusions. Ideas of community are particularly difficult, given the tensions between geographical communities, communities of interests or affiliations, and communities based on a shared cultural identity which may overlap spatially, though unevenly, with geographical communities (Prior et al., 1995). Each of the terms through which notions of the 'public' are represented, but especially the ideas of citizenship and community, has a deeply moral resonance. They are, therefore, particularly subject to appropriation in political discourse, as in the Citizen's Charter of the Conservatives or the communitarianism of the new Labour Party. The difficulties of definition are often subsumed under the weight of the moral imperatives that these terms carry.

Despite these difficulties, many academics and managers have sought to reassert a language of the public, whether of communicating with or consulting the public about specific areas of activity, or more broadly about reconstituting a public domain. This may be through the visions and leadership of community governance, through 'empowering' forms of service management, or through 'capacity building' in the way in which organisations relate to voluntary organisations, the independent sector and to those delivering informal care. For example, in the final chapter of *Management for the Public Domain* (1994), Ranson and Stewart talk of 'empowering a public culture'. They argue that 'A learning society requires an active citizenship as the basis for action in the public domain. Citizenship is given expression in the arena of public discourse' (1994: 249). It is the role of public organisations to foster and promote such discourse, and to ' involve the public as citizen as well as customer in the co-production of public services . . . The requirements upon management are then the management of co-production for citizenship as well as support for public discourse as citizenship' (1994: 252–3).

This vision takes us beyond notions of public consultation. It is much more constitutive and includes the redesign of organisations around a number of assumptions 'that carry the dominant values and functions of the public domain into the working practices of an organisation' (1994: 254). These values and functions include 'to convene the public discourse, the debate about need and thus to constitute the public as a critical public; to enable the public to be a public' (1994: 254). This argument actively reconstructs notions of the public – the public realm, the public domain, public service, public learning, public choice, a public culture, public management. Its importance lies in its attempt to construct a discourse in which we are not 'lost for words' but can express notions of values and purpose, and see a vision of how relationships between institutions, individuals and the polity might be constituted in new ways. However, there is also a need to acknowledge the limitations of public organisations' capacity to actively reshape a public realm, not least because of the realignments that have accompanied the formation of the 'managerial state'.

Reconstituting the public in public management reopens a number of problems that arise from the processes of change discussed in earlier chapters. We want to highlight three sets of issues. The first concerns the *dispersal of power* involved in the reconstruction of the state following the dismantling of the economic/political settlement. This raises the problem of public access to and control of state institutions. The second concerns the *power of organisational discourses and practices* in reconstituting the public as individuated consumers. This raises the problem of expressing collective interests in the new managerial forms of organisational settlement that are emerging in the public, private and voluntary sectors. The third concerns the *increasing significance of social differentiation* that has followed the dismantling of the old social settlement.

The political and economic realm and the dispersal of power

As we argued in Chapter 2, the processes of state restructuring have fundamentally altered the balance of power between a public realm (represented in public institutions) and the private realm. The binary distinction between public and private realms has taken on greater salience with the concern over forms of privatisation in relation to public services. However, the reshaping of the public/private divide is a complex, not a simple process. While the state has withdrawn in some ways, its powers and apparatuses have been extended in others – transferring responsibilities but simultaneously creating the capabilities of surveillance and enforcement to ensure that such responsibilities are being fulfilled. This has involved the *dispersal* of state power across a range of locales and sites. This dispersal has implications for any attempt to construct a unitary notion of the public or the public realm. Each of these dispersed sites constructs its own relationships with individuals and groups (users, stakeholders, clients, communities, customers, complainants, volunteers, supporters, funders, providers) in a particular way, drawing on different sets of discourses and practices. The public, then, is positioned in a field of multiple relationships with the state through which it is constituted in a range of different ways. The public sector no longer has a monopoly of interactions with the public. There are many potential interactions, involving a variety of organisations, which resist being reduced to a simple distinction between public and private. The inclusion of the 'informal' sector – outside state provision but increasingly subject to state scrutiny – compounds the complexity. These processes of dispersal make public access to and control over state institutions more problematic. They also raise significant theoretical and practical issues for how the public as a whole – rather than particularised service users – can be consulted, involved, or empowered by organisations acting in the public realm.

The organisational domain: managerialism and consumerism

The processes of dispersal, resulting in the disempowerment of a collectivist version of the public, have been accompanied by a process of empowerment of the public as individual consumers. As we have argued, the consumer has been a central reference point in the drive for public sector reform from the mid 1980s onwards. The figure of the consumer symbolises the crisis of the old organisational settlement of bureau-professionalism, and of the social democratic politics on which it was based. In the process, many of the defining features of 'public service values' – neutrality, impartiality, fairness, equity – have become disarticulated from the organisational regimes in which they were enshrined. We have yet to see the emergence of new values that go beyond those of flexibility, responsiveness and quality of service which are embedded in the couplet of managerialism and consumerism. At the same time, however, the institutional embeddedness of the old values has been weakened. Although language is powerful, simply speaking the values of fairness, equity, probity and so on is not enough in situations where they have become disarticulated from the *regimes of power* that sustained them.

The processes of dispersal of power across a range of state and non-state bodies (quangos, agencies, regional offices, private and voluntary sector organisations) has broken up the old institutional embodiments of a social democratic public, diminishing the role of elected government and reducing the powers of local government and other 'representational' institutions. The fragmentation of organisations into discrete businesses and services means that these points of involvement are dispersed both within and across a range of organisations. By focusing on responding to difference among service users, then, the institutions of the public realm constitute a fragmented public, and fail to deal with issues of differential access to power and control of the public realm as a whole.

New institutional arrangements are accompanied by discourses and practices through which the public comes to see itself and think of itself in different ways. They create new subject positions in which people may come to think of themselves as consumers (with certain sets of entitlements and expectations) rather than as citizens (with rights and responsibilities). In the droughts of the summer of 1995, appeals to voluntarily restrict the use of water were countered by calls for recompense and redress for poor or interrupted services from the consumers of the privatised water companies. People began to use the discourse of contracts and entitlements to resist appeals to 'responsible citizens' with a wider duty to the state in a time of difficulty. Media interviews with John Gummer (then Secretary of State for the Environment) illustrated the interplay of these conflicting discourses. Interviewers repeatedly deployed consumerist language ('surely people have the right to expect to get the service they are paying for, and to be compensated for deficiencies'), while the Minister utilised the language of the 'public' to call on a broader sense of duties and responsibilities. New practices, then, bring with them new discursive strategies and a potential reconfiguration of relationships between state and citizen. However, there is also evidence that the public have not yet adopted the consumer identity in any widespread way. A survey for the Public Management Foundation (*Guardian*, 27 March 1996: 7) indicated a popular reluctance to be addressed or identify themselves as 'customers' and a strong preference for an identity as 'members of the public'.

Paradoxically, the narrowing of social democratic notions of the public to a nation of consumers has had the effect of opening up representational spaces in which increasing numbers of groups and agencies have attempted to lay claim to being able to speak for the 'public interest'. For example, in the NHS, education and elsewhere, professional associations and public sector unions have repeatedly laid claim to defending the public interest as the guardians of services and of cherished institutions. Groups of users have campaigned against some forms of change (and especially resource constraints) both in their own interests, but also in the name of a wider public interest. Campaign groups (on transport and the environment for example) have developed more expansive conceptions of the public through speaking in the name of future and trans-national publics.

The increasing adoption of consumerist discourse involves the dismantling of notions of a collective public in favour of individualised users of services. It is the very power of this symbolism that leads to attempts to incorporate other formulations alongside it, as in organisational mission statements which talk of 'serving communities' as well as 'serving customers', and the deployment of the language of 'citizens' to fill the spaces in the impoverished individualism of the discourse. In attempts to counter the discourse of consumerism at an organisational level with notions of citizenship, public and community, the dislocations of the third form of post-war settlement – the social settlement – are confronted. It is precisely in attempting to construct forms of collective representation that notions of diversity and differentiation become most pertinent (Thompson and Hoggett, 1996; Williams, 1994, 1996).

The social domain: differentiation and diversity

The dismantling of the old social settlements on which the welfare state was based has led to significant challenges to notions of citizenship and community. This means that the debates about empowering the 'public realm' raise rather troubling questions about the nature of 'the people' who are constituted within it. The politics of pluralism embedded in the post-war settlement meant that the state had a key role in reconciling differences through the institutional arrangements of the public sector. The professional power of the NHS was, in theory, tempered by the representational power of community health councils and MPs. Particular interests were debated and compromises reached through the mechanisms of councillors and committees in local government. Each set of institutions has, however, traditionally acted as a filter through which particular interests are defined as 'legitimate' or 'illegitimate'. Changes in the social settlement have challenged this filtering effect, sometimes successfully (for example local authorities now encompass more or less comfortably debates about women and public safety, child sexual abuse, racial harassment on housing estates and so on). But new filtering mechanisms are emerging: for example the processes of user involvement, consumer consultation and community participation are obvious sites in which selective notions of the public are reproduced, and in which the practices of representation may need to be challenged. In particular the devolution of power to 'communities' raises a host of questions about how differences of interests within geographically defined communities are to be resolved, and indeed about how community based organisations may themselves operate informal exclusionary practices through which differential access to the public realm is reproduced. What is at stake is the possibility of notions of citizenship which fully acknowledge the shifting relationships of family, work and nation *and* the differential access to, and capacity to speak in, the public realm which these entail.

There is a danger of drawing on pluralist notions of diversity which are attentive to difference, but not to issues of inequality of access to the public realm itself. As we have argued (Chapters 1 and 4), the distinction between public and private realms is highly gendered, and ideas of citizenship are racialised, with ongoing legislative and ideological struggles around who is to be included in a British public. There are also struggles by disability movements for full citizenship rights, as well as debates around social care about better access to decision making for people with learning difficulties and for young people in care. It is important to go beyond ideas of diversity within a pregiven construction of the public realm to look at how a particular conception of the public can reproduce such deeper patterns of inequality.

The discourses of consumerism and decentralisation to communities both articulate concepts of diversity. The rise of consumerism was linked to New Right critiques of public services as insensitive, undynamic and unresponsive. At the same time consumerism embraces a particular conception of diversity. While the old regime of universal and standardised provision, delivered through bureaucratic regimes, had flattened the diversity of individual needs, consumerism linked to a business ethos of 'serving the customer' reworked notions of diversity in the formulation of 'niche markets'. While this has led to some important developments in service provision (care homes for black elders, sports provision for women, Muslim schools), it has been limited by the differential market power of specific groups of customers, only some of whom organisations wish to attract as service users. The development of 'managed diversity' (see Chapter 6) involved a greater responsiveness to some dimensions of social diversity. However what counts as *legitimate diversity* – and how it is to be managed – remains the continuing focus of struggles both within and outside state institutions.

Reinventing the public, then, raises a series of dilemmas (Newman, 1996a). There is a desire to call on notions of the public (public service values, serving the public, consulting the public and so on) in order to rectify the 'value deficit' of managerialism. In doing so, however, there is a risk of drawing on nostalgic images of the public based on a social settlement which has been dismantled. The public is constituted in a field of tensions arising from the complex shifts of notions of public and private across all three settlements (political–economic, organisational and social) as a result of the changes of the 1980s and 1990s. The representation of notions of the public through a series of dualities – public realm/private realm, public values/business values, and citizen/customer – is unhelpful. In many cases what we have witnessed is not a simple shift from one to the other side of these dualities. The relationship between 'old' and 'new', 'public' and 'private' is not linear, but dynamic. There may indeed be dangers in thinking in terms of dualities at all: the realignments we are witnessing often involve a shift in the relations of power which such a dualistic discourse conceals. Talking of public through an opposition with private replicates a discourse which masks a political realignment of state power that works both across and through these distinctions. In the process, ideas of the public that carry a form of citizenship based on historical exclusionary imageries and practices may be both idealised and reproduced.

Putting the public back into the institutions and practices of the managerial state is, then, no easy task. It cannot be accomplished by attempting to speak to the public at the margins of organisational and management practices through a questionnaire here, a consultation document there, and a mission statement expressing good intentions. The public cannot be injected into a set of discourses and practices from which it is structurally excluded. To put this another way, the continuing crisis of the *social* settlement that underpins this problem of the public resists attempts to resolve it at the level of the organisational settlement. The problem has to be understood in a broader analysis concerned with the development of what we have termed the 'managerial state' and the spaces within it in which political cooption or adaptation might be possible. The dynamic interaction between management and politics in the context of dispersed state power means that the tendency is for the problem of the public to be posed either in very general – and undifferentiated – terms or in organisationally particularised ways. The former can only grasp a socially differentiated public as a diversity of individual needs and wants. The latter can only imagine a public whose differences map on to the forms of organisational fragmentation. Neither addresses the reconfigurations of power which have taken place in the social realm as well as in the process of state restructuring. The problem for these attempts to reinvent the public in these managerialised forms is that the public is not what it used to be.

Reinventing community: towards a more civil society?

The rediscovery of 'community' has also emerged in the context of the impoverishment of the public realm effected by New Right ideology and policy. Community addresses the sense of loss created by the claim that there is 'no such thing as society' and the consequent break-up of collective institutional arrangements. It identifies the realm of the 'social', insisting that society is composed of more than an aggregate of self-willed individuals and their families. From this point of view, people are defined by their attachments – to places (geographical communities); to localised social relationships (neighbourhood communities) or to social groupings (communities of identity). Such attachments mobilise or motivate people to act in particular ways – collectively as well as individually. It is this sense of the social – as networks of social relationships in which people are embedded – that forms the core of what Tony Blair has called 'social-ism' and of 'communitarianism' as a political ideology. The New Labour interest in communitarianism is not very surprising given that they both share this underlying conception of what might best be termed civil society – a field of social relationships which is neither the state nor the market.[1] There are other points of connection to which we will return later, but it is first worth paying some attention to the attractions of community as an organising focus for political ideologies in the late 1990s.

Communitarianism is presented as an answer to the problems created by the failures of the old (statist) left and the new (marketising) right, promising the prospect of a 'third way'. In relation to the state, communitarians appear to have accepted the burden of the New Right critique that the state is both over-powerful and inappropriately interventionist: it does things to people rather than enabling them to do things for themselves. However, communitarianism also suggests that the market has its limitations. Over-reliance on the market makes people behave like consumers – pursuing their narrow self-interest at the expense of any wider social or public interests. These wider interests are to be found in 'communities'. Community is presented as the neglected force which could fill the gap left by consumerist individualism, revitalising a civil society which can be reduced to neither the nation state nor the marketplace. Communitarianism generously assumes that both state and market have roles to play in social life but that primary attachments, motivations and identities are formed and mobilised else-where.

Communitarianism has a multi-faceted appeal, drawing on diverse sets of images. The first is a nostalgic sense of sturdy and self-reliant communities. One source of such imagery is drawn from Britain's proletarian past: dense networks of solidaristic and self-regulating localities, based on local indus-tries (such as steel, mining, shipbuilding). This imagery of 'traditional working class communities' has been most explicitly articulated in the attempt to define a contemporary 'ethical socialism' in the work of Norman Dennis and A.H. Halsey (1988). It has increasingly come to focus on the relationship between the decline of the traditional family and growing moral disorder (Dennis, 1993; Dennis and Erdos, 1993). The nostalgic imagery of communities is also drawn from a rural past – stable and self-managing village communities based in networks of mutual dependence, obligation and deference. Where 'traditional working class communities' provide a point of reference for some contemporary Labourist approaches, the 'village community' is a more explicit imagery for neo-conservative appropriations of community, for example, in John Major's bucolic invention of a nation playing cricket on village greens supported by an ample supply of warm beer. Both sets of imagery, however, are profoundly nostalgic and have at their centre the idea of community as reproducing tradition – the community denotes networks of relationships that sustain established ways of being and behaving: community as a *moral order*.

The second address of communitarianism is to the field of community activism. Community here is identified as a mobilising focus for collective action – in defence of local interests and institutions (schools, roads, hospitals) and, more expansively, in the creation of new collective resources through self-provisioning. Again, this has both a traditional and a contem-porary imagery, linking the sturdy 'self-reliance' of the past to the 'active citizenry' of community action in the present. Such conceptions also draw on the increasing visibility of the voluntary sector in shaping a welfare pluralism alongside state and market forms, assisting in welfare provision, sustaining a diversity of needs and playing a role in community regener-ation. For example, Stoker and Young talk of 'third force organizations' which are 'independent and outside government like a pressure group, but also get involved in implementation and in carrying out projects' (1993: 3).

The final form of address in communitarianism is to a conception of communities of *common identities or interests*. Here, communities are affective or identity based rather than bounded spatial entities, though they may overlap in places. So, for example, communities can be based in ethnicity or culture ('minority ethnic communities') or in other forms of socialised identity (the 'gay and lesbian community', the 'Deaf community', etc.). These images of community may be passive (simply defined by distinguishing characteristics) or active (the basis for collective mobilis-ation). Such images are one way of registering the impact of the public realm of collective action or new social movements that are both based on and produce common identities.

Activist conceptions of community (whether locality or identity based) overlap with some of the developments around local governance, for example in arguments about the spatial decentralisation of public services ('community based' facilities) and in the reinvention of local government as an 'enabler' rather than a provider (e.g., Burns et al., 1994; Cochrane, 1993b, 1994). The idea of enabling was rooted in New Right views about a minimalist role for local government which would create the conditions for others to engage in service provision (Brooke, 1989). However, as local government has experienced reductions in both its functions and resources, there have been attempts to create more expansive conceptions of enabling. Some of these involve the development of a role in producing the 'strategic vision' that will guide the development of communities, often to be implemented through partnerships (Mackintosh, 1992). Some involve the attempts to build the capacity of local communities to engage in participation and self provision. A still more expansive conception has been the 'community empowerment' view developed in the work of John Stewart and others (e.g., Stewart, 1989; Ranson and Stewart, 1994). These arguments start from the limitations of both traditional and consumerist models of local governance and aim at constructing participatory democracies alongside representative ones in order to shape both local services and the use of local resources.

> As community government, local authorities' primary role is concern for the problems and issues faced by local communities. They are the means by which communities confront and resolve these problems and issues that are beyond the scope of individuals or of other modes of social action ... It recognises within communities many differing interests and values. Conflicts exist as well as shared purposes. Community government is achieved through political processes that express different interests and values and seek their resolution in political action. (Stewart, 1989: 240–1)

Although it is appropriate to talk about the *rediscovery* of community in terms of representations of the public in political ideology, it is also important to remember that, in some senses, the language has never gone away. It has remained part of the vocabulary of local government, health and other providers, referencing communities whose needs are to be served. So, for example, the idea of 'minority ethnic communities' has been a very salient one for welfare services – identifying distinctive cultural patterns and practices which need to be addressed in service planning and delivery. This has been true both at the level of national policy development (for example, in the 1989 Children Act's attention to 'race, religion, language and culture') and in local settings, such as social service departments. Community provides a recurrent reference point across a range of public services – in Community Health Councils, community care and the tendency to define policing as 'community safety', for example.

We suggested earlier that part of the potency of community as a political idea derived from the impact of New Right ideology and policy on the public realm. But community as an idea is also able to draw on the fact that it is a term which is already actively in use as one way in which different social groups interpret their own social situation. People do talk about the particular place in which they live as a community – or may regret the loss of a 'sense of community'. Others may identify themselves as part of communities of identity or affinity – based in social or cultural difference. Local politicians speak of themselves as representing their local community, while managers and workers involved in service provision see themselves as addressing the needs of different communities. There are, of course, problems about reconciling the different understandings and meanings of community, but there is little doubt that a significant part of the effectiveness of community as a political symbol derives from its status as a practical concept in the way social groups make sense of their worlds.

Communitarianism both draws on and addresses these varieties of community, imagining a civil society populated by a citizenry which is active but particularised (spatially or culturally). The proper role for the state in such circumstances appears as 'investor', 'enabler' and 'empowerer'. As investor, public funds (potentially in partnership with private investment) are to be spent by the state to improve quality (of skills, capacities and life).[2] As enabler the state's role is to provide the conditions for other agencies to provide services (in some form of mixed economy of welfare) rather than engaging in the direct provision of public services. As empowerer, the state's role is to use resources to create the conditions in which people can act collectively – as communities. But, in moving beyond such generalised imagery of the new relationships between the state and the people, the ambiguities in the conception of community start to become apparent.

The first – and most obvious – problem is associated with the identification of community with moral regulation, providing a stable base of conceptions of order, rights and duties. The community here is seen as the generational transmitter of tradition, identity and attachment. It is this conception that has made questions of parenting and the family so central to the ideology of communitarianism. As a result, the recent enthusiasm for community also embraces the attempt to restore the traditional – and patriarchal – set of family relations. This is visible across a range of arguments about the need to overcome the 'parenting deficit' (Etzioni, 1993); the need to deal with 'families without fathers' (Dennis and Erdos, 1993); and the need to deal with problems of illegitimacy and immorality in the 'underclass' (Murray, 1984, 1990). As Campbell (1995) has pungently argued, this conception of community as the basis of moral order hinges on a neo-conservative dream of reinventing the traditional family and patriarchal structures of authority within it:

> Communitarianism celebrates a holy trinity of family, community and nation, as if community represented a halcyon pasture, small but perfectly formed, an immaculately conceived domain of homogeneous kinships, shared interests and

common histories. This notion of community enlarges the fantasy of family life that was shaken by feminism's scrutiny of its secret life. (1995: 51)

She goes on to argue that this project of restoration is flawed, given its distance from the realities of power, inequality and social dynamics that both bear on communities from the outside and are visible in their internal relationships. Despite this, it is clear that this imagery has considerable political attractions – resonating with the (doomed) attempt to define Majorite Conservatism as a 'back to basics' movement, with the wider neo-conservative obsession with 'traditional values' and with New Labour images of families and communities as the foundation for 'responsible citizens' and 'good neighbours'.

At the same time, there are difficulties about the image of communities as the basis of 'sturdy self reliance', engaged in the activities of self-provisioning that make them not dependent on the state. This is not to underestimate the real achievements of communities – whether local neighbourhoods or national/international communities of identity (e.g., Mayo, 1994). There are many examples of communities making things happen, but there are also dangers of making a virtue out of necessity. Much self-provisioning, whether by local groups or social movements, has occurred because of perceived failures of the state to provide. Thus, the active response of the 'gay and lesbian community' to the impact of AIDS/HIV derives in large part from the perception of government initiatives as, at best, inadequate and, at worst, downright hostile (Weeks, 1996: 79). The rise of community care – and its emphasis on care by, rather than in, the community – indicates very clearly the limitations of viewing communities as infinitely elastic sources of labour supply. The happy assumption that communities represent untapped sources of energy, ready and waiting to be directed into DIY versions of social provision is increasingly running into the real limits embodied in the distribution of time, commitments and distance. Yet it is this view of communities as potentially self-provisioning that underpins both communitarianism and Osborne and Gaebler's view of government as needing to be strategic – engaging in 'steering not rowing'. With the ship of state's bridge full of captains and navigators, communities are increasingly expected to provide the galley slaves who will do the rowing.

The issue of 'steering' – the establishment of strategic directions – identifies further problems about community, particularly in relation to community activism. Such activism is generically treated as one of the strengths of communities – embodying their role in the creation of a 'civic culture' or a more independent civil society (e.g., Green, 1993). Nevertheless, such activism is frequently not an alternative to the state but a movement to make demands on it – for redress or resources that only the state can provide. As a result, community activism is engaged with, rather than separate from, the state. That engagement is usually structured by state definitions of what constitutes legitimate demands *and* legitimate forms of activism. Some demands – and some forms of activism – regularly fall outside such definitions (for example, many aspects of contemporary environmental activism). In these ways, far from being a source of reduced public provision or spending, communities are often the source of extended public spending, either in the form of meeting new demands or policing the limits of legitimacy.

Finally, there are tensions between the image of stability associated with community and the forms of social organisation that have created greater fluidity (in terms of social and spatial mobility and of forms of identification and attachment). Traditional communities were defined in part by their exceptional density of social relationships and by their relative homogeneity, not least in respect of class and ethnicity. Such mono-cultural communities may have sustained a moral order, but it was often through highly repressive and coercive means. They were not particularly tolerant of 'deviations' from the moral order around sexualised or ethnic identities. This is, of course, precisely why the imagery is so attractive to neo-conservative concerns, but it does pose problems about how to make sense of multiple, overlapping and contested communities. Social identities and identifications are not stable or so spatially specific. They are what Hall (1996b: 44–8) has called 'diasporic' patterns of identity: mobile, plural and contradictory. Essentialising these in terms of place or one dimension of identity leaves the tensions of social differentiation unresolved or forces them to be internalised by the communities themselves. As Weeks (1996) has recently argued in relation to sexuality, communities may be 'necessary fictions' that provide points of attachment and mobilisation but to forget that they are fictions – temporary and conditional – risks compartmentalising them and leaving the structures of difference and division underlying them untouched by public action.

The diverse sources of interest in and enthusiasm for community mean that it will continue to serve as an organising idea for social and political action in different ways. But the wish to see it as the foundation of a more civil society and an alternative to the problems of state provision moves community from being a necessary fiction to the realm of a dangerous dream (Clarke, 1997). Civil society is itself structured in difference. It is not simply peopled with happy families, energetic DIYers, freely associating to solve problems and improve their lot. It is contested, unequal, differentiated and demanding. As a consequence, it cannot make the problem of the state go away.

Buddy, can you spare me a stake? Towards social inclusion

Where the rediscovery of community restates rather than resolves the crisis of the social settlement, shifting it from the terrain of the state to that of civil society, the next 'big idea' – the stakeholder society – addresses the crisis more directly. It does so through the increasingly influential imagery of social exclusion and marginalisation (Levitas, 1996). These ideas direct attention to the way in which recent economic and social dynamics have pushed specific social groups out of the mainstream of social development, leaving them behind or outside of the experience of economic progress.

In terms of stakeholding, social groups have been – intentionally or inadvertently – dispossessed of their 'stake' in society. The marginalisation of the old, the young and the poor is represented as both an affront to human dignity and a danger to social order or the 'social fabric' and manifests itself in a decline of civility. Those without a stake are also those without social obligations. These concerns mark the revival of a social democratic imagery of society, inflecting neo-conservative concerns about moral order in a different way from the obsessive and voyeuristic fears of a new urban 'underclass' (Murray, 1990; see also Morris, 1993; Mann, 1994). Nevertheless, this is a social democratic imagery attuned to the new realism of a tougher and more competitive world in which even hypothetical and conditional rights come with their full burden of responsibilities.

As Levitas has argued (1996: 7–8), the concern with social exclusion and marginalisation is at the core of an emerging European consensus on economic and social policy, traceable in European Commission white papers and the Social Chapter as well as in the more local deliberations of the Commission on Social Justice (1994). Stakeholding has been articulated with this analysis both in the writings of Will Hutton (1995, ch. 12) and in recent speeches by Tony Blair as leader of the Labour Party. It has provided the symbolism of re-integration – the means of eliminating exclusion or of moving people in from the margins – by providing a stake or point of attachment between individuals, families, groups and the society as a whole. This stake is primarily conceived of in economic terms – the ability to participate in the labour force, although it has also been used to think about new relationships of citizenship in the fields of education and welfare benefits and services.

At this point, it is worth noting the peculiar trajectory of 'stakeholding'. Although Hall et al. (1996: 8–10) identify its linkages to nineteenth century political discourses about the nation state and the relationship between the propertied and the propertyless, its recent life has been spent in rather different circumstances. It has been an influential idea in the fields of strategic management and corporate governance, associated with a view that organisations are enmeshed in a complex set of relationships which influence their destinies and are not simply driven by the objectives and interests of shareholders. In these terms, stakeholders are individuals or groups who can make a claim on or are affected by an organisation's attention or resources (Freeman, 1983). Stakeholders may include employees, customers, competitors, partners as well as owners. Mapping the field of stakeholder interests – and their power to affect the organisation in return – has become one of the techniques of strategic management. The phrase has entered the literature of corporate governance, associated with arguments that it is not only 'enlightened' but also 'successful' organisations who take account of stakeholder interests in developing their corporate strategies. It is this route that connects the term back to Will Hutton's writing, forming part of his critique of the short-termism and share-holder dominated character of British corporate life:

> Stakeholding is a genuine departure; it attempts to offer a set of guiding principles that could organise a reformist political programme in five chief areas: the workplace, the welfare state, the firm and the City, the constitution and economic policy more generally ... The unifying idea is inclusion; the individual is a member, a citizen and a potential partner. But inclusion is not a one-way street; it places reciprocal obligations on the individual as well as rights – and in every domain and in every social class. (Hutton, 1996: 2)

The radicalism of Hutton's use of the stakeholder idea lies in the insistence that it connects reform of these 'five areas'. It extends an approach to corporate governance to the network of economic, social and political relationships. At present, the Blairite use of the idea has been both more tentative and more tenuous. This view of stakeholding – and its enlargement to a new Labour vision of a stakeholding society – raises the problem of power: how can stakeholders enforce their claims on the attention or the resources of the organisation (or the nation). Some stake-holders have a greater capacity to attract attention and resources than others – by itself a stake is not enough. In the context of the political imagery of exclusion and inclusion, this raises issues not just about the redistribution of income, wealth or opportunities to provide the 'marginalised' with their stake. It also raises problems about the redistribution of power that could enable would-be stakeholders to make their claims stick. One major problem about the creation of stakeholders centres on how exclusion and inclusion are understood.

The primary mechanism of re-integration is paid work. As Levitas remarks 'the terms social exclusion and exclusion from the labour market are used virtually interchangeably' (1996: 9). This returns us to the old – albeit updated – Beveridge problematic of full employment understood in conventional and masculine terms. Exclusion from the labour market is differentiated, subject to different processes across gendered positions, disablement, ethnicity and age. As Levitas suggests these differential exclusions are also inclusions into other social positions. Women's exclusion from the labour market – and even much of their participation in it – is structured around their 'other' identities as wives, mothers, carers. Equally, the growing European 'exclusion of migrant workers from benefit rights is their integration as a flexible pool of low paid workers' (1996: 19). Although the language of social exclusion and marginalisation is formally attentive to the 'multi-dimensional' nature of such processes, the centring of re-integrative strategies of paid employment undercuts any systematic attention to social differentiation and to forms of inequality, which are more than unequal access to employment. As Hall et al. observe, 'Labour's evocation of a unified, consensual national community (''One Nation Socialism'') has not been moving the party in the direction of a celebration of diversity and difference. On the contrary, there is a worry about who might turn out to be excluded from Labour's community, like Harold Wilson's earlier ''national interest'', and how coercively this idea might be deployed against future dissenters' (1996: 7–8).

The unsettled social question

This observation returns us once again to the crisis of the social settlement and the inability of the traditional formations of family, work and nation to sustain an expansive conception of welfare citizenship. The New Right project may have failed to install a 'nation of welfare consumers' in its place but it has shifted the conditions of possible new economic and social settlements. There is a peculiar oscillation between 'modernisation' and 'tradition' at the point where the economic and social meet. It is as if modernisation of the economy, organisations, working patterns and employment conditions must be countered by the preservation of the 'traditional way of life' – despite the social and cultural diversity that has undercut that tradition. Just as there is 'no going back' on the centrality of markets to economic life, so there is no 'going forward' beyond the conventionalising imagery of communities, traditions and families within the nation. It is this mix of economic and institutional reform and social authoritarianism that Hall captured in describing the New Right programme as one of 'regressive modernisation' (1988: 164). The variety of attempts to reinvent the public in the last decade have been persistently hamstrung by this nostalgia for the 'old way of life'. Its effects exemplify perfectly Marx's observation that tradition 'weighs like a nightmare on the brains of the living' (1968: 96). Despite the symbolic attractions of the old (not least in a society subjected so relentlessly to the imperative of change), attempts to resolve the crisis of the social by restoring 'authority', 'responsibility' and the patriarchal family form that embodies them will sustain the crisis rather than make it go away. 'The people' – in all their unequal and complex diversity – cannot be reunited as such a public.

Notes

[1] Civil society is another rather elusive concept. In this context, it is usually taken to refer to a realm of 'free association' among individual citizens in which they form social (and familial) relationships.

[2] On the investor role, see the report of the Commission on Social Justice (1994) which distinguishes between a 'Deregulators' Britain', a 'Levellers' Britain' and an 'Investors' Britain'.

8

An Unstable State?

This book has treated the changes of the past two decades in terms of a movement towards a 'managerial state'. This process is still being played out, with a great deal of political and media attention focusing on issues concerning the form and nature of the state. For example, 1996 witnessed political storms over the findings of the Scott and Nolan inquiries, signalling that the legitimacy of government and the conduct of its business remains problematic. The workings of various Agencies, from Child Support to the Prison Service, have indicated the instability of the new arrangements of political and managerial accountability. The reshaping of welfare around marketised and insurance based forms of provision has been the focus of discussion about the relationship between state and citizen, which some have seen as marking (again) the end of the welfare state. The emergence of the 'big idea' of stakeholding suggests continued attempts to reshape a new settlement between state and civil society. Arguments about the future of the state continue, and it is tempting to define a set of 'scenarios', identifying different possible futures. Equally, it often seems to be a responsibility of authors (particularly in the managerialised world) to set out a list of prescriptive injunctions: what we need is more of this and less of that. We think our analysis leads to a rather different sort of conclusion: one which uses the concepts we have developed to see how the future is framed by the limits of the 'settlements' being constructed and the forms of contradiction and conflict which they produce.

In the course of this book we have concentrated on the remaking of the state in terms of a shift from a regime dominated by bureau-professionalism to one dominated by managerialism, embedded in processes of both the dispersal and concentration of power. We have shown how the words 'welfare' and 'state' have been taken apart and placed in a new relationship: one which does not imply an integrated institutional form. We have tried to suggest both the dominant trends and tendencies and the ways in which these are uneven, contradictory and contested. Sustaining this dual perspective has been important as a means of avoiding simplifying analyses or over-unified views of past and future. In the introduction, we cited Gramsci's view of the state as passing through a series of 'unstable equilibria'. That conception seems to us to define the task of analysing the restructuring of the state perfectly. It draws attention to how 'equilibria' – or temporary settlements and accommodations – are formed, while recognising that both the external conditions and internal relationships of such points of equilibrium are contradictory and contested, creating instabilities.

In the preceding chapters, we developed an analysis of the reshaping of the state that has treated managerialism as the basis of a new equilibrium, while identifying those features of the process which make it less than stable. In this concluding chapter, we return to the problem of placing the analysis of changing regimes in a wider political and social context. We take as our starting point the crises in the multiple settlements that had supported the creation and development of the post-war welfare state – the political–economic, the organisational and the social. The processes of restructuring can best be seen as attempts to resolve these multiple crises and to create new settlements that sustain a new form of state. What follows examines the attempts to construct new alignments in political–economic, organisational and social settlements and traces their implications for both a new equilibrium and new instabilities.

'No turning back': the political–economic settlement

Writing in mid-1996, there are particular difficulties attached to assessing the character of the political–economic settlement. In the context of a Conservative Party imploding under the weight of its internal divisions and the different interpretations of its Thatcherite legacy, and the still elusive shape of the 'newness' of New Labour, even to talk about a settlement may seem to underestimate the dynamic mood swings of contemporary party politics. But the issue of a political–economic settlement is not simply a matter of measuring party political agreement and disagreement. Just as the period between 1945 and 1975 contained different party political stances and policies within an overall consensus around the welfare state, so it is possible to discern some elementary forms of a new managerialised settlement that frames the current political perspectives on the relationship between state and citizen.

At its most basic, there is a profound sense in which the parties now inhabit a landscape whose main political and economic features have been defined by the New Right. Most obviously, this involves the relocation of where the 'centre ground' of politics is to be found. The effect of the self-consciously ideological politics of the New Right has been to shift what is conventionally called the political 'spectrum' rightwards so that the centre is now to be contested around a series of issues established by Thatcherism in relation to the economy, the state and social welfare. In this sense, there is a fundamental agreement that 'there is no going back' to the political economy of the post-war period. The liberation of the dynamism of the market is essential and the old regulatory, monolithic and corporatist state of social democracy is a monster that has been vanquished. As Hall et al. have succinctly observed, 'The Left lost the battle to resolve this crisis [of the 1970s], with the consequences of this defeat felt most severely in the United States and Britain' (1995: 8). The consequences have been both national and

international, visible in the restructuring programmes of New Right governments in both countries and in the free trade, global economy, low public
spending prescriptions for economic health promulgated by supra-national
organisations like the International Monetary Fund and the World Bank.

In Britain, these terms of reference form the basis of a new political–
economic settlement which, as Hay has argued, positions the main political
parties in a conflict that is about how to accommodate to the Thatcherite
legacy (1996: ch. 8). Hay traces the paradoxes that this situation has
generated, noting that 'we live, then, not in a *one party state* . . . but in a *one
vision democracy*', where we face the 'unenviable choice between different
modes of consolidating the post-Thatcher settlement' (1996: 159–60). He
also suggests that this new foundation for a form of consensus politics is
simultaneously associated with an intensification of confrontational politics
of 'personnel and personality', itself the legacy of the New Right's ideological form of politics. The problems of consolidation of, and accommodation to, the restructuring of the relationships between state, society and
economy that characterised the 1980s and early 1990s now form the
framework within which political choices are to be made. Hay helpfully
takes this further by insisting that this is not just a matter of making the new
settlement work but of dealing with the economic and political contradictions that it has brought into being. In particular he focuses on the
tensions involved in the process of restructuring in terms that recall Hall's
idea of 'regressive modernization' (1988: 164). He speaks of:

> the co-existence of two very different conceptions of state and economic
> restructuring: the first, a regressive, ideologically driven, neo-liberal project; the
> second, a more pragmatically oriented, modernizing strategy . . . Closer scrutiny
> reveals that these twin conceptions of social and economic restructuring are found
> to be both mutually incompatible and internally contradictory. (Hay, 1996: 171)

Hay deals with these contradictions in terms of economic and political
restructuring, but we want to develop them later in this chapter by examining
the problems of the social settlement to which Hay pays rather less attention.
Nevertheless, it is clear that the remaking of the state is bound up in this new
political–economic settlement. The move away from the post-war conception of an integrated and universalist welfare state is now firmly established,
despite the continued rhetorical presence of the phrase 'the welfare state'.
The grounds for this shift – the pressures of demography, the problems of
cost and public spending, the inability of the old regime to deliver efficient
and user friendly services – are all firmly established as political truths (but
see Hills, 1993). There are, of course, continuing disputes about how to
make the new regime work most effectively and how to make it publicly
acceptable, but these are framed by assumptions about the necessity and
inevitability of a new order.

Just as there is 'no going back' on the economic restructuring driven
through by the New Right, so the new relationship between the state and

welfare is not to be undone. The elementary forms of mixed economies, markets, mothers and managers are installed as the framework within which political manoeuvring can take place. The creation of a 'welfare pluralism' involving multiple sectors, primarily linked by contracting mechanisms, forms the basis for a new consensus (Rao, 1996: 179–80). The shift towards more 'responsible' communities and families providing forms of care is established. The importance of 'well managed organisations' in making this new order work is taken for granted. The basic forms of this political–economic settlement lead Hay to conclude that we are seeing the revival of what used to be called 'managerial politics' – the competition between parties about who can best manage British capitalism (1996: ch. 8). In the context of the arguments we have been pursuing in this book, we would want to suggest that what is emerging is better described as a *managerialised politics*. In part, this is to capture the sense that the promise by governments to 'manage the economy' means something very different in the 1990s than it did in the 1950s and 1960s. But more importantly, the term managerialised politics designates the changed relationships between government, the state and welfare in the 1990s in which managerialism has a distinctive role. There is considerable consensus on the need for government to draw on some of the new managerial technologies; for example to 're-engineer' the delivery of welfare benefits, to set standards for school pupil achievements, to produce league tables of schools and hospitals, to have purchaser/provider splits in the NHS, and so on. There may, of course, be disputes around the margins of these developments. For example, when Home Secretary Michael Howard announced that he intended to introduce performance related pay for probation officers based on re-offending rates of their probationers (April, 1996), the Labour Party response was to say that they were in favour of PRP, it was just that Howard had picked the wrong indicator. There is increasing political accord around the need for a managerially based process of modernisation of state institutions. It is not just that the main political parties compete about economic management but that the ordering of power in and through the state is articulated around the relationship between management and politics. It is this which makes the organisational settlement, constructed around managerialism, more than a technical matter of delivery systems.

An unstable state: the political and organisational settlement

We want to suggest that the state is engaged with a range of social and political problems that outrun the conception that still more and better management will resolve any residual difficulties. These problems are played out across the complex sets of relationships that make up the new regime. They are structured by the double movements of centralisation and decentralisation; by the construction of horizontal patterns of quasi-competitive relationships; by the dispersal of power through these processes; and by the form of managerialism itself. In particular, the problems transcend the conventional distinctions between politics, policy and management.

Politics and policy

One strong thread in the restructuring of the state has been the attempt to depoliticise decision making by making it a matter of 'operational management'. Hoggett suggests that 'There is a danger that naturalistic assumptions may guide policy makers and organizational analysts which obscure how the boundaries of the "operational" and the "strategic" are in fact socially constructed' (1996: 19). In the NHS, the Prison Service, social care and education, the government has consistently attempted to distance itself from crises and controversies by insisting that these are not questions of policy or the responsibility of Ministers. For example, the perceived crisis arising from the overload of Accident and Emergency facilities in 1996 was identified by Ministers as 'an issue for local management'. Du Gay suggests that the split between policy and delivery which underpinned the setting up of the Civil Service Agencies are 'the ideal organisational innovation for ministers. Because ministers still retain formal accountability to Parliament for the conduct of policy and yet are simultaneously able to decide what is and is not a policy issue, they are now in a position both to have their cake and eat it' (1995: 26). Nevertheless, what is striking about this and other attempts to de-politicise controversial issues is the relatively limited success they have achieved. Even where ministers and their representatives have attempted to shift responsibility to managers, the dominant public perception seems to have remained that these matters are the proper business of government, with the result that they are consistently re-politicised in an oscillating sequence of accusations and denials. This parallels the other oscillation – that between what Harrison et al. (1992) call 'hands-off and hands-on management' – where the nominal line between policy and operational management is more honoured in the breach than the observance.

Despite these instabilities, the dominant tendency has been to depoliticise decision making through the dispersal of power to managerially controlled organisations in both the private and public spheres. This process has been extensively discussed around the idea of a 'democratic deficit' (Stewart, 1993), a term used to identify the declining control of public services by elected representatives. It has been raised as a problem about the construction of Civil Service Agencies with a more 'arm's length' relationship to Parliament and about the shift of public services to more autonomous organisational forms which exclude or minimise democratic forms of accountability (Grant Maintained Schools, hospital trusts, etc.). This is also a central thread in concern about the role of new 'intermediate' institutions that have supplanted some of the traditional functions of local government, such as TECs and other quasi-public bodies, through which public money is channelled and directed. At the heart of this process is the belief that the combination of 'men of good sense' (the 'new magistracy') and managers empowered to manage will produce more efficient services, freed from the dogma of politics. The notion that this produces a democratic deficit is contested by those arguing that change has led to greater levels of transparency of decision making, and by enhanced patterns of direct accountability to the consumers of services (Waldegrave, 1993). Such debates suggest contestations and instabilities about the *forms of legitimation* of the new regime: in particular, whether the legitimation frameworks of 'good management' are an adequate substitute for those of 'good government'.

Issues about the dispersal of power across a range of state and non-state agencies point to a further problem in the relationship between policy and management. The growing complexity of social problems during the 1980s and 1990s has not been matched by any enhanced capacity on the part of the state to address such issues in a way that deals with their interrelationships coherently. The domain of policy formation itself has been the focus of a double edged process of change. One dimension has been the pressure of New Right ideological politics resulting in 'ideological policy'. The second is the reform of institutions of government themselves, particularly the Civil Service, in an effort to make them more effective 'implementers' of politicised policies. The mood seems to have shifted from valuing of the traditional deliberative processes enshrined in the Civil Service to one of 'can do' responsiveness to a succession of radical government initiatives. Jervis and Richards point to a 'cycle of decline' in the policy core of the Civil Service, which has 'reinforced the government's inability to tackle the key agenda items' (1996: 5). This is not just about the morale or effectiveness of the policy making arms of the Civil Service. It is rooted in a deeper problem of the shifting balance between the centralised control of, and the dispersal of power to, a range of agencies and organisations through whom policy is delivered. This has produced a simultaneous process of *policy proliferation* and the emergence of *policy vacuums*. The proliferation of policies stems from a government seeking to control an unstable field of policy delivery in which issues and problems repeatedly refuse to be depoliticised, and so require an ever increasing set of policy interventions designed to reassure the public that everything is under control. Policy proliferation is an indicator of the struggle for legitimacy of a government seeking short term survival, what Hay nicely terms the process of 'crisis mismanagement' (1996: 162). However, there is a contradiction between endless policy invention and the lack of coherence between them. It is in this space that policy vacuums emerge. The attempts to integrate a fragmented policy domain at an intermediate level through the newly established regional offices of central government are hampered by contradictory pressures:

> On the one hand, they have to pursue government objectives as set for them including the development of local partnerships to secure these objectives and contributing local views and experience to government policy formulation. At the same time, they have to resist pressures for a too open and dirigiste form of

regional administration and strategic planning, since they are the servants of Ministers and the Whitehall machine, for whom such an approach tends to be treated as anathema. (Spencer, 1996: 36)

Attempts to integrate policy at a local level (through local government, TECs and so on) are hampered by the contradictory injunctions of different policy initiatives flowing down government, and by the perverse incentives produced by centrally controlled funding arrangements and performance measures. Where the Civil Service has been recast in a 'can do' mould, we might suggest that other organisations have been placed in a 'must do' relationship to policy, such that the experience of delivering services is increasingly experienced as a 'make do' task – managing the tensions between delivering policy and coping with limited resources, and between central and local pressures.

The logics of managerialism

But managers are not just positioned by the tension between central control and the dispersal of power. The dispersal of power allows not just the possibility of managerial actors pursuing and delivering the goals which the process of reform intended, but also of actively shaping the new institutional arrangements.What has emerged in recent years is a dominant template for organisational design and management practice. We can talk about this in terms of 'isomorphism' – the tendency for organisations to adopt similar forms. In Chapter 5 we outlined three forms of isomorphism – coercive, mimetic and normative. We can trace each of these forms of isomorphism in terms of a range of pressures which have shaped the dominant patterns of change. Organisational design has itself become politicised, with government reconfiguring the Civil Service through the separation of agencies from the policy elements, and with bodies such as the Audit Commission specifying the changes that were expected in particular services (such as the introduction of purchaser/provider splits in social services departments). More subtly, the publication of league tables and new funding arrangements have served to focus organisations on the delivery of their 'core business' and to prioritise efficiency gains over other forms of output. There has been a decline in political tolerance of organisational diversity among agencies delivering public services.

The tendency towards isomorphism is not just a result of such coercive forces. Organisations come to internalise a range of external pressures as they seek legitimacy among their various stakeholders. So, for example, the adoption of organisational arrangements based on a process of fragmentation into business units, purchaser/provider splits, internal contracting and charging, is based on a particular 'logic of appropriateness' derived from the external environment. The flurry of activities around the search for the latest Charter mark or award (e.g., Investors in People, BS 5750) can be as much about external legitimacy as it is about internal effectiveness. In addition, normative processes of isomorphism flow from the growing dominance of particular models – and fashions – of management which are disseminated through management education programmes, conferences, professional bodies, and in the ideas of the latest management guru. Together these processes have produced a dominant template of organisational design and managerial practice. The main features of the organisational template can be summarised in a list of public management orthodoxies including decentralisation, devolution, internal purchasing and charging, divisions between strategic and operational management, and the re-engineering of organisations around notions of 'core business' with the outsourcing of activities defined as non-core. Internal management processes are dominated by the twin rubrics of business planning, linked to target setting and performance management, and the building of corporate commitment to a specific organisational 'mission' and purpose, linked to survival in a competitive environment.

This template is highly effective in delivering some things. It enables organisations to be focused and strategic, and to get the structures and systems which will help them to deliver their goals. It helps produce a performance based orientation in which outputs may be defined and measured. It concentrates attention on efficiency and effectiveness. The stripping away of organisational infrastructures may produce greater 'flexibility'. However, being goal-driven tends to mean a focus on short term goals since these are the ones against which outputs and performance are measured. The template focuses concern on outputs (on which funding is increasingly based) rather than outcomes, and on short term rather than long term planning processes. It does not have the capacity to enable organisations and managers to deal with complexity and uncertainty. Greater flexibility does not necessarily lead to improved responsiveness.

Most significantly, issues of strategy and purpose are posed in terms of a narrow sense of core business rather than a wider public purpose. This in turn means that being effective has a narrow definition – it is effectiveness in relation to a narrow set of goals. The focus on corporate culture can produce an 'us against the world' philosophy, which in turn means a lack of capacity to collaborate across boundaries and a number of deficits in terms of partnership working. There is an emerging body of research on the effectiveness of partnerships in the public domain (e.g., Hudson, 1987; Huxham, 1993; Huxham and Vangen, 1996; Mackintosh, 1992; Nocon, 1994). This work highlights not only the practical problems of partnership working, but identifies some of its disbenefits for the organisations concerned. Evidence about the costs of partnership working, and its limited effectiveness in developing coordinated strategies, is beginning to emerge (Huxham and Vangen, 1996). The growing emphasis on competitive positioning acts as an obvious barrier to collaboration. In addition, the focus on core business, linked to outputs and output based funding, means that there are a number of 'perverse incentives' which inhibit inter-organisational cooperation.

All of this means that the capacity of organisations and management processes to respond to critical issues facing public services is very limited.

Such issues have been termed 'wicked issues' (Stewart, 1994) and include crime, poverty, community safety, the care of the elderly and of people with disabilities, economic regeneration, environmental issues, transport, child protection and a host of others. They are 'wicked' in the sense that they are ill defined, complex, are subject to conflicting perspectives on the level and nature of the problem, and – most critically – do not fall within conventional policy divisions or the province of single organisations. The pursuit of unconnected initiatives as organisations or government departments pursue an ever narrowing agenda and set of programmes defined around their core business serves to exacerbate, rather than address, such complex social issues and problems. The combined managerial and policy deficits in a dispersed field of power militates against the development of a capacity to address issues which resist being neatly defined as managerial problems. The deficits in the policy domain are both mirrored and intensified by the dominant template of organisational design and by the internal logics of the managerial regime. As a consequence, the new regime compounds new formulations of old problems (e.g., the relationship between needs and resources or collaborative working) with new problems that are the direct effect of the new relationships (e.g., the impact of defining core businesses).

This is all linked to the dispersal of state power, but goes beyond that. Our term 'managerialised politics' does not just concern the effectiveness of institutions, but involves the managerialisation of the policy domain itself, which influences not only the structures and institutions, but the discourses and frameworks within which deliberation and evaluation take place. Managerial discourse offers particular representations of the relationship between social problems and solutions. It is linear and oriented to 'single goal' thought patterns. It is concerned with goals and plans rather than with intentions and judgements. It is about action rather than reflection. It draws on analysis (breaking problems down) rather than synthesis. It sets up boundaries between 'policy' and 'delivery', 'strategy' and 'implementation', thought and action. It offers a technicist discourse which strips debate of its political underpinnings, so that debate about means supplants debate about ends. It is this 'technical' quality of managerialism that makes it attractive to diverse social and political interests. In particular, its application to solving the problems of an 'obstructive' and old-fashioned model of bureaucratic administrative system engages support from both political representatives (promised more effective implementation of their policies) and a range of other would-be modernisers (who seek more rational systems of governance).

These characteristics limit what is thinkable within managerial discourse. Part of the phenomenon of being 'lost for words' that we discussed in Chapter 3 relates to the shrinking purposes of public services associated with managerialism. The emphasis on improving 'service delivery' has bracketed wider questions of social and public purpose. The managerialisation of public services has attempted to resolve the contradictions between rising need and shrinking resources by turning this into a management problem – the production of 'more for less'. As a result, one of the dominant tasks for public sector management is the management of demand – expressed in terms of defining core business, prioritisation of need, the rationalisation of resource allocation and so on. This political contradiction has been managerialised and turned into the 'business' of specific organisations. As a consequence, it is not surprising that managerialism is experienced as a series of dilemmas and tensions. Public service managers are subjected to the interplay of multiple and competing objectives – or different 'stakeholder' interests. Local variants of these are framed by what remain contested views about the nature and proper role of the public sector and about the balance of power between organisations and politicians.

Managing welfare: squaring the circle?

The promise at the heart of these processes of restructuring was that good management could square the circle between rising demands for welfare and the pressures to reduce the costs of welfare. Good management meant the capacity to match resources and demand by increasing efficiency and productivity and by focusing organisational attention on the core business. This promise has been the escape route for governments attempting to negotiate the contradictions between promises to contain or reduce public spending and public anxiety over the future standards and availability of welfare services (concerning the NHS, in particular). The ways in which it has been delivered in practice account for the apparent paradox between evidence of 'increasing efficiency' and perceptions of 'declining services' that have been central to public arguments about the reforms.

The pursuit of economy and efficiency has involved a range of strategies. The quasi-market mechanism and the accompanying division between purchasers and providers has used the imitation of market competition to drive down costs in 'provider' organisations as they compete for contracts. Since purchasing agencies possess limited funding, this tends to place the cost of contracting services as the dominant priority. This, in turn, sets the agenda for provider agencies, unless they can define themselves as providing a 'niche' service which carries a financial premium. The competitive mechanism has effects alongside instilling cost consciousness: for example, through the way competitors strive to control the conditions that affect their costs and performance (Le Grand and Bartlett, 1993; Mackintosh, 1995a; Salter, 1993). For example, schools exclude 'difficult' pupils or attempt to 'skim the cream' of the most educable; private health insurers exclude costly medical conditions or 'bad risk' customers; health providers limit the range of services that they offer in order to avoid 'inefficient' operations or shift patients (and their costs) from health care to care in the community. For such reasons, what might be called *boundary management* has been an increasingly important managerial skill. Involved are decisions about what or who constitutes legitimate demands on an organisation's resources; processes of collaboration and partnership to share burdens or increase resources and the transfer of costs to other people's budgets.

Boundary management is not only an inter-organisational issue – although it is particularly visible in the disputes about the long term care needs of the elderly on the boundary between the NHS and social services (Vickridge, 1995). It is also an inter-sectoral matter – both through the 'creaming' and 'dumping' strategies in relation to good and bad risks and through the transfer of costs via contracting (for example, using lower cost labour in voluntary sector organisations). Most strikingly, however, it involves shifts between the organised sectors and the informal world of the household. This has been extensively discussed in relation to social care and to a lesser extent in relation to health care (with faster throughput transferring convalescence to the home setting). But it is also true of other efficiency gains in state welfare provision. Education has increasingly come to rely on supplementation from familial resources. This includes paying for extra-curricular provision or topping up student grants in higher education. It also involves using parental and other unpaid labour more intensively both within the curriculum (listening to children read) and in school management (in governing bodies and fund raising). Reductions in benefit levels and the increase in means testing for benefits and some services transfer the costs of living to private resources (using savings, practising better 'household management', borrowing and so on).

The wider political agenda of targeting welfare benefits and services is also mirrored in the expansion of organisational forms of discretionary judgement. The concern with targeting has been linked to the quest for efficiency, based on the argument that universal benefits and services are fundamentally wasteful of resources and unnecessary in a situation where more and more individuals are making private arrangements for their own welfare needs. Targeting has led to an increase in means testing for a variety of benefits and services in the place of access as of right. Although this has been most visible in the movement away from insured benefits to income support in the income maintenance system, it is also a strand in community care, education (as school provision narrows to the core curriculum), access to transport and leisure facilities, and aspects of health care. Such policies have been legitimated on the basis of concentrating resources on the most needy in ways that have revived older debates about need and moral worth – ranging from the 'undeserving' character of lone mothers to the denial of health resources to those who 'don't look after themselves' or are a 'bad investment'. Rationing – on the basis of matching limited resources to rising demands – has become a more visible and more significant process, ranging from the definition of health priorities to the requirement on local authorities to define those 'in need' of support through personal social services in both the Children Act of 1989 and the NHS and Community Care Act of 1990.

These issues suggest that the pursuit of organisational efficiency in social welfare has involved complex processes of cost transfers. Some of these involve shifting costs to work forces (through changed conditions of employment and different sectoral distributions). Some involve inter-sectoral transfers. But many involve shifting the costs of welfare from the public to the private realm – requiring workers, users, citizens and communities to meet the financial and social costs of survival. The processes of producing organisational efficiencies 'externalise' many of the costs of welfare, thus adding to (rather than reducing) the social problems to which the state is asked to respond. Reducing labour forces increases demands on the benefit system, as does low waged employment. Speeding up hospital throughput generates demand for other forms of care. The 'not our business' calculus of efficiency may improve organisational performance at the same time as diminishing the welfare of the public as a whole.

In crude terms, the restructuring of welfare has added to the wider processes of deepening resource inequalities that characterised the social dynamics of Britain during the 1980s and the first half of the 1990s – with widening gaps between rich and poor, growing numbers of poor people and changes in the social composition of poverty (Cochrane, 1993a). Welfare reform has contributed to these tendencies both in terms of the effects of the more targeted approach to income maintenance and through the growth of private welfare which has allowed those with money to gain access to services and benefits beyond the public sector. Reform has also intensified them through the efficiency gains involving cost transfers to the private realm. Such consequences are not particularly surprising given that both the neo-liberal and neo-conservative ideologies from which Conservative governments in the period have drawn much of their inspiration are committed to a view of social inequalities as both necessary and desirable for their motivational effects. But it does mean that assessments of the improved efficiency resulting from 'better management' in social welfare should not be limited to the narrow evaluation of organisational performance.

Expanding the right to manage

As we argued in Chapter 5, the process of institutional change has been complex, uneven and contested. The dispersal of power means that managerialism is enacted and produced in multiple ways across different sectors and sites, and is underpinned by a range of commitments as old and new regimes interact. Indeed, this is one of the points of instability in the new arrangements. Managers are not just the technical conduits through which policies are implemented. The process of institutional elaboration means that the outcomes of reforms are unpredictable. March and Olsen suggest that 'it is easier to produce change through shock than to control what new combinations of institutions and practices will evolve from the shock' (1989: 65). The 'empowerment' of managers in a dispersed set of organisational arrangements exacerbates this unpredictability. The New Public Management contains an expansionist logic that suggests that management should be empowered further. Here we want to highlight two versions of this that are particularly significant for the way that they address some of the contradictions and tensions that we have discussed in this chapter.

The first deals with the problems of policy and operational management. It suggests that the current situation is messy, compromised and unstable. Most of the blame for this can be laid at the door of politicians (whether in national or local government). They remain prone to 'interfering' (in operational matters); tend towards 'short termism' in policy initiatives; lack the capacity or will to set clear objectives and, most of all, fail to recognise what a powerful tool they have in management. Derek Lewis, the sacked Chief Executive of the Prison Service Agency, has been one of the most articulate proponents of this conception of 'setting the servants free' (*Guardian*, 13 May 1996: 13). Here, managerialism threatens to be 'a knife that turns in the hand'. Deployed to rationalise the old regime, it also turns its rationalising logic (and its claims to power) on the political centre which is identified as falling short of (managerial) rationality. In short, it demands that the rhetoric of 'the freedom to manage' be delivered in practice.

The second version addresses the problems of legitimacy and the delivery of effective services that are responsive to public needs. It suggests that over-centralised policy formation, the problems of limited accountability and service disintegration may have produced cost efficiency but have done little for the effectiveness of public services. It argues that, in practice, the potential for disaster of these problems has been minimised by the efforts of public service managers. Despite the government's worst efforts, managers have sustained public service values and embedded them in new organisational forms and practices. It is they who have built networks, collaborative relationships and partnerships that try to overcome the 'perverse effects' of fragmentation. It is they who have listened to users and customers to make services responsive to local needs and who have sought ways of enabling and empowering users and communities. As a result, what is needed is more freedom for managers to build on these qualities and capacities to create better public services.

These claims articulate different aspects of public management: the first is about 'knowing the business'; the second about 'knowing the public'. But both are about enlarging the right to manage and this is the final instability of the new organisational settlement. It is built on a regime that is inherently centred on claims to power, legitimated by a rationalist and universalising ideology which insists that managers be given the freedom (that they define as) necessary to 'do the right thing'. This expansionist character of managerialism itself is at the heart of our reluctance to treat management either as a set of neutral techniques and technologies or as the 'tool' of the New Right. It has an imperialist logic of its own which turns the problems of the new organisational settlement into opportunities for its own enlargement. Nevertheless, we remain sceptical about the claims that knowing the business and knowing the public provide the basis for resolving the contradictions of the new relationship between welfare and the state, not least because the unresolved nature of the crisis in the social settlement cannot be solved within the new organisational regime.

More than two nations? The social settlement

We argued in Chapter 7 that attempts to 'reinvent the public' had failed to engage with the challenges of social diversity – and it is this issue which continues to haunt the creation of a managerial state. The trinity of 'family, work and nation' that formed the social settlement of the post-war welfare state became unsustainable in the face of the twin pressures of social change and social challenges (Chapter 1). In the remaking of the relationship between the state and welfare, the dominant tendencies for responding to diversity have been those identified by Fiona Williams (1996: 73) as the 'individualist/choice' formation and 'managerialist diversity' which are embodied in the marketised and managerialised forms of restructuring. There have been particular initiatives that 'take account of' different needs and interests – shaped by local struggles and alliances to define needs and how they are to be met. The possibility of these is, in some ways, enhanced by the processes of dispersal. The multiplication of sites of decision making means that there are more points of connection with civil society that may be 'captured' by active articulations of Williams's third version of difference – as the basis of political identity and action, whether in the form of user groups, local community interests or social movements.

Despite this, the consumerist and managerialist versions of diversity have been the principal forms through which social differentiation has been addressed and embedded in the new regime. In the process, the social structuring of inequalities, divisions and antagonisms becomes flattened in their representation as either individual wants or categories of 'special' needs. This does pose a problem about what has happened to these structured differences as a result of the new regime. Has it reproduced existing inequalities? Has it redressed them? Or has it created new forms of differentiation and inequality? In some respects, this is a difficult question to answer precisely because of the processes of dispersal. For example, writing about inequalities in the NHS, Powell has commented that 'the NHS has always been a multi-tier service, and the reforms may merely have made old inequalities *appear* more visible, whether or not they have added to them' (1996: 39). This identifies a more general problem about assessing the social effects of the new regime – which is the changing visibility and invisibility of some forms of inequality in the shift to organisation based calculations of effectiveness. For example, while the increase in school exclusions has been widely reported, it is difficult to trace the social content of the organisational categories. Studies of earlier professional categories – like Coard's work (1971) on 'educationally subnormal pupils' – suggest that what proportion of 'difficult pupils' are black might be of relevance.

The intensification of social inequalities, divisions and problems is associated not just with the policy intentions of New Right governments but also with the new 'delivery systems' for social welfare we described in the previous section. Hay has referred to the growth of social polarisation and deepening inequality as a core component of Thatcherism as a 'two-nation Toryism' (1996: 145–6). While highlighting deepening income inequalities, the 'two nations' imagery obscures the complexity of social differentiation. This matters for an understanding of who is being consigned to the nation of 'have nots': the changing social composition of poverty which has involved an intensification of the intersection of gender, 'race' and disability, for example (Oppenheim, 1993). But it also matters for those dimensions of inequality which are simply income based – access to services, benefits and social rights – which are also the terrain of social difference. In this sense, there are more than 'two nations'. More accurately, there is one nation whose formation is multiple, contradictory and contested. As Hall et al. have suggested:

> Beyond the frame of the merely economic, both right-wing and social-democratic governments found themselves virtually mute in the face of a whole range of social movements organised around gender and sexuality, ethnicity and the environment. The old political establishments attempted to cast these as 'local', special issue causes not to be integrated into, and certainly not to affect, the 'real business of politics'. (1995: 9)

Despite the rise of consumerism, these have remained bracketed as 'special issues' – particular interests to be added to the 'real business' of providing welfare. For example, they appear as extra sets of 'stakeholders' whose demands may be assessed and traded off against other demands by managers in the processes of strategic planning and objective setting. As distinct stakeholders they are usually added on to 'the public' or 'service users' which remain undifferentiated categories. What is striking is that the old trinity of 'family, work and nation' continues to exert a stranglehold on attempts to imagine what the 'social' means in social welfare, despite its increasing disengagement from lived realities. The different variants that have been on offer over the past two decades – a nation of consumers, the revival of little Englanderism, a nation of communities, or the Blairite vision of 'social-ism' – continue to circle around these core images of a domesticated and mono-cultural nation. Even the recent concern with 'social inclusion' and the concern to overcome the problem of 'two nations' means inclusion into *this* nation: enterprising, responsible and thoroughly fam-ilialised. This is the profound sense of 'regressive modernisation' – the remaking of the economy, the institutions of the state, the relationship between the state and welfare takes place alongside an insistence that the traditional character of the social settlement must be sustained. Nowhere do the discourses of Change, Transformation or the 'New' manage to break out of this cycle of regression.

As a result, the social question remains unsettled. Attempts to restore the old – whether in all its phobic glory as little England or in its 'kinder, gentler' formulation of a more civil society – recurrently founder on the question of difference, unable to imagine a nation or its citizens which 'break the mould'. The imagery of the nation is constantly being interrupted by questions of the care of 'black elders', by the question of pension benefits for non-married couples and gay or lesbian partners, by employment tribunals confronted by evidence of the racist, sexist or homophobic organisational cultures of public services, by disability activists demanding citizenship rights, and by the long running – and multi-faceted – 'crisis of the family'. In these and many more ways, the unresolved crisis of the social settlement ensures that the formation of a new relationship between the state and the public will remain embattled – and unstable.

In search of the public?

The conditions of each of the three settlements intersect in uncomfortable ways that are peculiarly visible in the continuing problems of defining, representing and pursuing the 'public interest'. Chapter 4 explored managerialism as a regime of power based on a particular form of calculus which privileges efficiency goals. This calculus of efficiency and its association with organisational performance also raises wider questions about the role of the state in promoting the public interest. The dispersal of public services into a multiplicity of 'core businesses' has had a contradictory effect. It has simultaneously multiplied the number of organisations, groups and agencies which claim to 'speak for' the public – and produced them in fragmented forms as 'our' customers, users, patients, parents, communities, etc. At the same time the disintegration of the state means that none of these 'owns' the public interest as a whole. Each organisation pursues its 'core business' more or less single-mindedly, with wider conceptions of the public realm or public good disappearing into the spaces between them.

As a result, there has been a growing anxiety about the disintegrative social effects of the managerial state. To a large extent, these have been laid at the door of Thatcherite individualism and its hostility to 'socialism' but they also imply questions about whether the new political–economic and organisational settlements can find ways of addressing them. At the centre of these problems are the material and symbolic roles of welfare states in promoting social cohesion, providing integrative forms of citizenship in a public realm. This has primarily been posed in terms of the dislocation of the cross-class alliances that sustained social democratic conceptions of welfare citizenship (e.g., Esping-Anderson, 1990; Hutton, 1995; Mishra, 1990). The disentangling of the middle classes from the old regime by addressing them as 'taxpayers' carrying an unreasonable burden, supplemented by offering them the choice to 'buy themselves out' of residualised public services, has been an essential feature of welfare restructuring. Self-provisioning through private services, personal insurance and pensions undercut the ties of mutuality that implicated different social interests in the citizenship of the old regime. Nevertheless, the spread of social and economic insecurity beyond the original victims into sectors of the middle class has made the question of 'social security' a more urgent one than it appeared in the 1980s, not least because of growing doubts about the capacity of private arrangements to deliver.

The social fracturing promoted in and through the managerial state has exacerbated this issue. The deepening of social inequalities and divisions and the simultaneous spread of economic insecurity has brought questions of social cohesion back to the centre of the political stage. These questions are currently articulated around three axes: insecurity; social order; and social justice. *Insecurity* is the manifest and experienced effect of the project of economic restructuring of the 1980s and 1990s. Intended to reposition 'UK plc' in the new global economy, the processes of de-industrialisation, de-regulation and low wage/low tax competitiveness have produced what Hay has called 'a race for the bottom' (1996: 173). While the primary victims were 'excess labour', this strategy commanded sufficient electoral support. As its effects have widened to include the 'excess middle classes' in the experience of redundancy and labour intensification, it has proved less attractive.

Social order is the focus for the multiple anxieties about the effects of these changes on the 'social fabric'. It links the problems identified by neo-conservatives and new social democrats about the collapse of civility, rising disorderliness, de-moralisation and the behaviour of 'marginalised' and 'excluded' populations. While the perceptions and definitions of the problem vary, they overlap in the concern with social dis-integration (Levitas, 1996). As we argued in Chapter 7, they also share some common threads in their perceptions of the importance of 'community' and 'family' as re-integrative social institutions. In the new social democracy, however, this concern with dis-integration is also linked to the re-emergence of *social justice* as an organising theme. This is visible in both the Commission on Social Justice's conception of an 'Investors' Britain' (1994) and Blairite visions of a 'stakeholder society'. Although in these forms older social democratic concerns with equality and redistribution have been relatively marginalised, the idea of the state promoting social integration and cohesion has been central.

While these emerging concerns place the 'social' in a much more central role by comparison with the individualism of a nation of consumers, they do so in ways that are both partial and contradictory. One central limitation is the way that they de-differentiate the social. They address a nation of 'stakeholders' who are not positioned by social difference – or where the only difference is between 'society' and the 'excluded'. The complexity and instability of divisions and inequalities and the linked problems of the conditions of access to welfare rights, benefits and services disappear. At the same time, they address a de-gendered private realm in which the 'wives and mothers' of Beveridge's day are replaced by 'parents and carers'. The deepening contradictions of the gendered division of labour in paid and unpaid work remain invisible while the conventional form of the family is both taken for granted and championed as the foundation of a 'healthy' society.

As a result, it is not surprising that the shifting boundary between public and private which we discussed in Chapter 2 remains the focus of intense concern and confusion. The 'privatization' of roles and responsibilities, particularly in the context of reduced public support, has been paralleled by the escalating public interest in what were previously conceived of as 'private matters'. So, the state of the family obsesses political debate – with divorce, parenting, the rights of fathers, the problem of lone mothers and the rights and wrongs of intervention into abusive families being constant threads. For other reasons, the question of sexuality oscillates backwards and forwards across the public–private divide. Here it appears in the form of sexual discrimination in public organisations or the Church; there in the prosecutions of gay men for sado-masochistic sex 'in private'; now in arguments about the age of consent; next in arguments about gay or lesbian couples as adoptive parents. Small wonder, then, that an editorial in the *Independent* should articulate this as a sense of being 'morally confused':

> partly because the line between the public and private is shifting so fast. So much of what we formerly thought were private matters – the grounds we use to justify divorce, the lifestyles of single mothers – have been turned into public and often political issues, while much of what was traditionally dealt with through the public sector now depends on competition, the market and regulation to satisfy citizens who have become consumers. (26 December 1995: 7)

To which we might add that confusing the private as personal and the private as economic sector only makes matters worse. But such a conflation of the two meanings does raise again the issue of the capacity of the managerial state to resolve – or even address – these instabilities. This is not a question of whether, within the political–economic settlement, politicians are capable of generating more or less engaging visions of the nation and its citizens. Clearly, the imageries of communities, stakeholders, social inclusion and even little Englanderism attempt to provide new points of popular political attachment. Rather, it is a question of whether such visions of the public and the public interest can be embedded within the new organisational settlement. We have already suggested that the new form of the state – with its dispersal into core businesses – seems ill-equipped to do so, either symbolically (providing points of attachment between state and citizen) or materially (addressing 'public' problems effectively).

This gap between the form of the state and the representation of the public interest has been manifested in a variety of what Gramsci (1971: 276) called 'morbid symptoms'. At a mundane level, there is the continuing downwards slide in the public's perception of politicians as 'trustworthy'. The growing cynicism about both the motives and capacity of government has clearly been intensified by evidence and allegations of corruption, the equation of national interest with party interest and the exploitation of increased powers of patronage. The Nolan and Scott inquiries (and the political finangling that surrounded their publication) and the District Auditor's investigation into Westminster Council's housing policy (1996) have both intensified this perception of politicians and traced its corrosive effects into the administrative (or managerial) machinery of government. Such concerns are paralleled by suspicion about the impact of managerialising reforms on public services – most obviously in the case of the NHS. Whether true or not, there is anxiety about the perceived dominance of the 'business culture' and its effects on the availability of health care through cost calculations dominating 'clinical judgement' in highly publicised cases. In other service areas, there are concerns about the impact of funding constraints, contracting arrangements and the apparent lack of coordination on the outcomes of provision, for example in community care. Whatever else it may have achieved, the discourse of efficiency – even tempered by the discourse of quality – has not accomplished an effective means of institutionalising the public interest.

As a result, there has been a growing use of and interest in the processes of external review and evaluation. This is reflected in the use of legalistic inquiries and judicial review of particular events and cases, including the growing significance of the European Court, particularly in relation to issues of discrimination. It is also involved in the growing roles of evaluative and regulatory agencies, ranging from the Audit Commission through to the education Funding Councils. Such processes are one way of addressing the perceived decline of 'trust'. By being 'independent' of government, they offer a different mode of embodying the public interest. Nevertheless, we would suggest that they are better seen as part of the problem of the managerial state rather than solution. They are, as Hoggett (1996) has argued, integral to the way in which the limited autonomy of organisational agencies has been framed and the 'excessive formalization' involved 'has proved to be organisationally dysfunctional, creating new layers of bureaucracy engaged in contract specification and monitoring, quality control, inspection, audit and review' (1996: 27–8). Regulation and evaluation are elements of the process of managerialised dispersal, linking government, regulatory agencies and 'local' organisations in the managerial specification and achievement of performance. These are an essential part of the 'transaction costs' of the new regime and intensify the problem of the politics of information that we discussed in Chapter 6, as organisations strive to manage their information (if not their activities) into the forms required for evaluation.

They are also part of the managerialisation of the policy-implementation process that we discussed earlier. While regulatory and evaluation agencies address the 'operational' part of this process, the process is framed by the managerial calculus of how to assess performance and by the managerial preoccupation with organisational design – whether this is the Audit Commission's view of how to implement community care or the Office for Standards in Education (OFSTED)'s obsession with the 'leadership' role of head teachers in creating the corporate culture of schools. But in a world of self-consciously ideological politics and ideologised policy, the independence of such agencies is always prone to being compromised. This is not simply a matter of 'bias' on the part of the agencies, though OFSTED's enthusiasm for 'teacher bashing' has raised doubts about its distance from both the government and New Right think tanks despite its claim to represent the interests of 'parents'. Rather, this is a matter of there being no 'innocent' positions after the end of consensus politics. It may be that the new political–economic settlement will see regulation and evaluation as the technicist solution to managing the performance of public services (in the maintenance or improvement of standards and quality as de-politicised objectives). But the politics of representation that we discussed in Chapter 6 suggests that the role of this 'new judiciary' will remain a focus of both social and organisational contestation in terms of who is represented in them. They have a specific (and all too predictable) social composition which may – but how would we know? – lead to systematic patterns of partiality. Such (hidden) inclinations may have consequences for their views of the public and how they are to be served. But how are we to know whether OFSTED, HEFCE, the Audit Commission and the rest have 'social' rather than merely 'political' biases? The issue of representation is necessarily a source of difficulty for public service bodies in the context of a fractured and divided social realm. This social realm constantly eludes the attempts to capture it in the characteristic discourses of the managerial state. The construction of technicised discourses that speak in the name of undifferentiated consumers, users or stakeholders simply pretends that 'this is not our business'. But getting on with 'business as usual' always implies some conception of a social settlement: a normative view of the social order. As a result, the managerial state lives out this tension between the rational–technical paradigm of managerialism and the unresolved crisis of the social settlement.

The problems which the managerial state is intended to resolve derive from contradictions and conflicts in the political, economic and social realms. But what we have seen is the managerialisation of these contradictions: they are redefined as 'problems to be managed'. Terms such as 'efficiency' and 'effectiveness', 'performance' and 'quality' depoliticise a series of social issues (whose efficiency? effectiveness for whom?) and thus displace real political and policy choices into series of managerial imperatives. As a consequence, we can see a trend towards major social contradictions and conflicts being experienced at the front line of service delivery organisations. This is uncomfortable for those working there, but more importantly it points to the limitations of the capacity of new organisational regimes to cope with these problems. This incapacity is most serious in terms of how far the new regime can provide an institutional form for rearticulating the relationship between state and citizens. The instabilities, gaps and legitimacy problems that both led to and resulted from the demise of the social democratic state cannot be resolved in this way. Where champions of the managerial state have celebrated its dynamism, our analysis leads us to a different view. What we see is the unstable oscillations of a form of state that cannot reconcile the social contradictions and conflicts of contemporary Britain within a managerial calculus.

Bibliography

Ackroyd, S., Hughes, J. and Soothill, K. (1989) 'Public sector services and their management.' *Journal of Management Studies*, 26(6), pp. 603–619.

Ahmad, W.I.U., ed. (1993) *'Race' and Health in Contemporary Britain*. Buckingham, Open University Press.

Anthias, F. (1992) 'The problems of ethnic and race categories and the anti-racist struggle.' In N. Manning and R. Page, eds., *Social Policy Review 4*. Canterbury, Social Policy Association.

Audit Commission (1988) *The Competitive Council*. London, HMSO.

Audit Commission (1992) *The Community Revolution: Personal Social Services and Community Care*. London, HMSO.

Bacon, R. and Eltis, W. (1976) *Britain's Economic Problem: Too Few Producers*. Basingstoke, Macmillan.

Barnes, M. (1997) *Care, Communities and Citizens*. London, Longman (in press).

Barnes, M. and Prior, D. (1995) 'Spoilt for choice? How consumerism can disempower public service users.' *Public Money and Management*, July–September, pp. 53–59.

Beresford, P. and Croft, S. (1993) *Citizen Empowerment: A Practical Guide for Change*. London, Macmillan.

Beveridge, W. (1942) *Social Insurance and Allied Services* (The Beveridge Report). London, HMSO, Cmnd 6404.

Birchall, I., Pollitt, C. and Putnam, K. (1995) 'Freedom to manage? The experience of NHS trusts, grant-maintained schools and voluntary transfers of public housing'. Paper presented to the UK Political Studies Association Annual Conference, York, April.

Blackwell, T. and Seabrook, J. (1993) *The Revolt Against Change: Towards a Conserving Radicalism*. London, Vintage.

Bluestone, B. and Harrison, B. (1982) *The Deindustrialization of America*. New York, Basic Books.

Bouckaert, G. (1995) 'Concluding reflections.' In C. Pollitt and G. Bouckeart, eds., *Quality Improvement in European Public Services*. London, Sage.

Brooke, R. (1989) *Managing the Enabling Local Authority*. London, Longman.

Brown, H. and Smith, H. (1993) 'Women caring for people: the mismatch between rhetoric and women's reality.' *Policy and Politics*, 21(3), pp. 185–193.

Burns, D., Hambleton, R. and Hoggett, P. (1994) *The Politics of Decentralisation: Revitalising Local Democracy*. London, Macmillan.

Burr, V. (1995) *An Introduction to Social Constructionism*. London, Routledge.

Burrows, R. and Loader, B., eds.(1994) *Towards a Post-Fordist Welfare State?* London, Routledge.

Butcher, T. (1995) *Delivering Welfare Services*. Buckingham, Open University Press.

Campbell, B. (1995) 'Old Fogeys and Angry Young Men: a critique of communitarianism.' *Soundings*, Issue 1, Autumn, pp. 47–64.

Carabine, J. (1992) ' ''Constructing Women'': women's sexuality and social policy.' *Critical Social Policy*, 34, pp. 23–39.

Carpenter, M. (1994) *Normality is Hard Work: Trade Unions and the Politics of Community Care*. London, Lawrence and Wishart.

Charlesworth, J., Clarke, J. and Cochrane, A. (1996) 'Tangled webs? Managing local mixed economies of care.' *Public Administration*, 74, pp. 67–88.

Clarke, J. (1991) *New Times and Old Enemies: Essays on Cultural Studies and America*. London, Harper Collins.

Clarke, J. (1993) 'The comfort of strangers.' In J. Clarke, ed., *A Crisis in Care? Challenges to Social Work*. London, Sage.

Clarke, J. (1995) 'Doing the right thing? Managerialism and social welfare.' Paper presented to ESRC seminar on 'Professionals in Late Modernity', Imperial College London.

Clarke, J. (1996a) 'After social work?' In N. Parton, ed., *Social Theory, Social Change and Social Work*. London, Routledge.

Clarke, J. (1996b) 'The problem of the state after the welfare state.' In M. May, E. Brunsdon and G. Craig, eds., *Social Policy Review 8*. London, Social Policy Association.

Clarke, J. (1996c) 'Capturing the customer? Consumerism and social welfare.' *Self and Agency*, 1 (in press).

Clarke, J. (1997) 'Public nightmares and communitarian dreams: the crisis of the social in social welfare.' In S. Edgell, P. Hetherington and A. Warde, eds., *Conceptualising Consumption*. Keele, Sociological Review Monograph (in press).

Clarke, J., Cochrane, A. and McLaughlin, E., eds., (1994a) *Managing Social Policy*. London, Sage.

Clarke, J., Cochrane A. and McLaughlin, E. (1994b) 'Mission accomplished or unfinished business? The impact of managerialization.' In *Managing Social Policy*. London, Sage. pp. 226–242.

Clarke, J., Cochrane, A. and Smart, C. (1987) *Ideologies of Welfare*. London, Routledge.

Clarke, J. and Newman, J. (1993a) 'The right to manage: a second managerial revolution?' *Cultural Studies*, 7(3), pp. 427–441.

Clarke, J. and Newman, J. (1993b) 'Managing to survive: dilemmas of changing organisational forms in the public sector.' In N. Deakin and R. Page, eds., *The Costs of Welfare*. Aldershot, Avebury.

Coard, B. (1971) *How the West Indian Child is made Educationally Sub-Normal in the British School System*. London, New Beacon Books.

Cochrane, A. (1993a) 'The problem of poverty.' In R. Dallos and E. McLaughlin, eds., *Social Problems and the Family*. London, Sage.

Cochrane, A. (1993b) *Whatever Happened to Local Government?* Buckingham, Open University Press.

Cochrane, A. (1994) 'Managing change in local government.' In J. Clarke, A. Cochrane and E. McLaughlin, eds., *Managing Social Policy*. London, Sage.

Cochrane, A. and Clarke, J., eds. (1993) *Comparing Welfare States*. London, Sage.

Collinge, C. and Hall, S. (1996) 'Hegemony and regime in urban governance'. In N. Jewson and S. Macgregor, eds., *Transforming Cities: Contested Governance and New Spatial Divisions*. London, Routledge (in press).

Commission on Social Justice (1994) *Social Justice: Strategies for National Renewal*. London, Vintage.

Corvellec, H. (1995) *Stories of Achievements: Narrative Features of Organisational Performance*. Malmo, Lund University Press.

Cousins, C. (1987) *Controlling Social Welfare*. Brighton, Wheatsheaf Books.

Cousins, C. (1988) 'The restructuring of welfare work: the introduction of general management and the contracting out of ancillary services in the N.H.S.' *Work, Employment and Society*, 2, pp. 210–228.

Cutler, T. and Waine, B. (1994) *Managing the Welfare State*. London, Berg.

Davies, C. (1995a) 'Competence versus care? Gender and caring work revisited.' *Acta Sociologica*, 38, pp. 17–31.

Davies, C. (1995b) *Gender and the Professional Predicament in Nursing*. Buckingham, Open University Press.

Deakin, N. (1994) *The Politics of Welfare: Continuities and Change*. Hemel Hempstead: Harvester Wheatsheaf.

Deakin, N. and Parry, R. (1993) 'Does the Treasury have a social policy?' In N. Deakin and R. Page, eds., *The Costs of Welfare*. Aldershot, Avebury.

Dennis, N. (1993) *Rising Crime and the Dismembered Family*. London, IEA Health and Welfare Unit.

Dennis, N. and Erdos, G. (1993) *Families without Fatherhood*. London, IEA Health and Welfare Unit (2nd edition).

Dennis, N. and Halsey, A.H. (1988) *English Ethical Socialism*. Oxford, Oxford University Press.

DiMaggio, P. and Powell, W. (1991) 'Introduction.' In W. Powell and P. DiMaggio, eds., *The New Institutionalism in Organisational Analysis*. Chicago, University of Chicago Press.

Djilas, M. (1957) *The New Class*. London, Allen and Unwin.

Douglas, M. (1987) *How Institutions Think*. London, Routledge and Kegan Paul.

du Gay, P. (1994a) 'Colossal immodesties and hopeful monsters: pluralism and organisational conduct.' *Organization*, 1 (1), pp. 125–148.

du Gay, P. (1994b) 'Making up managers: bureaucracy, enterprise and the liberal art of separation.' *British Journal of Sociology*, 45(4), pp. 655–674.

du Gay, P. (1995) *Office as a Vocation: 'Bureaucracy' but Not as We Know It*. Cultural Policy Paper no. 4, Australia Key Centre for Cultural and Media Policy, Faculty of Humanities, Griffith University.

du Gay, P. (1996) *Consumption and Identity at Work*. London, Sage.

du Gay, P. and Salaman, G. (1992) 'The Cult(ure) of the Customer.' *Journal of Management Studies*, 29(5), pp. 615–633.

Dunleavy, P. (1991) *Democracy, Bureaucracy and Public Choice*. London, Harvester Wheatsheaf.

Dunleavy, P. and Hood, C. (1994) 'From old public administration to new public management', *Public Money and Management*, July–September, pp. 9–16.

Escott, K. and Whitfield, D. (1995) *The Gender Impact of CCT in Local Government*. Manchester, Equal Opportunities Commission.

Esping-Anderson, G. (1990) *The Three Worlds of Welfare Capitalism*. Cambridge, Polity Press.

Etzioni, A. (1993) *The Spirit of Community: Rights, Responsibilities and the Communitarian Agenda*. New York, Crown.

Fergusson, R. (1994) 'Managing education.' In J. Clarke, A. Cochrane and E. McLaughlin, eds., *Managing Social Policy*. London, Sage.

Finch, J. (1987) *Family Obligations and Social Change*. Cambridge, Polity Press.

Finch, J. and Groves, D., eds. (1983) *A Labour of Love: Women, Work and Caring*. London, Routledge and Kegan Paul.

Fitzgerald, L., Ashburner, L. and Ferlie, E. (1995) 'Professions, markets and managers: empirical evidence from the NHS'. Paper for the Professionals in Late Modernity seminar series, Warwick, April.

Flynn, N. (1990) *Public Sector Management*. Hemel Hempstead, Harvester Wheatsheaf.

Flynn, N. (1994) 'Control, commitment and contracts.' In J. Clarke, A. Cochrane and E. McLaughlin, eds., *Managing Social Policy*. London, Sage.

Flynn, N. and Strehl, F. (1996) *Public Sector Management in Europe*. Hemel Hempstead, Harvester Wheatsheaf.

Foster, A. (1996) 'Stroll on, Dixon.' *Guardian*, 29 February, p. 17.

Fraser, N. and Gordon, L. (1994) 'Civil citizenship against social citizenship?' In B. van Steenbergen, ed., *The Condition of Citizenship*. London, Sage.

Freeman, R. (1983) 'Strategic management: a stakeholder approach.' *Advances in Strategic Management*, vol. 1, pp. 31–60.

Fuller, L. and Smith, V. (1991) 'Consumers' reports: management by customers in a changing economy.' *Work, Employment and Society*, 5(1), pp. 1–16.

Garson, B. (1989) *The Electronic Sweatshop*. New York, Penguin.

Gaster, L. (1996) *The 'Citizen Question': Re-thinking Service Design*. School of Public Policy Working Paper, University of Birmingham.

Glennerster, H. (1992) *Paying for Welfare: the 1990s*. Hemel Hempstead, Harvester Wheatsheaf.

Graham, H. (1993) *Hardship and Health in Women's Lives*. Hemel Hempstead, Harvester Wheatsheaf.

Gramsci, A. (1971) *Selections from the Prison Notebooks*. London, Lawrence and Wishart.

Gray, A. and Jenkins, B. (1993) 'Markets, managers and the public service: the changing of a culture.' In P. Taylor-Gooby and R. Lawson, eds., *Markets and Managers: New Issues in the Delivery of Welfare*. Buckingham, Open University Press.

Green, D. (1993) *Reinventing Civil Society: Rediscovering Welfare without Politics*. London, Institute of Economic Affairs.

Green, J. and Armstrong, D. (1995) 'Achieving rational management: bed management and the crisis in emergency admissions.' *Sociological Review*, 43 (4), pp. 743–764.

Griffiths, R. (1988) *Community Care: Agenda for Action. A Report to the Secretary of State for Social Services*. London, HMSO.

Grocott, M. (1989) 'Civil Service management.' In I. Taylor and G. Popham, eds., *An Introduction to Public Sector Management*. London, Unwin Hyman.

Hall, S. (1984) 'The rise of the representative/interventionist state.' In G. McLennan, D. Held and S. Hall, eds., *State and Society in Contemporary Britain*. Cambridge, Polity Press.

Hall, S. (1988) *The Hard Road to Renewal: Thatcherism and the Crisis of the Left*. London, Verso.

Hall, S. (1996a) 'Gramsci's relevance for the study of race and ethnicity.' In D. Morley and K-H. Chen, eds., *Stuart Hall: Critical Dialogues in Cultural Studies*. London, Routledge.

Hall, S. (1996b) 'New ethnicities.' In D. Morley and K-H. Chen, eds., *Stuart Hall: Critical Dialogues in Cultural Studies*. London, Routledge.

Hall, S. and Jacques, M., eds. (1983) *The Politics of Thatcherism*. London, Lawrence and Wishart.

Hall, S., Massey, D. and Rustin, M. (1995) 'Editorial: Uncomfortable times.' *Soundings*, Issue 1, Autumn, pp. 1–18.

Hall, S., Massey, D. and Rustin, M. (1996) 'Editorial: What's at stake?' *Soundings*, Issue 2, Spring, pp. 5–16.

Hambleton, R. and Hoggett, P. (1988) 'Beyond bureaucratic paternalism.' In P. Hoggett and R. Hambleton, eds., *Decentralisation and Democracy*. Occasional Paper no. 28, School for Advanced Urban Studies, University of Bristol.

Hammer, M. and Champy, J. (1993) *Reengineering the Corporation: a Manifesto for Business Revolution*. London, Brearley.

Handy, C. (1989) *The Age of Unreason*. London, Arrow.

Harden, I. (1992) *The Contracting State*. Buckingham, Open University Press.

Hardy, C. (1994) *Managing Strategic Action: Mobilising Change*. London, Sage.

Harris, H. (1996) 'He who pays the piper calls the tune – a consideration of management issues of voluntary and not for profit agencies in the contracting process.' Paper presented to the International Research Symposium on Public Services Management, University of Aston (March).

Harrison, S. and Pollitt, C. (1994) *Controlling Health Professionals*. Buckingham, Open University Press.

Harrison, S., Hunter, D., Marnoch, J. and Pollitt, C. (1992) *Just Managing: Power and Culture in the National Health Service*. Basingstoke, Macmillan.

Harrow, J. and Talbot, C. (1994) 'Central Government: the Changing Civil Service.' In Jackson, P. and Lavender, M., eds., *The Public Services Yearbook 1994*. London, Chapman & Hall.

Hay, A.C. (1996) *Re-stating Social and Political Change*. Buckingham, Open University Press.

Hills, J. (1993) *The Future of Welfare: a Guide to the Debate*. York, Joseph Rowntree Foundation.

Hirst, P. and Thompson, G. (1996) *Globalization in Question*. Cambridge, Polity Press.

HM Treasury (1991) *Competing for Quality: Buying Better Public Services*. London, HMSO.

Hoggett, P. (1990) 'Modernisation, political strategy and the welfare state.' *Studies in Decentralisation and Quasi-Markets*. Occasonal Paper no. 2. School for Advanced Urban Studies, University of Bristol.

Hoggett, P. (1994) 'The politics of the modernisation of the UK welfare state.' In R. Burrows and B. Loader, eds., *Towards a Post-Fordist Welfare State?* London, Routledge.

Hoggett, P. (1996) 'New modes of control in the public service'. *Public Administration*, 74, pp. 9–32.

Hollway, W. (1991) *Work, Psychology and Organisational Behaviour*. London, Sage.

Hopfl, H. (1992) 'The making of the corporate acolyte: some thoughts on corporate leadership and the reality of organisational commitment.' *Journal of Management Studies*, 29(13), pp. 23–34.

Hopfl, H. (1994) 'Empowerment and the managerial prerogative.' *Empowerment in Organisations*, 2(3), pp. 35–44.

Hudson, B. (1987) 'Collaboration in social welfare: a framework for analysis.' *Policy and Politics*, 15(3), pp. 175–182.

Hudson, B. (1994) *Making Sense of Markets in Health and Social Care*. Sunderland, Business Education Publishers.

Hudson, R. (1988) 'Labour markets and new forms of work in "old" industrial regions.' In D. Massey and J. Allen, eds., *Uneven Development: Cities and Regions in Transition*. London, Hodder and Stoughton.

Humphrey, C. and Scapens, R. (1992) 'Whatever happened to the liontamers? An examination of accounting change in the public sector.' *Local Government Studies*, 18(3), pp. 141–147.

Hutton, W. (1995) *The State We're In*. London, Cape.

Hutton, W. (1996) 'Raising the stakes.' *Guardian 2*, 17 January, pp. 2–4.

Huxham, C. (1993) 'Collaborative capability: an intra-organisational perspective on competitive advantage'. *Public Money and Management*, July–September, pp. 21–28.

Huxham, C. and Vangen, S. (1996) 'Key themes in the management of relationships between public and non-profit organizations.' Paper presented to the International Research Symposium on Public Services Management, Aston Business School, March.

Jackson, P. (1994) 'Curbing promiscuity: constructing total quality in an Acute Hospitals NHS Trust.' Paper presented to the Employment Research Unit Conference on The Contract State, Cardiff, September.

Jervis, P. and Richards, S. (1995) 'Strategic management in a "re-invented government": Rowing 1, Steering 0'. Paper presented to the strategic management Society 15th Annual Conference, Mexico City, October.

Jervis, P. and Richards, S. (1996) 'The three deficits of public management'. School of Public Policy Working Paper, University of Birmingham.

Jessop, B. (1993) 'Towards a Schumpeterian workfare state? Preliminary remarks on post-fordist political economy.' *Studies in Political Economy*, 40, pp. 7–39.

Jessop, B. (1994) 'The transition to post-Fordism and the Schumpeterian workfare state.' In R. Burrows and B. Loader, eds., *Towards a post-Fordist Welfare State?* London, Routledge.

Johnson, N. (1990) *Reconstructing the Welfare State*. Hemel Hempstead, Harvester Wheatsheaf.

Johnson, N., ed. (1995) *Private Markets in Health and Welfare: an International Perspective*. Oxford, Berg.

Johnson, T. (1973) *Professions and Power*. London, Macmillan.

Kane, P. (1996) 'The company we keep', *Guardian Weekend*, 25 May, pp. 22–29.

Keat, R., Whitely, N. and Abercrombie, N., eds. (1994) *The Authority of the Consumer*. London, Routledge.

Kirkpatrick, I. and Martinez-Lucio, M., eds. (1995) *The Politics of Quality in the Public Sector*. London, Routledge.

Kitchener, M. and Whipp, R. (1994) 'Professionals, quality and the marketing change process.' Paper presented to the Employment Research Unit Conference on The Contract State, Cardiff, September.

Land, H. (1995) 'Families and the law.' In J. Muncie, M. Wetherell, R. Dallos and A. Cochrane, eds., *Understanding the Family*. London, Sage.

Lane, J-E. (1993) 'Economic organisation theory and public management.' In K. A. Eliassen and J. Kooiman, eds., *Managing Public Organizations*. London, Sage.

Langan, M. and Clarke, J. (1993a) 'The British welfare state: foundation and modernization.' In A. Cochrane and J. Clarke, eds., *Comparing Welfare States: Britain in International Context*. London, Sage.

Langan, M. and Clarke, J. (1993b) 'Restructuring welfare: the British welfare regime in the 1980s.' In A. Cochrane and J. Clarke, eds., *Comparing Welfare States: Britain in International Context*. London, Sage.

Langan, M. and Clarke, J. (1994) 'Managing in the mixed economy of care.' In J. Clarke, A. Cochrane and E. McLaughlin, eds., *Managing Social Policy*. London, Sage.

Le Grand, J. and Bartlett, W., eds. (1993) *Quasi-Markets and Social Policy*. Basingstoke, Macmillan.

Legg, B. (1994) *Civil Service Reform: a Case for More Radicalism*. London, European Policy Forum.

Levitas, R., ed. (1986) *The Ideology of the New Right*. Cambridge, Polity Press.

Levitas, R. (1996) 'The Concept of Social Exclusion and the New Durkheimian Hegemony.' *Critical Social Policy*, 16 (1), February, pp. 5–20.

Lewis, G. (1997) 'Difference, what difference? Ethnicity and social work texts.' In F. Williams, ed., *Social Policy: a Critical Reader*. Cambridge, Polity Press (in press).

Lewis, J. (1993) 'Developing the mixed economy of care: emerging issues for voluntary organisations.' *Journal of Social Policy*, 22(2), pp. 173–192.

Ling, T. (1994) 'Case study: the Benefits Agency: claimants as customers.' In H. Tam, ed., *Marketing, Competition and the Public Sector*. London, Longman.

Loney, M. (1985) *The Politics of Greed*. London, Pluto Press.

Loney, M. et al., eds. (1986) *The State or the Market?* London, Sage.

Lowndes, V. (1996a) 'Varieties of new institutionalism: a critical appraisal.' *Public Administration*, 74 (2), pp. 181–197.

Lowndes, V. (1996b) 'Change in public service management: new institutions and management regimes.' Paper for *La journee d'etude 'Local Governance'*, Paris, February.

Lowndes, V. et al. (1996) 'The new management, citizenship and institutional change in local governance.' Unpublished ESRC research report, School of Public Policy, University of Birmingham.

MacInnes, J. (1987) *Thatcherism at Work: Industrial Relations and Economic Change*. Milton Keynes, Open University Press.

Mackintosh, M. (1992) 'Partnerships: issues of policy and negotiation.' *Local Economy*, 7(3), pp. 210–224.

Mackintosh, M. (1995a) 'Competition and contracting in selective social provision.' *European Journal of Development Research*, 7(1), June, pp. 26–52.

Mackintosh, M. (1995b) 'Putting words into people's mouths? Economic culture and its implications for local governance.' Open Discussion Paper in Economics, no. 9, Faculty of Social Sciences, Open University.

Maddock, S. (1995) 'Is macho management back?' *Health Services Journal*, 23 February, pp. 26–28.

Maile, S. (1995) 'Managerial discourse and the restructuring of a district authority.' *Sociological Review*, 43 (4), pp. 720–742.

Mann, K. (1994) 'Watching the defectives: observers of the underclass in the U.S.A, Britain and Australia.' *Critical Social Policy*, Issue 41, Autumn, pp. 79–99.

March, J. and Olsen, J. (1989) *Rediscovering Institutions: the Organizational Basis of Politics*. New York: Free Press.

Mark, A. and Brennan, R. (1995) 'Demarketing: managing demand in the UK National Health Service.' *Public Money and Management*, July–September, pp. 17–21.

Marshall, J. (1995) *Women Managers Moving On*. London, Routledge.

Marx, K. (1968) 'The Eighteenth Brumaire of Louis Bonaparte.' In *Marx and Engels Selected Works*. London, Lawrence and Wishart.

Mayo, M. (1994) *Communities and Caring: the Mixed Economy of Welfare*. London, Macmillan.

Metcalfe, L. (1993) 'Conviction politics and dynamic conservatism: Mrs Thatcher's Managerial Revolution.' *International Political Science Review*, 14 (4), pp. 351–371.

Metcalfe, L. and Richards, S. (1990) *Improving Public Management*. London, Sage (2nd edition).

Meyer, J. and Rowan, B. (1991) 'Institutionalized organizations: formal structure as myth and ceremony.' In W. Powell and P. DiMaggio, eds., *The New Institutionalism in Organisational Analysis*. Chicago, University of Chicago Press.

Mintzberg, H. (1983) *Structure in Fives: Designing Organisational Effectiveness*. London, Prentice-Hall.

Mishra, R. (1990) *The Welfare State in Capitalist Society*. Hemel Hempstead, Harvester Wheatsheaf.

Mohan, J. (1995) *A National Health Service? The Restructuring of Health Care in Britain since 1979*. Basingstoke, Macmillan.

Moody, K. (1987) 'Reagan, the business agenda and the collapse of labour.' In R. Miliband, L. Panitch and J. Saville, eds., *The Socialist Register 1987*. London, Merlin.

Morris, L. (1993) *Dangerous Classes*. London, Routledge.

Moss Kanter, R. (1989) *When Giants Learn to Dance: Mastering the Challenges of Strategy, Management, and Careers in the 1990s*. London, Unwin.

Murray, C. (1984) *Losing Ground: American Social Policy 1950–1980*. New York, Basic Books.

Murray, C. (1990) *The Emerging British Underclass*. London, IEA Health and Welfare Unit.

Murray, R. (1991) 'The state after Henry.' *Marxism Today*, May, pp. 22–27.

Nadler, D. and Tushman, M. (1989) 'Organisational framebending: principles for managing reorientation.' *Academy Executive*, 3, pp. 194–202.

Newman, J. (1994) 'The limits of management: gender and the politics of change.' In J. Clarke, A. Cochrane and E. McLaughlin, eds., *Managing Social Policy*. London, Sage.

Newman, J. (1995) 'Gender and cultural change.' In C. Itzin and J. Newman, eds., *Gender, Culture and Organisational Change: Putting Theory into Practice*. London, Routledge.

Newman, J. (1996a) *In Search of the Public*. School of Public Policy Working Paper, University of Birmingham.

Newman, J. (1996b) *Shaping Organisational Cultures in Local Government*. London, Pitman.

Newman, J. and Clarke, J. (1994) 'Going about our business? The managerialisation of public services.' In J. Clarke, A. Cochrane and E. McLaughlin, eds., *Managing Social Policy*. London, Sage.

Newman, J. and Williams, F. (1995) 'Diversity and change: gender, welfare and organisational relations.' In C. Itzin and J. Newman, eds., *Gender, Culture and Organisational Change: Putting Theory into Practice*. London, Routledge.

Niskanen, W.A. (1971) *Bureaucracy and Representative Government*. New York, Aldine-Atherton.

Nocon, A. (1994) *Collaboration and Community Care in the 1990s*. Sunderland, Business Education Publishers.

North, D. (1990) *Institutions, Institutional Change and Economic Performance*. Cambridge, Cambridge University Press.

Oliver, M. (1990) *The Politics of Disablement*. Basingstoke, Macmillan.

Oliver, M. and Barnes, C. (1991) 'Discrimination, disability and welfare: from needs to rights.' In I. Bynoe, M. Oliver and C. Barnes, eds., *Equal Rights for Disabled People*. London, Institute for Public Policy Research.

Oppenheim, C. (1993) *Poverty: the Facts*. London, Child Poverty Action Group.

Osborne, D. and Gaebler, T. (1992) *Reinventing Government: How the Entrepreneurial Spirit is Transforming the Public Sector*. Reading, MA, Addison–Wesley.

Parker, H. (1982) *The Moral Hazard of Social Insurance*. Research Monograph no. 37, London, Institute of Economic Affairs.

Peters, G. (1993) 'Managing the hollow state.' In K. Eliassen and J. Kooiman, eds., *Managing Public Organisations: Lessons from Contemporary European Experience*. London, Sage.

Peters, T. (1987) *Thriving on Chaos: Handbook for a Management Revolution*. London, Pan.

Peters, T. (1993) *Liberation Management*. New York, Knopf.

Peters, T. and Waterman, R. (1982) *In Search of Excellence: Lessons from America's Best-Run Companies*. New York, Harper and Row.

Peterson, P. (1981) *City Limits*. Chicago, University of Chicago Press.

Pfeffer, N. and Coote, A. (1991) 'Is quality good for you?' Social Policy Paper no. 5, London, Institute for Public Policy Research.

Pierson, C. (1993) *Beyond the Welfare State?* Cambridge, Polity Press.

Pinch, S. (1994) 'Labour flexibility and the changing welfare state: is there a post-Fordist model?' In R. Burrows and B. Loader, eds., *Towards a Post-Fordist Welfare State?* London, Routledge.

Pollitt, C. (1993) *Managerialism and the Public Services*. Oxford, Basil Blackwell (2nd edition).

Pollitt, C. (1994) 'The Citizen's Charter: a preliminary analysis.' *Public Money and Management*, April–June, pp. 9–14.

Porter, M. (1989) 'How competitive forces shape strategy.' In D. Asch and C. Bowman, eds., *Readings in Strategic Management*. Basingstoke, Macmillan.

Posner, B. and Rothstein, L. (1994) 'Reinventing the business of government: an interview with change catalyst David Osborne.' *Harvard Business Review*, May–June, pp. 133–143.

Potter, J. (1994) 'Consumerism and the public sector: how well does the coat fit?' In D. McKevitt and A. Lawson, eds., *Public Sector Management: Theory, Critique and Practice*. London, Sage.

Powell, M. (1996) 'Granny's footsteps, fractures and the principles of the NHS.' *Critical Social Piolicy*, 47, pp. 27–44.

Power, M. (1994) *The Audit Explosion*. London, Demos.

Prior, D. (1993) 'Review Article: In search of the new public management.' *Local Government Studies*, 19(3), Autumn, pp. 447–460.

Prior, D., Stewart, J. and Walsh, K. (1995) *Citizenship, Rights and Community Participation*. London, Pitman.

Ranson, S. and Stewart, J. (1994) *Management for the Public Domain: Enabling the Learning Society*. Basingstoke, Macmillan.

Rao, N. (1996) *Towards Welfare Pluralism: Public Services in a Time of Change*. Aldershot, Dartmouth Publishing Company.

Reed, M. (1995) 'Managing quality and organizational politics: TQM as a governmental technology.' In I. Kirkpatrick and M. Martinez-Lucio, eds., *The Politics of Quality in the Public Sector*. London, Routledge.

Reich, R. (1984) *The Next American Frontier*. New York, Penguin.

Rhodes, R. (1987) 'Developing the public service orientation.' *Local Government Studies*, May–June, pp. 63–73.

Rhodes, R. (1994) 'The hollowing out of the state: the changing nature of public services in Britain.' *Political Quarterly*, Spring, pp. 138–151.

Rose, N. (1989) *Governing the Soul: the Shaping of the Private Self*. London, Routledge.

Rustin, M. (1989) 'The politics of post-Fordism, or the trouble with New Times.' *New Left Review*, no. 175, pp. 54–77.

Rustin, M. (1994) 'Flexibility in higher education.' In R. Burrows and B. Loader, eds., *Towards a Post-Fordist Welfare State?* London, Routledge.

Salter, B. (1993) 'The politics of purchasing in the National Health Service.' *Policy and Politics*, 21(3), July, pp. 171–184.

Sayer, A. and Walker, D. (1992) *The New Social Economy: Reworking the Division of Labour*. Oxford, Blackwell.

Secretaries of State (1989) *Caring For People: Community Care in the Next Decade and Beyond*. Cm 8849, London, HMSO.

Skelcher, C. (1996) 'Public service consumerism: some questions of strategy.' *Community Development Journal*, 31(1), January, pp. 66–72.

Smith, R. J. (1994) *Strategic Management and Planning in the Public Sector*. Harlow, Longman.

Spencer, K. (1996) 'Place, people and local policy.' Inaugural lecture, University of Birmingham, March.

Stewart, J. (1989) 'A future for local authorities as community government.' In J. Stewart and G. Stoker, eds., *The Future of Local Government*. Basingstoke, Macmillan.

Stewart, J. (1993) *Accountability to the Public*. London, European Policy Forum.

Stewart, J. (1994) *Issues for the Management of Local Government*. Birmingham, School of Public Policy, Birmingham University.

Stewart, J. and Ranson, S. (1994) *Management for the Public Domain: Enabling the Learning Society*. London, Macmillan.

Stewart, R., (1996) 'Divided loyalties.' *Health Service Journal*, 21 Mar., pp. 30–1.

Stoker, G. (1989) 'Regulation theory, local government and the transition from Fordism.' In D. King and J. Pierre, eds., *Challenges to Local Government*. London, Sage.

Stoker, G. (1990) 'Creating a local government for a post-Fordist society: the Thatcherite project?' In J. Stewart and G. Stoker, eds., *The Future of Local Government*. Basingstoke, Macmillan.

Stoker, G. and Mossberger, K. (1994) 'Urban regime theory in comparative perspective.' *Environment and Planning C: Government and Policy*, 12, pp. 195–212.

Stoker, G. and Young, S. (1993) *Cities in the 1990s*. London, Longman.

Stone, C. (1989) *Regime Politics*. Lawrence, KA, University Press of Kansas.

Swann, D. (1988) *The Retreat of the State: Deregulation and Privatisation in the UK and the US*. New York and London, Harvester Wheatsheaf.

Taylor, G. (1993) 'Challenges from the margins.' In J. Clarke, ed., *A Crisis in Care? Challenges to Social Work*. London, Sage.

Taylor-Gooby, P. and Lawson, R., eds. (1993a) *Markets and Managers: New Issues in the Delivery of Welfare*. Buckingham, Open University Press.

Taylor-Gooby, P. and Lawson, R. (1993b) 'Where we go from here; the new order in welfare.' In P. Taylor-Gooby and R. Lawson, eds., *Markets and Managers: New Issues in the Delivery of Welfare*. Buckingham, Open University Press.

Thompson, S. and Hoggett, P. (1996) 'Universalism, selectivism and particularism: towards a postmodern social policy.' *Critical Social Policy*, 16 (1), February, pp. 21–44.

Townley, B. (1994) *Reframing Human Resource Management; Power, Ethics and the Subject at Work*. London, Sage.

Vickridge, R. (1995) 'NHS reforms and community care – means tested health care masquerading as consumer choice?' *Critical Social Policy*, 43, pp. 76–80.

Waine, B. (1992) 'The voluntary sector – the Thatcher years.' In N. Manning and R. Page, eds., *Social Policy Review 4*. Canterbury, Social Policy Association.

Walby, S. and Greenwell, J. (1994) 'Managing the National Health Service.' In J. Clarke, A. Cochrane and E. McLaughlin, eds., *Managing Social Policy*. London, Sage.

Waldegrave, W. (1993) *The Reality of Reform and Accountability in Today's Public Services*. London, Public Finance Foundation.

Walker, A. (1993) 'Community Care Policy: from consensus to conflict.' In J. Bornat, C. Pereira, D. Pilgrim and F. Williams, eds., *Community Care: a Reader*. Basingstoke, Macmillan.

Walker, A. and Walker C., eds. (1987) *The Growing Divide: a Social Audit 1979–87*. London, Child Poverty Action Group.

Walsh, K. (1995) *Public Services and Market Mechanisms: Competition, Contracting and the New Public Management*. Basingstoke, Macmillan.

Weeks, J. (1996) 'The Idea of a Sexual Community.' *Soundings*, Issue 2, Spring, pp. 71–84.

Wetherell, M. and Potter, J. (1994) *Mapping the Language of Racism: Discourse and the Legitimation of Exploitation*. Hemel Hempstead, Harvester Wheatsheaf.

Whitley, R. (1992) 'The social construction of organizations and markets: the comparative analysis of business recipes.' In M. Reed and M. Hughes, eds., *Rethinking Organizations: New Directions in Organizational Theory and Analysis*. London, Sage.

Whittington, R., McNulty, T. and Whipp, R. (1994) 'Market-driven change in professional services: problems and processes.' *Journal of Management Studies*, 31(6), November, pp. 829–845.

Williams, F. (1989) *Social Policy: a Critical Introduction*. Cambridge, Polity Press.

Williams, F. (1992) 'Somewhere over the rainbow: universality and diversity in social policy.' In N. Manning and R. Page, eds., *Social Policy Review 4*. Canterbury, Social Policy Association.

Williams, F. (1993) 'Gender, "race" and class in British welfare policy.' In A. Cochrane and J. Clarke, eds., *Comparing Welfare States: Britain in International Context*. London, Sage.

Williams, F. (1994) 'Social relations, welfare and the post-Fordism debate.' In R. Burrows and B. Loader, eds., *Towards a Post-Fordist Welfare State?* London, Routledge.

Williams, F. (1996) 'Postmodernism, feminism and the question of difference.' In N. Parton, ed., *Social Theory, Social Change and Social Work*. London, Routledge.

Williamson, C. (1995) 'Gender gap.' *Health Services Journal*, 30 March, pp. 27–29.

Wilson, E. (1977) *Women and the Welfare State*. London, Tavistock.

Wilson, J. (1995) 'Charters and public service performance.' In J. Wilson, ed., *Managing Public Services: Dealing with Dogma*. London, Tudor (Hodder and Stoughton).

Winstanley, D., Sorabji, D. and Dawson, S. (1995) 'When the pieces don't fit: a stakeholder power matrix to analyse public sector restructuring.' *Public Money and Management*, April–June, pp. 19–26.

Wistow, G., Knapp, M., Hardy, B. and Allen, C. (1994) *Social Care in a Mixed Economy*. Buckingham, Open University Press.

Witz, A. (1992) *Professions and Patriarchy*. London, Routledge.

Index

accountability 64, 66, 145
Ackroyd, S. 100
activism, community 132, 135–6
agency 21, 23, 25, 26, 29, 30, 31
agenda setting power 63–5
Anthias, F. 10
Armstrong, D. 66
audit 80–1, 101, 118–19
Audit Commission 39, 53, 59, 80, 90, 146, 158, 159

Barnes, M. 109, 110, 113, 121
Bartlett, W. 114
Benefits Agency 19, 120
Beresford, P. 110
Beveridge, W. 3
Birchall, I. 30, 98–9, 99–100, 101, 102
Blackwell, T. 52–3
Blair, Tony 131, 137, 138
Bouckaert, G. 121
boundary management 79–80, 81, 149–50
Brennan, R. 113
Brooke, R. 133
bureau-professional regimes
    decision-making, agenda setting and
        normative power 63–4
    modes of attachment 62–3
    relations of power 68–70
    reshaping by managerialism 75–7
    see also bureaucratic administration;
        professionalism and professionals
bureaucratic administration
    contrast with managerialism 65
    contrast with professionalism 6–7
    hostility towards 15, 45
    in welfare state 5–6, 8, 12–13
Burns, D. 112
'business agenda' 57–8
Butcher, T. 22

Campbell, B. 134–5
Caring for people 109
Carpenter, M. 51
centralisation, and state power 23

Champy, J. 44, 49
change
    affinities between managerialism and
        New Right 45, 46, 49
    cultural change 36–9, 98–9
    difficulties of opposition and dissent
        50–5
    globalisation narratives 46–8
    impact of the discourse on consent 50–5
    and institutional theory 87–8, 101, 103
    tensions in the process of 101–3
    transformational discourse 42–3, 45
Charlesworth, J. 26, 80, 89
Child Support Agency 24, 28
citizens as consumers 121–2, 123, 127–8
Citizen's Charter 37, 109–10, 125
citizenship 3–4, 9–10, 125, 129
Civil Service 36, 47, 145
Civil Service Agencies 19, 23, 60, 140, 144
civil society 131, 134, 136, 154
Clarke, J. 3–4, 6, 8, 14, 15, 24, 28, 30, 35,
        50, 56, 59, 77, 79, 101, 114, 115, 136
class relations, in bureau-professional
        regimes 68
Coard, B. 153
Cochrane, A. 23, 24, 32, 59, 151
Collinge, C. 61
Commission on Social Justice 137, 156
communitarianism 131–3, 134
community and communities 125, 128, 129,
        131–6
community care 28, 29, 114, 115, 133, 135,
        150
competitive organisational orders 70–2
compulsory competitive tendering 70–1
consensus politics 1, 2, 9, 142
consumerism
    application of principles to public service
        108–9
    critiques of old welfare state 12, 109–12
    discourse 128
    limitations of in welfare services 121–2
    market mechanisms in public services
        112–16

see also citizens as consumers; customers; markets; public choice theory
Coote, A. 120
'core business' concept 78–9, 146, 147, 148, 155
corporate culture
  cultural change 36–9, 98–9
  modes of attachment 62–3
  results of focus on 147
corporate governance 69, 137
Corvellec, H. 88
Cousins, C. 6
Croft, S. 110
cultural change 36–9, 98–9
  see also corporate culture
customer focus 45
customers
  accountability of managerial regimes to 66
  competing claims to represent needs of 116–18
  as focal point of conflict 112, 122
  relationship with services 121–2
  see also consumerism; 'needs'
Cutler, T. 28, 48, 58, 80

Davies, C. 69, 71, 74
Deakin, N. 23, 83
decentralisation
  constraints and possibilities 105
  embedding of managerialism 77
  erosion of central power 96
  and state power 23
  see also dispersal
decision-making
  de-politicisation of 144
  power in organisational regimes 63–5
demand, management of 113, 149
'democratic deficit' 66, 144–5
demoralisation 15, 156
Dennis, N. 132, 134
'dependency culture' 15
DiMaggio, P. 86, 89–90, 103
disability 4, 11, 124, 129
discontinuous change 43–4
discourse theory 94–5
discourses
  of change 34–55
  of consumerism 127–8
  of human resource management 94
  of managerialism 76, 91–5, 97, 101, 148
  of quality management 93–4
  tensions between managerial discourses 101

dispersal 25, 29–32, 60, 66, 81, 123, 126–7, 144–6
displacement 76
dissent 52–5
diversity 111, 124, 153
  colonisation of term 52
  and consumerism 111, 122, 129–30
  managerialist conception of 111, 115, 130
  see also social differentiation
Douglas, M. 91
du Gay, P. 5, 38, 45, 47–8, 58, 74, 92, 93, 107, 144
Dunleavy, P. 21, 85

education services 6, 7, 23, 98, 128, 150
  see also Office for Standards in Education; schools
empowerment 31, 64, 72, 151
  colonisation of term 52
  of communities 133, 134
  of the public 121, 125, 127
enabling by local government 133, 134
equal opportunity processes 69, 71
equitable treatment, and bureaucracy 5, 11
Erdos, G. 132, 134
Escott, K. 71
ethical socialism 132
ethnicity 3–4, 9–10
  see also minority ethnic groups
Etzioni, A. 75, 134
European Commission 137
European Court 158
evaluation of performance *see* performance
excellence 35, 72–3, 93, 107, 112
exclusion *see* social exclusion

Fabian ideology 7
family
  communitarianism and 134–5
  impact of managerial labour on 74–5
  sexual division of labour in 3, 28, 156
  shift of responsibilities to 28–9, 150
  and the social settlement 2–3, 10, 139, 156
'feminisation' of management 73
Fergusson, R. 23
financial management, increased significance of 58–9
Financial Management Initiative 20, 59
Finch, J. 3
Fitzgerald, L. 77
flexibility 22, 70, 147
Flynn, N. 51, 75
Fordist mass production, analogy with welfare delivery 23–4
Foster, A. 79

Foucault, M. 30–1
fragmentation 25
  see also dispersal
'freedom to manage' 30, 56, 81, 98, 152
Freeman, R. 137
full employment 3, 9, 138
Fuller, L. 62

Gaebler, T. 21, 37, 49, 107, 135
Garson, B. 162
Gaster, L. 121
gay community 132, 135, 136
gender
  division of labour within families 3, 10,
    28, 156
  divisions within bureau-professional
    regimes 69
  implications of partnership model 72–3
  and state welfare 3, 4, 10–11
globalisation narratives 46–8
Graham, H. 3
Gramsci, A. 1, 140, 157
Gray, A. 80
Green, J. 66
Greenwell, J. 117, 118
Griffiths, R. 40
Grocott, M. 46
Gummer, John 128

Hall, S. 5, 14, 16, 61, 136, 137, 138, 139,
    141, 154
Halsey, A.H. 132
Hambleton, R. 110
Hammer, M. 44, 49
Handy, C. 35, 43–4
Harden, I. 117–18
Hardy, C. 41–2
Harris, H. 89
Harrison, S. 78, 144
Harrow, J. 37
Hay, A.C. 1, 18, 142, 143, 145, 154, 156
health service *see* National Health Service
Heseltine, Michael 34
Hills, J. 142
Hirst, P. 46
Hoggett, P. 13, 25, 30, 80, 105, 110, 128,
    144, 158
Hollway, W. 94
Hood, C. 21
Hopfl, H. 44, 62, 93
housing associations 98
Howard, Michael 143
human resource management 72, 94
Humphrey, C. 59
Hutton, W. 137–8

Huxham, C. 147
'hybrid' formations 77

impartiality 5, 11
incentives
  and new institutional theory 86–7
  'perverse' incentives 15, 114, 146, 147
  and public choice theory 84–6
  response to market incentives 95–6, 97
industrial relations 57
inequality 18, 151, 153–4
insecurity 156
instability, as structural feature of
    managerialised dispersal 31–2, 140–53
institutional theory 86–91, 101, 103–6
International Monetary Fund 9, 142
isomorphism 47–8, 89–90, 146–7

Jackson, P. 76
Jacques, M. 16
Jenkins, B. 80
Jervis, P. 20, 145
Jessop, B. 22
Johnson, N. 18
Johnson, T. 12

Kane, P. 42
Kirkpatrick, I. 94, 119

labour, and the 'right to manage' 56–7
Labour Party 125, 131, 135, 137, 138, 143
Land, H. 3
Lane, J-E. 86
Langan, M. 3–4, 8, 15, 114, 115
language, and legitimation 91–2
  see also discourses; radical vocabularies
Lawson, R. 23, 112
Le Grand, J. 114
league tables 80–1, 85, 89, 119, 143, 146
Legg, B. 47
legitimacy of managerialism 65–7
legitimating practices 88–91
Levitas, R. 14, 136, 137, 138, 156
Lewis, Derek 152
Lewis, G. 69
Lewis, J. 26
Lilley, Peter 44
Lilley, Roy 118
Ling, T. 112, 116, 120
local government
  and community 133
  cultural change 38
  customer centred initiatives 112
  decentralisation of power 23
  increased role of financial and
    performance management 59

neo-conservatives, views of 15–16
response to market incentives 96–7
Local Government Management Board 89
logic of appropriateness 87, 90, 91, 146
Lowndes, V. 86, 87, 100, 101, 103, 104,
  105
loyalties 62–3, 102

'machine bureaucracy' 6
'macho' management 70–2, 73
MacInnes, J. 57
Mackintosh, M. 91, 96–7, 100, 101, 102,
  103, 133
McNulty, T. 95–6, 100, 101, 102
Maddock, S. 71
Maile, S. 53, 92
management of demand 113, 149
managerial regimes
  accountability to users 66
  decision-making, agenda setting and
    normative power 64–5
  intersection with professionalism 102–3
  and modes of attachment 62–3
  sources of legitimacy 65–7, 145, 146
  see also managerialism
managerialisation of politics 122, 143, 148
managerialism
  affinities with New Right 45, 46, 49
  claims to represent needs of customers
    116–18, 152
  discourses 91–5, 97, 101, 148
  and dispersal 30–2, 60, 81
  expansionist character of 151–2
  growth of transformational managerialism
    35–6
  internalisation of 78–81
  legitimacy and rationalism of 65–7
  as process of legitimation 88–91
  and quality 119–20
  and reform of machinery of government
    20–2
  reshaping of bureau-professional regimes
    75–7
  and the 'right to manage' 56–8
  role in legitimising transformation of the
    state 34, 36–9
  in semi-autonomous public service
    organisations 60
  as a set of institutions 86–7
  variability between and within
    organisations 99–100
  see also managerial regimes
March, J. 87–8, 151
marginalisation 136–7, 138
Mark, A. 113

markets
  and the business agenda 57, 58
  and consumerism in public services
    112–16
  introduction in machinery of government
    20, 21, 149
  naturalising legitimations 91
  neo-liberal economics 14
  response in local government 96–7
  response of professionals 95–6
  see also incentives
Marshall, J. 75
Martinez-Lucio, M. 94, 119
Marx, K. 139
Massey, D. 137, 138, 141, 154
Metcalfe, L. 20, 166
Meyer, J. 88, 91–2, 101
military imagery 41–2
minority ethnic groups
  in bureau-professional regimes 68–9
  communities 132, 133
  implications of partnership model 72–3
  see also ethnicity
Mintzberg, H. 6
Mishra, R. 1
mixed economy of welfare 19, 25–7, 134
Mohan, J. 23, 24, 83
Moody, K. 57
Moss Kanter, R. 44, 46, 78
Mossberger, K. 61
Murray, C. 15, 134, 137
Murray, R. 23
myths 88–9, 90–1

Nadler, D. 50
National Health Service 20, 21, 23, 31, 128,
  144, 158
  corporate governance 69
  decentralisation 98–9
  enthusiasm for Trust status 38
  extent of privatisation 28
  inequalities in 153
  management style 71
  managers' conflicts of loyalty 102
  medical power in 6, 7, 8
  representation of customer needs 114,
    117, 118
  response of professionals to market
    incentives 95–6
naturalising analogies 91
'needs' 63, 76, 114–16
  competing claims to represent 116–18
neo-conservatism 14–15, 124, 132, 134,
  135, 136, 151
neo-liberalism 14–15, 46, 123, 124, 151

neo-Taylorism 20, 51, 58, 62, 119
neutrality
    of bureaucracy 5, 15
    Fabian view of the state 7
    of professionalism 7, 15
    of welfare state 11, 12
New Public Management 21–2, 100, 104,
    151
New Right
    affinities with managerialism 45, 46, 49
    ideology and objectives 14–17, 18, 28,
        123–4, 139, 141–2
'new social movements' 11, 51
Newman, J. 11, 50, 51, 56, 67, 69, 71, 72,
    77, 79, 101, 124
Nocon, A. 115
normative power 63–5
North, D. 87

Office for Standards in Education 158–9
Olsen, J. 87–8, 151
operational management, separation from
    policy 81, 144, 145–6, 152
Oppenheim, C. 18, 154
oppositions
    discourse of change 48–50
    representations of 'public' 124–5, 130
organic imagery 40–1
organisational development 41
organisational orders
    competitive orders 70–2
    traditional orders 68–70
    transformational orders 72–3
organisational regimes 60–1
    see also bureau-professional regimes;
        managerial regimes
organisational settlement 4–8, 12–13,
    143–53
organised labour, and the business agenda
    57
Osborne, D. 21, 37, 38, 49, 107, 135
outsourcing 20, 147
ownership 79–80

parenting 15, 75, 134
    see also family
Parker, H. 15
Parry, R. 23, 83
partnership model, transformational
    organisations 72–3
partnerships 20, 133, 134, 147
performance 64, 88
    evaluative and regulatory agencies 158–9
    growth of audit 80–1, 118–19
    management 59, 147
    measurement 62, 79

perverse incentives 15, 114, 146, 147
Peters, G. 23
Peters, T. 21, 35, 38, 43, 46, 54, 57–8, 67,
    72, 107
Peterson, P. 61
Pfeffer, N. 120
Pierson, C. 11
police forces 78–9
policy
    disciplining by bureaucratic
        administration 6
    separation from service delivery 81, 144,
        145–6, 152
political-economic settlement 1–2, 8–9,
    141–3
politicians, public's perception of 157–8
politics
    of information 116–18, 122, 158
    managerialisation of 122, 143, 148
    of quality 118–20, 122
    of representation 116–20, 122, 159
Pollitt, C. 20, 21, 28, 34–5, 56, 58, 76, 78,
    98–9, 99–100, 101, 102, 109, 110
Porter, M. 41
post-Fordism 22–5, 57
Potter, J. 108–9
Powell, M. 153
Powell, W. 86, 89–90, 103
Power, M. 80
power
    centralisation and decentralisation 23
    in mixed economy of welfare 25–7
    in organisational regimes 60–75
    relational power 67–75
    strategic dispersal of 25, 29–32, 126–7
Prior, D. 109, 113, 121, 125
Private Finance Initiative 20, 28
privatisation 27–9
probation officers 143
professionalism and professionals 6–7, 8,
    11–13
    attacks on by New Right 15
    constraint by managerial concerns 114–15
    contrast with managerialism 65
    intersection with managerial regimes
        102–3
    knowledge of the 'customer' 117, 118
    managerial colonisation of discourse 76
    modes of attachment 62–3
    and quality 76, 119, 120
    response to market incentives 95–6
    see also bureau-professional regimes
proxy customers 114, 122
'public'
    definitions and concepts 124–6, 130

distinguished from 'private' 27–9, 74–5, 157
public administration
  and bureaucracy 5–6
  contrast with New Public Management 21–2
public choice theory 14, 84–6, 108, 109
Public Management Foundation 128
public sector workers, as political force 16
public service 4–5, 8, 62, 127
public spending 9, 13
Putnam, K. 98–9, 99–100, 101, 102

quality 118–20, 121
  and disciplining of professional autonomy 76, 119
  discourse of 93–4
  tensions between managerialism and professionalism 119–20

'race' *see* ethnicity; minority ethnic groups
radical vocabularies 38–9, 50, 52, 54
rankings *see* league tables
Ranson, S. 125–6
Rao, N. 143
rationing 64, 66, 150
Rayner, Sir Derek 36
re-engineering 44, 49
Reed, M. 93–4
regimes *see* organisational regimes
regulatory agencies 158–9
Reich, R. 57
reinvention of government 37–8, 44, 49
relational power 67–75
representation, politics of 116–20, 122, 159
Rhodes, R. 23
Richards, S. 20, 36, 145
'right to manage' 56–8, 64, 98, 151–2
Rose, N. 31, 62
Rowan, B. 88, 91–2, 101
rules, and institutional theory 86, 87
Rustin, M. 24, 57, 137, 138, 141, 154

Salaman, G. 107
Salter, B. 114
Sayer, A. 25, 57
Scapens, R. 59
schools 77, 78, 98, 153
Schumpeterian Workfare State 22
'scroungers' 14–15
Seabrook, J. 52–3
sexual division of labour *see* gender
sexuality 11, 157
  see also gay community
Skelcher, C. 111
Smith, V. 162

Social Chapter 137
social cohesion 155–6
social differentiation 154–5
  and community 136
  destabilisation of post-war social settlement 9–11, 139
  and exclusion 138, 154
  see also diversity
social exclusion 136–7, 138, 154
social inequality *see* inequality
social justice 156
social order 156
social policy studies 18–19
social services departments 26, 97, 100, 114, 133, 146, 150
social settlement 2–4, 9–12, 124, 139, 153–5, 159
Spencer, K. 145–6
stakeholding 136–8, 154, 156
state welfare
  neo-conservative views 15
  neo-liberal critique 14–15
Stewart, J. 66, 125–6, 133, 144, 148
Stewart, R. 102
Stoker, G. 61, 132
Stone, C. 61
subjection 30–1
  and discourse of change 54
  and managerial discourse 93–5
Swann, D. 27, 35

Talbot, C. 37
targeting 66, 113, 150
taxation 14
Taylor-Gooby, P. 23, 112
tensions, in the process of change 101–3
Thompson, G. 46
Thompson, S. 128
Townley, B. 94
trade unions 57
transformational discourse 42–3, 45, 51–2
transformational organisational orders 72–3
turbulence, discourse of 43–4
Tushman, M. 50

unionised labour 57
users xiii, 63–4, 102, 107–22, 125–8, 151–2
  as citizens 3–4
  as consumers 14–15, 31–2, 107–9, 112–16, 123–4, 127–8
  representation of 116–18, 159
  and social diversity 9–11, 111, 129–31, 153–5
  as stakeholders 137–8, 156

variability in development of managerialism
99–100
Vickridge, R. 80, 150
vocabularies *see* discourses; language;
radical vocabularies
voluntary organisations 26, 89, 132

Waine, B. 26, 28, 48, 58, 80
Walby, S. 117, 118
Waldegrave, W. 145
Walker, A. 18, 113
Walker, D. 25, 57
Walsh, K. 84, 85, 91, 112
Waterman, R. 21, 35, 107
Weeks, J. 135, 136
welfare pluralism 19, 125, 132, 143
see also mixed economy of welfare
welfare state
challenge by New Right 15–17
crisis in 8–13
neutrality of 11
organisational settlement 4–8, 12–13,
143–53
political-economic settlement 1–2, 8–9,
141–3

post-Fordist analyses of changes in 22–5
social settlement 2–4, 9–12, 124, 139,
153–5, 159
'value base' 8
Whipp, R. 95–6, 100, 101, 102
Whitfield, D. 71
Whitley, R. 91
Whittington, R. 70, 95–6, 100, 101, 102
Williams, F. 2, 10–11, 18, 24, 32, 51, 111,
115, 124, 128, 153
Williamson, C. 69
Wilson, E. 10
Wilson, J. 110
Witz, A. 74
women
exclusion from labour market 138
impact of competitive management
strategies upon 70–1
impact of intensification of managerial
labour upon 74–5
see also gender
Working for Patients 109
World Bank 142

Young, S. 132